The Cold War

Blackwell Essential Readings in History

This series comprises concise collections of key articles on important historical topics. Designed as a complement to standard survey histories, the volumes are intended to help introduce students to the range of scholarly debate in a subject area. Each collection includes a general introduction and brief contextual headnotes to each article, offering a coherent, critical framework for study.

Published

The German Reformation: The Essential Readings
C. Scott Dixon

The Counter-Reformation: The Essential Readings
David M. Luebke

The English Civil War: The Essential Readings
Peter Gaunt

The French Revolution: The Essential Readings
Ronald Schechter

The Russian Revolution: The Essential Readings
Martin Miller

The Third Reich: The Essential Readings
Christian Leitz

The Cold War: The Essential Readings
Klaus Larres and Ann Lane

In Preparation

The Italian Renaissance: The Essential Readings
Paula Findlen

The Enlightenment: The Essential Readings
Martin Fitzpatrick

Stalinism: The Essential Readings
David Hoffmann

The Crusades: The Essential Readings
Thomas Madden

Cromwell and the Interregnum: The Essential Readings
David Smith

The Cold War

The Essential Readings

Edited by Klaus Larres and Ann Lane

Editorial Adviser   Robert MacMahon

BLACKWELL
Publishers

First published 2001

2 4 6 8 10 9 7 5 3 1

Blackwell Publishers Ltd
108 Cowley Road
Oxford OX4 1JF
UK

Blackwell Publishers Inc.
350 Main Street
Malden, Massachusetts 02148
USA

British Library Cataloguing in Publication Data

A CIP catalogue record for this book is available from the British Library.

Library of Congress Cataloging-in-Publication Data
The Cold War : the essential readings / edited by Klaus Larres and Ann Lane.
    p.   cm. — (Blackwell essential readings in history)
    Includes bibliographical references and index.
    ISBN 0–631–20705–8 — ISBN 0–631–20706–6 (pbk. : alk. paper)
    1. Cold War—Sources.   2. World politics—1945-—Sources.   3. Europe—Foreign relations—1945-—Sources.   4. United States—Foreign relations—1945–1989—Sources.   5. Soviet Union—Foreign relations—1945–1991—Sources.   I. Larres, Klaus.   II. Lane, Ann.   III. Series.
    D843 .C577323   2001
    909.82—dc21

                                                        2001025676

Typeset in 10.5 on 12 pt Photina
by Best-set Typesetter Ltd., Hong Kong
Printed in Great Britain by Antony Rowe, Chippenham, Wilts

This book is printed on acid-free paper.

Contents

Acknowledgements

The authors and publishers gratefully acknowledge the following for permission to reproduce copyright material:

Extracts from "Economics, Power and National Security" from *A Preponderance of Power: National Security, the Truman Administration, and the Cold War* by Melvyn P. Leffler, © 1992 by the Board of Trustees of the Leland Stanford Junior University. Reprinted with permission of the publishers, Stanford University Press;

Extract from *We Now Know: Rethinking Cold War History* by John Lewis Gaddis, published by Oxford University Press UK, © John Lewis Gaddis 1997. Reprinted by permission of Oxford University Press;

Extract from *Inside the Kremlin's Cold War: From Stalin to Khrushchev* by Vladislav Zubok and Constantine Pleshakov, published by Harvard University Press, © 1996 by the President and Fellows of Harvard College. Reprinted with permission of Harvard University Press;

Extract from "The Vietnam War and the Superpower Triangle", *The Fifty Years War: the United States and the Soviet Union in World Politics 1941–1991*, by Richard Crockatt. Published by Routledge. Reprinted with permission of Taylor & Francis;

Extract from "The Failure of the Détente of the 1970s" from *Détente and Confrontation: American–Soviet Relations from Nixon to Reagan*, revised edition by Raymond L. Garthoff, published by The Brookings Institution, 1999. Reprinted with permission of the publisher;

Extract from "Some Lessons from the Cold War" by Arthur Schlesinger Jr., from *The End of the Cold War: Its Meaning and Implications*, by

M. J. Hogan, published by Cambridge University Press, 1992. Reprinted with permission of the publisher;

Extract from *The Devil We Knew: Americans and the Cold War* by H. W. Brands, published by Oxford University Press, New York, © 1993 H. W. Brands. Used with permission of Oxford University Press Inc.

The publishers apologize for any errors or omissions in the above list and would be grateful to be notified of any corrections that should be incorporated in the next edition or reprint of this book.

1

Introduction: The Cold War as History

Ann Lane

The term "Cold War" refers to the state of tension, hostility, competition and conflict which characterized the West's relations with the Soviet Union, and more particularly, Soviet–American relations for much of the post-war period. The Cold War was not premediated in the way that Hitler's war had been, nor prepared for as was the case before the First World War. Rather it emerged as a consequence of a stand-off between the Western Powers and the Soviet Union whose wartime alliance had broken down amid a welter of suspicion, distrust and conflicting interests once the war against the Axis was over and the common enemy defeated. One of the fascinating things about Cold War history is that, despite the endless debate, there is little agreement about when it started or even where. Some would say that it began in eastern Europe; others argue that it was in Germany or the Near East; still others would say that the events which sealed the conflict occurred in the Far East.[1] Its clearest manifestation was the division of Europe into east and west by the Iron Curtain, the heavily guarded and fortified frontier which demarcated the boundaries between the western "liberal democracies" and the "people's democracies" of what we used to call eastern Europe. Most symbollic of all was the division of Germany and in particular the partition of the city of Berlin, deep in the eastern zone, by a wall constructed in 1961 on Khrushchev's instructions in order to stabilize the German Democratic Republic by halting westward migration.

1   See for example, W. Kimball, "Naked reverse right: Roosevelt, Churchill and Eastern Europe from Tolstoy to Yalta and a Little Beyond", *Diplomatic History*, vol. 3, no. 2, spring 1979; B. Kuniholm, *The Origins of the Cold War in the Near East: Great Power conflict and diplomacy in Iran, Turkey and Greece*, Princeton, NJ, 1980; W. Stueck, *The Road to Confrontation: American Foreign Policy Toward China and Korea, 1947–1950*, Chapel Hill, 1981.

As the ambitions and insecurities of West and East came up against each other in the Middle East, the Far East, the Indian subcontinent, Africa and Latin America, each provided a forum in which the two superpowers waged their struggle for political, economic and ideological hegemony which was conducted by all means short of open armed conflict between them for over forty years. However, there is a paradox at the heart of the history of this period: despite the intensity and bitterness of the struggle, each of the superpowers was wary of action which might provoke a direct retaliation from the other and for protracted periods, the Cold War was characterized by a concerted effort on the part of the United States and the Soviet Union to establish a modus vivendi for peaceful coexistence. Periods of détente occurred in the late 1950s and, with an interruption at the beginning of the Kennedy administration culminating in the Cuban missile crisis, resumed in the mid-1960s; an interval of renewed tension at the end of the 1970s preceded the de-escalation of the conflict as the Soviet leadership concluded that its domestic disarray could be ignored no longer. This "long peace", as John Gaddis named it, was the product of a vested interest in stability consequent on the existence of nuclear weapons, a near monopoly of knowledge of this technology by the major powers, and the doctrine of mutually assured destruction.[2] Having teetered on the brink of a nuclear exchange in October 1962, the superpowers directed ever increasing diplomatic resources to weapons limitations agreements and constrained their respective clients from action which would draw them into open conflict.

The voluminous literature on the Cold War contains many good (and occasionally conflictual) analyses of the historiography of the period and particularly that relating to the question of causation.[3] The objective here is to identify the principal strands and to discuss some of the more recent developments in the literature. The earliest attempts to offer an interpretation of Cold War origins were closely linked with, and defined by, the need to justify the creation in the United States of the national security state. During the 1950s considerable quantities of ink were spilt by commentators and officials in the attempt to define the

2 J. L. Gaddis, *The Long Peace: Enquiries into the History of the Cold War*, Oxford, 1987, pp. 215–45.
3 Of particular use are M. P. Leffler, "Interpretative Wars over the Cold War, 1945–60", in G. Martel (ed.), *American Foreign Relations Reconsidered, 1890–1993*, London, 1994, pp. 106–24; J. S. Walker, "Historians and Cold War Origins: The New Consensus", in G. K. Haines and J. S. Walker (eds), *American Foreign Relations: A Historiographical Review*, Westport, Conn., 1981, pp. 207–36; G. Lundestad, "Moralism, Presentism, Exceptionalism, Provincialism, and Other Extravagances in American Writings on the Early Cold War Years", *Diplomatic History*, vol. 13, no. 4 (1989), pp. 527–45; M. H. Hunt, "The Long Crisis in U.S. Diplomatic History: Coming to Closure", *Diplomatic History*, vol. 16 (1992), pp. 115–40.

enemy and thereby justify the vast and constantly increasing demands for expanding the defence budget. These accounts were heavily influenced by contemporary views of the Soviet political system and a conservative bias which predominated in intellectual circles in the immediate post-war period. Intrinsic to American political thinking since the late nineteenth century were assumptions about dictatorship and autocracy which held that such regimes could be characterized by oppression at home and aggression abroad, but the emergence of fascism and Nazism encouraged a conceptualization of totalitarian systems of government into which the Soviet Union under Stalin was readily fitted. This framework held that under totalitarian dictatorship power was indivisible and vested in the personality of its ruler; the system was incapable of change and its survival, moreover, was dependent upon pursuit of the goals identified in a messianic ideology by which the regime justified its existence. During the 1950s, this conceptualization provided the defining theoretical construct by which to justify American containment strategies.[4] At the same time two decades of international disharmony which had preceeded the Cold War, characterized by world depression, protectionism, the rise of the European dictatorships and renewed world war, led to the search for security and stability in the post-war period. The ideological fence-building which took place in the wake of the Second World War can be explained in part as a consequence of the insecurities of the interwar years.

The early accounts of Cold War origins were authored primarily by American scholars who drew heavily on published memoirs and diaries of serving officials as well as on such published diplomatic correspondence and state papers as were then available. Indeed, some writers such as Herbert Feis and William McNeil had been policy practitioners actively engaged in the events which they sought to explain. The questions which this school addressed were those about the policy process: who made policy, which policies did they choose and why, and once chosen, how were they implemented? The methodology was essentially hermeneutic and owed much to the nineteenth-century scholarship of Leopold von Ranke which presumed that "objective truth" could and should be established through perusal of diplomatic documents. Indeed, the process was not unlike that conducted in Europe during the 1920s and 1930s when the publication of state papers on the part of the First World War protagonists had informed a debate about the rightness or otherwise of the war guilt clause of the Paris Peace Treaties. The effect was not dissimilar. What emerged was an America-centric view

4   For an account of this concept's impact on twentieth-century historiography see A. Gleason, *Totalitarianism: The Inner History of the Cold War*, Oxford, 1995.

which explained the Cold War in terms of the impossibility of dealing with "the Soviets". Several strands can be identified: the conservative approach which sought to condemn the Roosevelt and Truman administrations, the former for yielding too readily to Soviet demands at Yalta, the latter for hesitancy and inexperience; the liberals on the contrary, justified American foreign policy as a bold and imaginative effort to deal at one and the same time with Soviet expansionism and residual American isolationism which reached its pinnacle with the Truman Doctrine.[5] A third strand which is also generally grouped with Orthodox accounts is Realism. This approach takes a deeply critical view of American foreign policy as being overly determined by moralistic and universalist ideals and unduly attentive to the ideological element in Soviet foreign policy at the expense of balance of power considerations. The Cold War, the realists argue, was inevitable because of the expansionist needs of both the Soviet and the American political systems.[6]

Therefore the "received wisdom" enshrined in orthodox history held that the breakdown of the Grand Alliance was due to Stalin's inherent suspiciousness of the West and, in the case of both liberals and conservatives, to Soviet expansionism legitimized by the teleological goals of Marxist–Leninist dogma. Among the key primary sources invoked for this thesis was the "Long Telegram" penned in the American Embassy in Moscow by the Chargé d'Affaires, George Kennan, which attempted to explain to the Truman Administration the sources of Soviet foreign policy in terms of domestic politics and ideological considerations.[7] Soviet demands arising from its concern for security were, he argued, insatiable. Moreover, he considered that "a permanent modus vivendi" existed in so far as Soviet foreign policy was founded on the belief that "it is desirable and necessary that the internal harmony of our society be disrupted, our traditional way of life be destroyed, the international authority of our state be broken, if Soviet power is to be secure". Kennan argued that Soviet foreign policy was ideologically determined, but he

5   For example, the conservative thesis is advanced in W. H. Camberlin, *America's Second Crusade*, Chicago, 1950; the liberal interpretation is exemplified by H. Feis, *Churchill, Roosevelt, Stalin: the war they waged and the peace they sought*, Princeton, 1957, and Feis, *Between War and Peace: the Potsdam Conference*, Princeton, 1960.

6   The classic statement of Realist interpretations of Cold War origins is that by H. J. Morgenthau, *In Defense of the National Interest: a critical examination of American Foreign Policy*, New York, 1951, p. 116. See also N. A. Graebner, *Cold War Diplomacy: American Foreign Policy 1945–1960*, Princeton, 1962 and G. F. Kennan, *Realities of American Foreign Policy*, Princeton, 1954. For an example of an interpretation of Soviet foreign policy viewed from the realist perspective see A. Ulam, *Expansion and Coexistence: the History of Soviet Foreign Policy 1917–67*, New York, 1963.

7   Department of State, *Foreign Relations of the United States, Diplomatic Papers, 1946* (cited hereinafter as *FRUS*), Washington, 1969, vol. vi, pp. 696–709.

also recognised a flexibility in the Kremlin's decision-making which could be invoked by demonstrations of American power.[8] While Kennan himself was later to modify his views, and took a dim view of the containment policies which evolved in Washington as a consequence of his commentary, this characterization of the motives of the Soviet leadership became the centrepiece of the emerging Cold War paradigm in Washington and one which determined American foreign policy for several generations.[9] The policy of containment was defined by the United States National Security Council in April 1950; this revealed that American policy makers, in the space of five years, had come to conceive of American national interests, and thus the Cold War, in global terms.[10] Conveniently, the National Security Council's suppositions seemed to be confirmed by the timely outbreak of the Korean War in June 1950 which served to legitimize military as opposed to the purely economic containment of the communist world which Kennan had identified. One liberal orthodox writer (and former White House aide), Arthur Schlesinger, argued in a classic formulation of the Orthodox approach published in 1967 that the Cold War could have been avoided "only if the Soviet Union had not been possessed by convictions both of the infallibility of the communist world and of the inevitability of a communist world".[11] He continued that these convictions "transformed an impasse between national states into a religious war, a tragedy of possibility into one of necessity".

By the time Schlesinger wrote these words, the bipolarity which this thesis assumed and which defined international politics following the breakdown of the Grand Alliance in 1945, was under challenge. The newly emerging nations, whose numbers at the United Nations Organisation had significantly increased in the early 1960s, were having a considerable impact on international politics. The disinclination of the Afro-Asian states to align with either of the communist or western blocs gave them the opportunity to hold the balance of power in a game which was defined by the possession of nuclear weapons. While the newly emerging states were essentially highly diverse, they were united not just by a disinclination to align in Cold War terms, but also by their

8 For a useful summary see J. S. Walker, "Historians and Cold War Origins", pp. 207–36.

9 See for example, G. F. Kennan, "Containment: Then and Now", *At a Century's Ending: Reflections 1982–1995*, New York, 1996, pp. 110–15 and the exchange of letters between G. F. Kennan and J. Lukacs in *American Heritage* (December 1995), p. 65.

10 See *FRUS 1950*, vol. 1, pp. 237–92, "NSC-68 United States Objectives and Programme for National Security", 14 April 1950. The full text was published in *Naval War College Review*, xxvii, 6/seq., N. 255 (May/June 1975), pp. 51–108; for a commentary see T. Etzold and J. L. Gaddis, *Containment: Documents on American Policy and Strategy, 1945–1950*, New York, 1978.

11 A. Schlesinger, "Origins of the Cold War", *Foreign Affairs*, vol. 46 (October 1967), p. 52.

relative underdevelopment and need for assistance to achieve economic development. Their experience of European colonialism predisposed these states to a distaste for western interference and, at least in the short term, they saw in the communist system a more attractive model for rapid modernization. The task of influencing the newly emerging states became a priority for both the eastern and western blocs which now extended their competition out of Europe, where the battle lines were stalemated, into Africa, Asia and Latin America where the boundaries to superpower influence remained more fluid.

In the meantime, the logic of containment doctrines had led to a steady increase in the American commitment to Vietnam. The origins of American involvement lay, or so it seemed, in the very conceptualization of the Soviet system and Soviet–American relations which had been adopted by orthodox scholars as justifications of containment. Such challenges to the received wisdom combined with a wider disillusionment with American ideals and their foreign policy expression among radicals who in time defined themselves as of the New Left, and provided the stimulus for the emergence of a body of scholarship on Cold War origins. In fact, a revisionist literature existed well before Vietnam gained centrality in contemporary debate: studies such as those of William Appleman Williams and Denna Frank Fleming published in 1962 and 1961 respectively, challenged the orthodox assumption of naïveté in American foreign policy and the conclusion that it was "reactive" to Soviet inspired antagonism.[12] Drawing on the progressive ideas which were experimented with by students of international relations in the 1930s, these authors argued that the economic system and the privileges derived from it by the elite were in control of the foreign policy process.[13] Thus, the requirement of market capitalism for constant expansion and non-interventionist political systems represented the driving forces behind the Wilsonian goal of making "the world safe for democracy" by which American actions were justified.

The revisionist school only really flourished, however, once the foreign policy consensus had broken down over the Vietnam War when the need was perceived to find an alternative explanation for world events than that offered by realism. This perhaps explains why it was the publication in 1965 of Gar Alperovitz's monograph on the decision-

---

12   W. A. Williams, *The Tragedy of American Diplomacy*, rev. edn, New York: 1962; D. F. Fleming, *The Cold War and its Origins 1917–60*, 2 vols, Garden City, New York, 1961. See also L. Gardner *Architects of Illusion: Men and Ideas in American Foreign Policy 1941–1949*, Chicago, 1970; D. Horowitz, *The Free World Colossus: A Critique of American Foreign policy in the Cold War*, New York, 1965; G. Kolko, *The Politics of War: the World and United States Foreign Policy, 1943–1945*, New York, 1968.
13   For example, C. A. Beard, *Roosevelt and the Coming of War*, New York, 1947.

making which led to the use of the atomic bomb to end the war with Japan which really provoked a revisionist debate about Cold War origins.[14] Alperovitz attacked the orthodox position in the most radical manner, arguing that the United States had used the bomb not out of military considerations but in order to impress its power upon Stalin so as to achieve a favourable post-war settlement. Subsequently, more sophisticated revisionist works sought to show how the United States had tried firstly to demand open access to eastern Europe and upon receiving a rebuff, had then sought to reconstruct western Europe and particularly the western zones of Germany in the liberal democratic mould. During the 1950s and 1960s this extended into the Third World as decolonization opened up these regions to economic penetration. The creation of multilateral organisations, such as the United Nations and the International Monetary Fund, in which the United States had the largest share of the votes because it provided the most substantial proportion of the funds, were held up as further evidence of a drive to establish an international world along capitalist lines. This thesis was stated most starkly by Gabriel and Joyce Kolko who de-emphasized the importance of the Soviet Union as a factor in American foreign policy and identified these policies as determined by the nature of its capitalist system and by recurrent fears of recession: "The United States' ultimate objective", they argued, "was both to sustain and to reform world capitalism".[15] Such socio-economic explanations were expanded upon by others such as Thomas Paterson who argued that the "national security and economic well-being of countries touched by the destructive force of World War II depended upon a successful recovery from its devastation . . . the United States alone possessed the necessary resources – the economic power – to resolve the recovery crisis". He adds that "Coercion characterised United States reconstruction diplomacy".[16]

With regard to the Soviet Union, the revisionists were influenced by theses currently being advanced by Sovietologists who were applying pluralist and bureaucratic models of politics to the Soviet system in order to elucidate these hitherto under-researched aspects of the one party state. This process was reflected particularly in the works of Gavriel Ra'anan and William McCagg who agreed that the United States was prepared to exploit the advantages inherent in its overwhelming military and economic strength to achieve leverage over the less pros-

---

14   G. Alperovitz, *Atomic Diplomacy: Hiroshima and Potsdam*, New York, 1965.
15   J. Kolko and G. Kolko, *The Limits of Power: the World and United States Foreign Policy, 1945–1954*, New York, 1972, p. 11.
16   T. G. Paterson, *Soviet–American Confrontation: Postwar Reconstruction and the Origins of the Cold War*, Baltimore, 1973, p. 260.

perous and developed Soviet Union; that the Kremlin was being forced into making concessions and thereby compromising its own national interests, in order to appease American demands.[17] They concluded, therefore, that the Soviet decision to impose its politico-economic model on its sphere in eastern Europe could be interpreted as essentially a reaction to American expansionism. Picking up on the inclination of Sovietologists to seek evidence of pluralist manifestations in Soviet domestic politics, revisionist scholars began to focus on the domestic sources of Soviet foreign policy. Thus, Stalin was not portrayed as a twentieth-century despot, but rather as *primus inter pares*, a leader whose policy options were constrained by the needs to balance infighting within the bureaucracies and amongst members of the Politburo. Furthermore, they argued that the Soviet Union was not unduly expansionist while Stalin himself was a pragmatic leader who was prepared to make concessions if only the Americans had been willing to compromise their ambitions and recognize his legitimate concerns. Accordingly, his policies of consolidation in eastern Europe were perceived as hesitant and only after the Marshall Plan conference held in Paris in July 1947, which seemed to clarify the hegemonic ambitions of the United States in Europe, did the Soviet Union consolidate its sphere of control.

The debate provoked by revisionism was bitter, public and at times vitriolic.[18] Like so many acrimonious disputes it was effective in provoking a new generation of scholars to critically reassess the evidence and explore new sources and fresh avenues of approach. In this task they were assisted by the release at the end of the 1960s and early 1970s of a great volume of official documentation pertaining to the mid-1940s. What emerged was a third school of interpretation, beginning with publication in 1972 of John Lewis Gaddis's masterly study of American foreign policy.[19] Gaddis's early works are interesting because they incorporate elements of the revisionist thesis while simultaneously making an argument which is not entirely dissimilar from orthodoxy, and in this preoccupation with the state demonstrated tendencies which are usually associated with Realism. He accepts that the United States made

17   W. O. McCagg, *Stalin Embattled, 1943–1948*, Detroit, Michigan, 1978; G. D. Ra'anan, *International Policy Formulation in the USSR: Factional "Debates" During the Zhadonovschina*, Hamden, Connecticut, 1983.
18   For a summary see N. Graebner, "Cold War Origins and the Continuing Debate: A Review of Recent Literature", *Journal of Conflict Resolution*, vol. 13 (1969), pp. 123–32; M. Leigh, "Is there a Revisionist Thesis on the Origins of the Cold War?", *Political Science Quarterly*, vol. 89, no. 1 (1994), pp. 181–206.
19   J. L. Gaddis, *The United States and the Origins of the Cold War 1941–1947*, New York, 1972; "Was the Truman Doctrine the Real Starting Point?", *Foreign Affairs*, vol. 52 (January 1974), pp. 386–402.

a significant contribution towards the onset of the Cold War and that American foreign policy was determined by economic and ideological motivations. Further, he concedes that Stalin's objectives were limited. But he criticises the revisionists for placing emphasis on economic factors to the exclusion of political considerations which, he argues, were critical determinants of foreign policy. Partisan politics, ethnic voting blocs and rivalries between the legislature and the executive, were, according to Gaddis, the critical factors in defining American foreign policy. While he is convinced by arguments that economic weapons were employed to extract concessions from those who stood in the way of achievement of America's long term and ideological objectives, Gaddis differs from the revisionists in arguing that economics was only the means and never the ends of American foreign policy. Moreover, he asserts that primary responsibility for the Cold War lay with Stalin who was "immune from the pressures of Congress, public opinion or the press" and thus was free to direct his foreign policy unfettered by domestic considerations. Nor does Gaddis accept that Stalin was constrained by ideology: rather "he was the master of communist doctrine, not a prisoner of it . . . his absolute powers did give him more chances to surmount the internal restraints on his policy than were available to his democratic counterparts in the West".[20] In a later and equally seminal work, Gaddis develops this thesis further. American containment of the Soviet Union in the Cold War, he argues, was designed to balance world power.[21] In effect this amounted to creation of an American empire, but the difference between this and earlier forms of imperialism as well as the Soviet variant, was that it was empire by invitation. America had been asked to extend its hegemony through economic aid to support liberal regimes which regarded themselves to be threatened by international communist subversion directed from Moscow.

The school of thought which this work spawned has been labelled post-revisionist, the central assumption of which is the liberal denial of the governance of politics by economics.[22] The post-revisionist consensus, which Gaddis famously declared as emerging in 1983, is rooted in a thesis that American hegemonic behaviour is more accurately described as defensive rather than offensive expansion, "of invitation

---

20   Gaddis, *The United States and the Origins of the Cold War*, pp. 360–1.
21   J. L. Gaddis, *Strategies of Containment: a critical appraisal of Postwar American National Security Policy*, Oxford, 1982.
22   B. Cummings, "'Revising Postrevisionism', or The Poverty of Theory in Diplomatic History", *Diplomatic History*, vol. 17, no. 4 (1993), p. 551, n. 35; J. L. Gaddis, "The Emerging Post-Revisionist Synthesis on the Origins of the Cold War", *Diplomatic History*, vol. 7 (1983), pp. 171–93. It is unclear who first coined the term "post-revisionism".

rather than imposition, or improvisation rather than careful planning". The post-revisionists also maintain that it was Stalin's ill-defined but relentless search for security at the expense of his neighbours combined with the failure of the western powers to recognize his ambitions and draw the lines firmly enough to deter him that led to the Cold War. This thesis was supported by several scholars of Soviet foreign policy who during the late 1970s and early 1980s produced studies of Stalin's foreign policy which utilized the still fragmentary Soviet and east European sources.[23]

Far from being consensual, post-revisionism has become the focus of particularly lively scholarly debate especially in the United States. Among its principal critics, Melvyn Leffler challenges the post-revisionist condemnation of Stalin's post-war foreign policy as the root cause of the Cold War.[24] Instead he argues that Soviet concerns were genuine and that it was testimony to the American preoccupation with geopolitical interests that no attempt (or very little) was made to consider what Soviet perceptions might be and to factor in the enormous losses suffered during the war in order to evaluate the motivations of Soviet demands for security on its frontiers. At the same time he agrees with Gaddis that the revisionists were incorrect in discounting American concerns about Soviet intentions, perceiving in the Truman Administration's policies a genuine preoccupation with Soviet strength and the Soviet Union's potential to exploit social and economic disruption to further its own interests.

More vigorous in their criticism of post-revisionism are those who have rooted their interpretations in more formal conceptual frameworks. Michael Hogan is among those who has employed the corporatist model as an analytical tool and demonstrates how self-interested collaboration among supranational organizations and public and private agencies formed the basis of a strategy which aimed to ensure capitalist expansion.[25] Secondly, there has been some experimentation with the world systems approach which purports to identify a structured world system, capitalist in nature, which effectively imposes limitations on attempts at socialist construction because of the distortions that the capitalist "reality" creates for non-capitalist states. Accordingly, scholars such as Bruce Cummings have explained American foreign policy in

23   V. Mastny, *Russia's Road to the Cold War: Diplomacy, Warfare and the Politics of Communism 1941–1945*, New York, 1979; W. Taubman, *Stalin's American Policy: From Entente to Détente to Cold War*, New York, 1982.
24   M. P. Leffler, "The American Conception of National Security and the Beginnings of the Cold War, 1945–48", *The American Historical Review*, vol. 89 (April 1984), pp. 346–81.
25   For example, M. J. Hogan, *The Marshall Plan: America, Britain and the Reconstruction of Western Europe, 1947–1952*, New York, 1989.

terms of a drive to revive world capitalism and to sustain the American position within that system.[26]

Cold War history was enriched during the 1980s as a result of a burgeoning European scholarship which focused for the first time on the perceptions of the superpowers from the perspective of the European states. The stimulus for these studies lay immediately in the opening of the archives in accordance with the thirty-year rule which governs the release of government records, but the published results undoubtedly reflect the contemporaneous growth of European self-confidence in its search for a role and the definition of its interests as distinct from those of the United States. In so doing, however, European scholarship largely accepts the parameters of American debate in so far as it was also most sharply focused on the debate about origins. The principal underlying theme was that Europeans were not mere bystanders at a superpower struggle for influence; rather they were actors with independent voices which had had some influence on this process. Despite the crippling effects of the war, the European powers in reality played an important part in the reordering of the international system during the 1940s and the history of the Cold War is incomplete without a proper assessment and acknowledgement of their role.[27] Collectively, this scholarship produced a body of evidence which confirmed that various of the European Governments had also harboured deep anxieties about a Soviet challenge and that these had a significant influence on American foreign policy.[28] The British in particular, appear to have been rather more anxious about Soviet intentions immediately after the war and they did much to alert the Americans to the perceived dangers.[29] Indeed, with few exceptions, orthodoxy in terms of the acceptance of Soviet expansionism, has dominated European scholarship. Revisionism has never had much impact on the writing of Europe's Cold War history which may be a testament to the extent to which the

26   For example, T. J. McCormick, *America's Half-Century: United States Foreign Policy in the Cold War*, Baltimore, MD, 1989.
27   A. L. DePorte, *Europe Between the Superpowers: the Enduring Balance*, Yale, 1979; D. Reynolds, "The Origins of the Cold War: the European dimension 1944–45", *The Historical Journal*, vol. 28, no. 2 (1985), pp. 497–515.
28   B. Kuniholm, *The Origins of the Cold War in the Near East: Great Power Conflict and Diplomacy in Iran, Turkey and Greece*, Princeton, 1979; G. Lundestad, *America, Scandinavia and the Cold War 1945–1949*, New York, 1989; Kuniholm, "Empire by Invitation? The United States and Western Europe 1945–1952", *Journal of Peace Research*, vol. 23 (1986), pp. 263–72; T. Anderson, *The United States, Great Britain and the Cold War, 1944–1947*, Columbia, MO; 1981; L. S. Kaplan, "Western Europe in the 'American Century': A Retrospective View", *Diplomatic History*, vol. 6, no. 2 (1982), pp. 213–26.
29   P. G. Boyle, "The British Foreign Office View of Soviet–American Relations, 1945–46", *Diplomatic History*, vol. 3 (1979), pp. 307–20; H. Thomas, *Armed Truce: the Beginnings of the Cold War, 1945–46*, London, 1986.

writing of history is affected by the wider intellectual fashion. By the time that the Europeans studied Cold War origins, new left thinking was already becoming passé.

The impact of the European contributions was to reveal a much more complex web of international relations than the quasi-political debate being conducted in the United States would allow and challenged both revisionism and post-revisionism in their assumptions that American foreign policy could be explained from domestic political sources alone.[30] One of the more penetrating critiques of earlier Cold War historiography and in particular its predisposition towards American exceptionalism appeared in *Diplomatic History* just as the Berlin Wall was being demolished.[31] In this article the Norwegian scholar, Geir Lundestad, took issue with a methodology which has, in presuming American exceptionalism, concentrated exclusively on the development of American foreign policy without reference to the external factors by which it has been shaped. Only by taking into account the latter, can American exceptionalism, and particularly the nature of that exceptionalism, be proved.

Throughout the Cold War, the greatest stumbling block to a contextualization of American foreign policy was the absence of access to a comparable archival database on the Soviet side. Much has been written about the perceptions of the United States and its allies of the motivations for Soviet actions, but only a few scholars have tackled the problem from Moscow's perspective. Since the end of the Cold War and the opening of Russian, and to a greater extent, east European archives, some progress has been made in filling this gap.[32] Two views of the problem emerge from recent literature. The first concerns the role of ideology. During the 1970s and 1980s, ideology had been regarded as a tool of limited value to students of Soviet foreign policy, except in the narrowest sense but the prominent role played by ideas in ending the Cold War has encouraged a re-examination of the ideological dimension in both American and Soviet foreign policy. In the Soviet context this has led to a fresh attempt to understand the complex relationship between Marxist–Leninist ideology, especially in its Stalinist variant, and the legacies of Russian imperial history to which the Soviet leaders

30 This point was made by D. Cameron Watt in "Rethinking the Cold War: a letter to a British Historian", *Political Quarterly*, vol. 49, no. 4 (1978), pp. 446–56.
31 G. Lundestad, "Moralism, Presentism, Exceptionalism, Provincialism and other extravagances in American Writings on the Early Cold War Years", pp. 527–45.
32 J. Haslam, "Russian Archival Revelations and Our Understanding of the Cold War", *Diplomatic History*, vol. 21, no. 2 (1997), pp. 217–28; see also W. C. Wohlforth, "New Evidence on Moscow's Cold War: Ambiguity in Search of Theory", pp. 229–42 and O. A. Westad, "Secrets of the Second World: The Russian Archives and the Reinterpretation of Cold War History", pp. 259–71, both in the same *Diplomatic History* journal.

were heirs.[33] Such interpretations emphasize the role played in the decision-making process of eschatalogical fears regarding the very survival of the regime. These were consequent on the experiences of intervention and isolation in the early years following the revolution, compounded by invasion and near defeat in 1941 and reinforced subsequently by the teachings of its founder who had much to say on the subject of capitalist encirclement. The task of protecting the regime only appears to have become a less pressing concern after Stalin's death. Similarly, the imperial tradition in Russian history was deeply ingrained in the post-revolutionary leadership: the Soviet leaders inherited a geopolitical entity acquired through imperial aggrandizement and the notion that the secession of territory amounted to a challenge to the regime's legitimacy was as firmly rooted in their minds as it had been in those who inhabited the Tsar's court. The objectives of furthering the cause of socialism, the triumph of which the Soviet leadership consistently believed to be inevitable, became inextricably linked with the preservation of territorial integrity and the Soviet Communist Party's leading role in the world communist movement. Believing the triumph of socialism to be unavoidable, the Soviet Union wished to assist communist parties abroad in furthering this end.

The second approach places renewed emphasis on Soviet security concerns.[34] While accepting that the Soviet Union was expansionist these scholars argue that this process was limited and determined by the perceived needs to secure Soviet borders from renewed German and Japanese aggression in particular but also, and by implication, from the hostile capitalist world. Some synthesis of both interpretations has been achieved by Vladislav Zubok and Constantine Pleshakov.[35] More generally, contemporary studies reveal that while the Soviet military establishment was indeed formidable, Soviet capabilities both military and domestic were nonetheless persistently overestimated by western

33 For an impression of the state of scholarship in 1991 see F. Fleron, E. P. Hoffman and R. F. Laird (eds), *Soviet Foreign Policy: Classic and Contemporary Issues*, New York, 1991; an overview of the Russian interpretation of Soviet history has been written by R. W. Davies, *Soviet History in the Yeltsin Era*, London, 1997. Examples of reinterpretations of Soviet foreign policy during the early Cold War which place emphasis on the ideological angle can be found in L. Gibianski, "The Soviet-Yugoslav Conflict and the Soviet Bloc" in F. Gori and S. Pons (eds), *The Soviet Union and Europe in the Cold War, 1945–1953*, London, 1996, pp. 222–45; D. T. MacDonald, "Communist Bloc Expansion in the Early Cold War: Challenging Realism, Refuting Revisionism", *International Security*, vol. 20 (winter 1995), pp. 152–88.
34 For example, S. N. Goncharow, J. W. Lewis and X. Litai, *Uncertain Partners: Stalin, Mao and the Korean War*, Stamford, 1993; M. N. Narinskii, "The Soviet Union and the Berlin Crisis, 1948–49", in F. Gori and S. Pons (ed.), *The Soviet Union and Europe in the Cold War*, pp. 57–75.
35 V. Zubok and K. Pleshakov, *Inside the Kremlin's Cold War: From Stalin to Khrushchev*, Cambridge, MA, 1996.

policy-makers. This points to either a failure of intelligence gathering or a disfunction in the process through which such material was processed and analysed. Consequently, the perceptions of the Soviet Union's strength and intent became essentially self-serving to western establishment interests. Similarly the scant work done on the Soviet economy indicates the extent to which the "political economy of illusions" distorted official estimations of Soviet economic performance suggesting that Soviet claims to modernization were far too readily accepted at or near face value by the West. As yet, Cold War history has not adequately explained these misperceptions.[36]

Just as there is no real consensus about the Cold War's origins, the question of how and why it ended remains similarly contentious. The events of the late 1980s were for the most part unforeseen and the Cold War's ending took students of international history, international relations and other branches of the social sciences by surprise. Several interpretations have emerged. The first argues that the timing indicates a triumph for the policies of the first Reagan administration which intensified the Cold War competition particularly in terms of military build-up and effectively overburdened the Soviet economic system, thereby forcing the Kremlin to admit that the Soviet economic system was so inherently flawed that it could no longer maintain even a pretense of keeping pace.[37] Acknowledging that the United States used its military power excessively at times, American military strength was perceived to have been fundamental to the containment of Soviet expansionism and in "forcing the Warsaw Pact to disintegrate and the Soviet Union to acknowledge the need for final reform". Accordingly, it followed that "containment" had been vindicated. This approach was given philosophical expression by Francis Fukyuama in an article published in 1989 which argued that the disintegration of communism represented "the end of history" in the Hegelian sense in so far as the search for political democracy had been finally realized and that "liberal democracy may constitute the end point of mankind's ideological evolution" and the "final form of human government" which could not be improved upon.[38] In short, liberal internationalism, democratic government and free markets had triumphed over state intervention and planning and coerced "progressivism" which had been the basis of communist structure. An alternative view argued that while contain-

36   O. Westad, *Diplomatic History*, vol. 21, no. 2 (1997), pp. 261–2.
37   S. Wells Jr., "Nuclear Weapons and European Security during the Cold War", M. Hogan (ed.), *The End of the Cold War: Its Meaning and Implications*, Cambridge, 1992, pp. 63–75.
38   F. Fukuyama, "The End of History?", *The National Interest* (summer 1989), pp. 3–18; Fukuyama, *The End of History and the Last Man*, Penguin, 1992, p. xi.

ment and the arms race had played an important part in hastening the Cold War's end, the primary catalysts were the domestic sources of the Soviet Union's demise and the voluntarism of its abdication from world power. While the Soviet system, as Kennan had observed forty years earlier, contained the seeds of its own destruction, it was Mikhail Gorbachev's attempts at reform which resulted in a revision of Soviet foreign policy objectives, in particular the abnegation of the Brezhnev Doctrine in April 1989. This released the People's Democracies from their obligations of obedience to the Soviet Communist Party and consequently brought the Cold War to a close.

Clearly, our knowledge of the Cold War as history rather than an ongoing process has to reopen the debate about its meaning and significance and this throws into relief research in the period between Stalin's death and Gorbachev's rise which is the background of historians' attempts to explain the Cold War's longevity. This process had been greatly enriched by the influence of new trends in the social sciences and experimentation with social science models of development in order to illuminate specific problems has become increasingly prevalent, particularly among scholars working with the post-1960s period for which there exists something of an historical vacuum in terms of secondary literature.[39] Similarly, there is some recognition of the instructive value inherent in the challenges to "traditional" historical writing raised by the new cultural history which, in placing emphasis on the social construction of memory postulates that historical memories are socially acquired and collective and are also constantly refashioned to suit present purposes. Michael Hogan, in a recent collection on Hiroshima has demonstrated how this approach can be used to stimulate fresh examination of old debates.[40] But even for those who have declined to incorporate postmodernist thinking in their research methodology, the preoccupations with domestic, social and economic issues have diluted the tendency of international history to focus on policy and policy-makers, while experiments with social science theories have blurred the distinctions between history as a discipline and political science as seems only appropriate given the interdependent nature of their relationship.[41] Nonetheless, the struggle continues to find a balance between oversim-

39   R. N. Lebow and J. G. Stein, *We All Lost the Cold War*, Princeton, 1994; B. Cummings, *The Origins of the Korean War*, vol. 2, *The Roaring of the Cataract 1947–50*, Princeton, 1990; G. A. Craig and A. L. George, *Force and Statecraft: Diplomatic Problems of Our time*, 3rd edn, Oxford, 1995.
40   An example of how this method can be employed to effect is that of M. Hogan (ed.), *Hiroshima in History and Memory*, Cambridge, 1996.
41   M. Hunt, "The Long Crisis in US Diplomatic History: Coming to Closure", *Diplomatic History*, vol. 16 (1992), pp. 115–40.

plification and historical reductionism on the one hand, and "mindless eclecticism" on the other.[42]

The study of the Cold War remains a thriving and vital area of historical endeavour, and access to new sources of documentary material as well as the provocations of the profession's sceptics provides every incentive for the reopening of old debates and the constant revision of interpretations of exactly what did happen and why. While Cold War history provides prime examples of the exploitation of history for contemporary political purposes, this is all the more reason why a decade after its passing, students should be encouraged to study the Cold War as history and demand access to the records which can shed light on the policy-making processes which gave this era its specific character. Only by these means can the many historical "myths" to which it gave rise be challenged, and absolute advances in knowledge achieved. In the words of one British historian, "if history is a constant re-writing and re-interpretation, it is also a cumulative development".[43] This process of accumulating knowledge about the Cold War and assessing the significance of new findings in the light of what is already known is still very much in its infancy.

42   See J. L. Gaddis, "New Conceptual approaches to the Study of American Foreign Relations: Interdisciplinary perspectives", *Diplomatic History*, vol. 14, no. 3 (1990), pp. 406–10. A contrasting view appears in B. Cummings, "Revising Postrevisionism: the Poverty of Theory in Diplomatic History", *Diplomatic History*, vol. 17, no. 4, pp. 539–69.
43   A. Marwick, *The Nature of History*, 3rd edn, London, 1989, p. 15.

Part I

Cold War Origins

Introduction to Part I

The debate about Cold War origins is one about perceptions and intentions. What were the driving forces of Soviet and Western foreign policies? To what extent was the Cold War a struggle rooted in an ideological clash? Or was it about a mere traditional contest for hegemony and the balance of power which had characterized earlier periods of colonialism? How far did economic or military needs determine political decisions and what impact, if any, did personalities have on the onset of the conflict? At the heart of this debate is the question of whether this struggle was in some sense "inevitable". Since the late 1940s determinists of various persuasions have sought to explain how the Cold War was preordained, and yet the very fact that there is still a "debate" about why the Cold War occurred implies that there could have been a different and possibly better outcome. Regardless of the emphasis scholars choose to adopt in explaining the onset of the Cold War, any reading of the papers of the protagonists in east and west reveals the extent to which all were seeking to get a clear understanding of the others intentions. Why then did this period of uncertainty crystallize into a Cold War in which each side conducted its planning on the basis that its worst assumptions about its adversary were correct?

Turning first to Soviet foreign policy, there are clear paradoxes which undoubtedly led to confused responses on the part of western governments. In 1945, the western powers understood that the Kremlin was preoccupied with post-war security and recognized that it had legitimate demands regarding its immediate neighbours and the former Axis powers. There was also an awareness that the Soviet Union required peace: the war had been immensely costly in human as well as material terms and, moreover, it had followed upon a period of intense and brutal industrial-ization. More ominously, however, the Soviet Union had re-emerged from its post-revolutionary isolationism to resume its role as a great power in Europe. The difference now was that only an enfeebled Britain remained to challenge the Soviet might on the continent, and the British govern-ment was far from sure that it was equal to that task.

While western diplomats pondered alternative explanations of Soviet actions, they focused increasingly on the nature of the Soviet system. The fact that it sought its legitimacy from pursuit of the teleological goals of the radical left in general and of world communism in particular was a persistent concern. It made it possible to interpret the actions of the Kremlin as determined by ideological needs to achieve that revolution which according to Marxist–Leninist dogma would alone ensure the secu-rity and the survival of the Soviet system. John Lewis Gaddis is firmly con-vinced of the need of the Soviet Union to expand. The poor economic foundations on which the Soviet system was based required this. More-over, Gaddis argues that the Soviet Union saw itself as the centre from which global socialism would emanate. Thus, according to Gaddis, the mainsprings from which Soviet foreign policy flowed was Moscow's belief that territorial acquisition rather than historically determined class struggle would achieve the goal of world revolution. Melvyn Leffler is in agreement that the "real imponderable was whether the Kremlin wanted more than just security". However, he is less convinced than Gaddis of the ideological motivations of Soviet foreign policy. Instead, he links the Soviet Union's immediate and justifiable peace conference demands, rooted in legitimate security interests in eastern Europe, with the pos-sibility that the Kremlin might have been motivated by traditional great power ambitions to maximize the opportunities for territorial expansion and control of resources.

Germany lay at the heart of the Cold War dispute because it was here that the Soviet vision of the post-war settlement came into conflict with that of the United States and its western allies. The United States, the mainland of which had no experience of direct assault let alone invasion, had justified the shedding of American blood with the argument that it was a war of liberating Europe from Hitler and a war which was fought for a post-war order to be built on the "four freedoms". The antithetical nature of this idealism with that of the Soviet Union explains in some measure the anxiety which pervaded the foreign ministries of the western powers as they sought to interpret the Kremlin's actions. After all, western liberal democracy was perceived as being vulnerably exposed to the rev-olutionary methods by which the Soviet leadership had acquired power and subsequently governed their state. American foreign policy, moreover, was also riven by internal contradictions. These existed between those who took a Europeanist and even universalist view and who sought for the United States the hegemony in Europe and the Pacific which flowed from its status as a superpower. Others argued for a prompt retreat, especially from Europe, and even a return to isolationism. Alongside this debate was the pressure for commercial expansion which the highly industrialized American economy appeared to demand as a result of its wartime prosperity. Similar pressure resulted from the symbolic American power of a formidable military establishment which alone in the world had custody of the atomic bomb.

Gaddis expresses a readiness to identify the expansionism inherent in American capitalism as a factor in explaining Cold War origins. Indeed he argues that the potential for Soviet–American conflict was established in 1918 with the defeat of European colonialism and the old order which created a vacuum which these two new ideologies could fill. The Second World War had forced the two societies to abandon their interwar isolationism and thereby brought them into a collision in Europe. However, he concludes that the United States was ultimately a reactive power and that the primary element in bringing about the Cold War was the personality of Josef Stalin. Paranoid, secretive and obsessive about the need for security, "it was Stalin's disposition", Gaddis writes, "to wage Cold Wars".

Leffler's interpretation, while sharing many of Gaddis's reservations about Soviet intentions, is rather more equivocal in its view of American foreign policy. Accepting the ambiguities of the Kremlin's actions and the sense of insecurity which pervaded the western European states in the aftermath of the war, Leffler argues that America perceived itself to be vulnerable and that the explanation for this is complex. Economic concerns, stemming from the recent experience of the Great Depression, anxieties about the possibility of military attack, albeit only a distant danger, and the possibility that a rival would develop comparable war-making capabilities were important aspects. These factors were compounded by a real fear of the politics of the left which sought to resist any restoration of the old order and evidence of the extension of Soviet power in Europe through consolidation of the Soviet system in the satellites.

By examining the sources of the perceptions and misperceptions on the part of the two most powerful states in the Cold War era, these two authors explore the connections between the ideological rivalry which gave this period its unique character. They also consider the underlying political, social and economic factors which both guided and constrained the policies of the two superpowers.

2

Economics, Power and National Security: Lessons of the Past

Melvyn P. Leffler

This brief discussion of fears and threats, which will be elaborated upon in the chapters to follow, illuminates the extent to which US officials defined their national security in terms of correlations of power. American power depended on the country's magnificently productive economic machine, its technological prowess, and its capacity to use strategic air power to inflict great damage on the economy of any enemy. Adversaries would be able to threaten US security only if they could undermine the American economy, attack it militarily, or develop comparable or superior industrial warmaking capabilities. These eventualities were most likely to occur if the Soviet Union gained direct or indirect control over the industrial infrastructure and skilled labor of advanced nations or if the Kremlin developed its own strategic air force, atomic bomb, and forward bases.

From the perspective of postwar Washington, a viable international economy was the surest way to defend the health of core industrial nations and to protect friendly governments from internal disorders and nationalist impulses that might impel them to gravitate eastward. American officials believed that they had to relieve the problems besetting the industrial democracies of Western Europe, integrate former enemies like Germany and Japan into the international economy, and insure that all these industrial core nations could find markets and raw materials in the underdeveloped periphery of the Third World. If they failed in these tasks, the correlation of power in the international system would be transformed. The Soviet Union would grow stronger, the United States weaker.[1]

This mode of thinking about national security was influenced by the rising popularity of geopolitics in the late 1930s and 1940s. In a world beleaguered by totalitarian regimes and ravished by global conflict, power became a central organizing concept for understanding behavior in the international system. Political philosophers, economists, and journalists as well as international relations experts and government officials believed that totalitarian states sought to monopolize internal power and to expand their external power. They did so by organizing their economies for warfighting purposes. Geopolitics sought to explain how nations mobilized their capabilities, acquired additional resources, and combined them with new forms of transport and weaponry for the pursuit of power politics. The Nazis popularized geopolitics. During the war the widespread appearance of maps in US newspapers and magazines helped to disseminate popular notions of geopolitics.[2]

Realistic statesmen had to be aware of correlations of power based on configurations of geopolitical influence and trade.[3] If an adversary gained control of Eurasia, Walter Lippmann reminded Americans in 1943, the United States would face a desperate situation.[4] At the time it was not clear to Lippmann and to most commentators whether Stalinist Russia would behave as an aggressive totalitarian power in the postwar world. But those who were certain of the Kremlin's malevolent intentions attributed to Stalin a fixed political ambition to dominate Eurasia. Soviet power, wrote James Burnham, flowed outward from the Eurasian heartland and lapped "the shores of the

1   Robert Gilpin, "The Politics of Transnational Economic Relations," *International Organization* 25 (Summer 1971): 398–419.
2   For geopolitical thinking, see Halford MacKinder, "The Round World and the Winning of the Peace," *Foreign Affairs* 21 (July 1943): 598–605; Hans W. Weigert, *Generals and Geographers: The Twilight of Geopolitics.* New York: Oxford University Press, 1955; For geopolitics in the popular media, see, e.g., "The Thousand Scientists Behind Hitler," *Reader's Digest* 38 (June 1941): 23–8; "The US and the World," *Fortune* 22 (Sep. 1940): 42–57; Robert Strausz-Hupe, "Geopolitics," *Fortune* 24 (Nov. 1941): 110–19; Joseph J. Thondike, Jr., "Geopolitics," *Life* (Dec. 1942): 106–12; see also the weekly sections "World Battlefronts: Strategy," *Time* (1941–2). For recent assessments, see Colin Gray, *The Geopolitics of Super Power.* Lexington: University of Kentucky Press, 1988; G. R. Sloan, *Geopolitics in United States Strategic Policy, 1890–1987.* New York: St. Martin's, 1988; David G. Haglund, ed. *The New Geopolitics of Minerals: Canada and International Resource Trade.* Vancouver: University of British Columbia Press, 1989, 3–34. For totalitarianism, see Thomas F. Lifka, *The Concept of "Totalitarianism" and American Foreign Policy 1933–1949.* New York: Garland, 1988.
3   MacKinder, "Round World and the Winning of the Peace."
4   Walter Lippmann, *United States Foreign Policy: Shield of the Republic.* Boston, Mass.: Little, Brown, 1943; Ronald Steel, *Walter Lippmann and the American Century.* Boston, Mass.: Little, Brown, 1980.

Atlantic, the Yellow and China Seas, the Mediterranean, and the Persian Gulf."[5]

Most illustrative of American thinking about national security at the end of the war was a Brookings Institution study in 1945 authored by a number of the nation's most prominent experts on international relations: Frederick S. Dunn, Edward M. Earle, William T. R. Fox, Grayson L. Kirk, David N. Rowe, Harold Sprout, and Arnold Wolfers. They concluded that it was essential to prevent any one power or coalition of powers from gaining control of Eurasia. The United States would not be able to withstand attack from an adversary who had subdued the whole of Europe or Eurasia. Like Lippmann, they aspired for good relations with Soviet Russia. Still, they insisted that the United States must not rely on assumptions about the Kremlin's good intentions. "In all the world only Soviet Russia and the ex-enemy powers are capable of forming nuclei around which an anti-American coalition could form to threaten the security of the United States." The indefinite westward movement of the Soviet Union, they added, must not be permitted "whether it occurs by formal annexation, political coup, or progressive subversion."[6]

Military planners got hold of this study, deeming it so important that they classified it as an official Joint Chiefs of Staff (JCS) document.[7] The ideas expressed in it accurately reflected US strategic thinking in the early postwar years. So much excellent writing has been focused on the development of American air power that it is often overlooked that military officials and their civilian superiors in the Pentagon operated from assumptions that attributed primacy to geopolitical configurations of power and to warmaking capabilities.[8] Military planners assumed that if war erupted it would be protracted; the side that had the superior industrial and technological capabilities would prevail. In peacetime, therefore, it was essential to thwart the Kremlin from gaining indirect control of critical industrial infrastructure, skilled labor, raw materials, and forward bases. The United States had to retain allies across the oceans, particularly in England, France, Germany, and Japan. "The potential military strength of the Old World [Europe, Asia, and Africa]," argued the JCS, "in terms of manpower and in terms of

5   James Burnham, "Lenin's Heir." Partisan Review 12 (Winter 1945): 66–7; Richard H. Pells, The Liberal Mind in a Conservative Age: American Intellectuals in the 1940's and 1950's. New York: Harper & Row, 1985, 76–83.
6   "A Security Policy for Postwar America," NHC, SPD, series 14, box 194: A1–2.
7   Fred Kaplan, The Wizards of Armageddon. New York: Simon & Schuster, 1983, 22.
8   For excellent books on air power, see, e.g., Michael S. Sherry, The Rise of American Air Power: The Creation of Armageddon. New Haven, Conn.: Yale University Press, 1987; Ronald Schaffer, Wings of Judgment: American Bombing in World War II. New York: Oxford University Press, 1985.

war-making capacity is enormously greater than that of [the Western Hemisphere]."[9]

These attitudes were especially pervasive in the Army. While writers usually dwell on the rivalries between the Air Force and the Navy when they seek to elucidate the threads of America's postwar defense posture, the Army probably had greater importance in shaping overall national security strategy in the early postwar years. The Army, after all, had occupational responsibility in Germany and Japan as well as Austria and Korea. Army officers in the Civil Affairs Division and the Operations Division (later Plans and Operations) and their civilian superiors like Howard C. Petersen and William H. Draper as well as proconsuls abroad like Generals Lucius Du Bignon Clay and Douglas MacArthur realized that their policies would shape overall correlations of power in the international system. They recognized, for example, that the Ruhr/Rhine industrial complex must not be allowed to support the military potential of a future adversary whether it be Germany or Russia or a combination of the two. Instead the region's resources had to be used to expedite recovery in Western Europe, undermine the appeal of local Communists, and bar the Kremlin from gaining preponderance in Europe.[10]

Subsequently, the most important National Security Council (NSC) papers of the Truman administration incorporated a geostrategic vision. National security was interpreted in terms of correlations of power. Power was defined in terms of the control of resources, industrial infrastructure, and overseas bases. In the autumn of 1948, NSC 20/4 became the first comprehensive strategy study to be adopted as national policy. "Soviet domination of the potential power of Eurasia," it emphasized, "whether achieved by armed aggression or by political and subversive means, would be strategically and politically unacceptable to the United States."[11]

The Central Intelligence Agency (CIA), formally established in 1947, used the same criteria when it identified threats and assessed vital interests. According to the CIA, nations could not become powerful if

---

9   JCS 1769/1, "United States Assistance to Other Countries from the Standpoint of National Security," 29 Apr. 1947, RG 165, ABC 400.336 (20 March 1947), sec. 1-A. For overall strategic thinking, see the PINCHER war plan studies, RG 218, CCS 381 USSR (3-2-46); see also some of the strategic studies of different countries and regions, RG 218, CCS 092 USSR (3-27-45).

10   See, e.g., Charles C. Bonesteel, "Some General Security Implications of the German Settlement" [ND], RG 107, SecWar, Robert P. Patterson Papers, Safe File, box 1; OPD and CAD, "Analysis of Certain Political Problems Confronting Military Occupation Authorities in Germany," 10 Apr. 1946, ibid., OASW, Howard C. Petersen Papers, Classified, 091 Germany; Patterson to Byrnes, 10 June 1946, *FRUS, 1946*, 2: 486–8.

11   *FRUS, 1948*, 1: 667.

they did not have adequate supplies of mechanical energy (coal, water power, or petroleum), raw materials for basic industries, skilled technicians, experienced managers, and a sophisticated social structure accustomed to producing surpluses beyond consumption for military purposes. The task of American policymakers, the CIA advised, was to keep "the still widely dispersed power resources of Europe and Asia from being drawn together into a single Soviet power structure with a uniformly communist social organization." Winning the loyalties of peoples on the periphery was part of a "sociological" security dilemma whose solution would thwart Communist inroads and Soviet efforts to gain domination over the "Eurasian littoral."[12]

The highest civilian officials in the United States shared this geopolitical perspective. They defined security in terms of correlations of power. When Dean Acheson became secretary of state in 1949, he used this framework of analysis to tackle the most important issues he encountered, including those decisions relating to the atomic stockpile and the hydrogen bomb. "The loss of Western Europe," he said, "or of important parts of Asia or the Middle East would be a transfer of potential from West to East, which, depending on the area, might have the gravest consequences in the long run."[13] But perhaps no one articulated these views better than did President Harry S. Truman. "Our own national security," he emphasized in his annual message to Congress in January 1951, "is deeply involved with that of the other free nations. . . . If Western Europe were to fall to Soviet Russia it would double the Soviet supply of coal and triple the Soviet supply of steel. If the free nations of Asia and Africa should fall to Soviet Russia, we would lose the sources of many of our most vital raw materials, including uranium, which is the basis of our atomic power. And Soviet command of the manpower of the free nations of Europe and Asia would confront us with military forces which we could never hope to equal."[14]

National security, however, meant more than defending territory. Truman, Acheson, and their advisers repeatedly emphasized that the Soviet Union did not have to attack the United States to undermine its security. "If Communism is allowed to absorb the free nations," said the president, "then we would be isolated from our sources of supply and detached from our friends. Then we would have to take defense measures which might really bankrupt our economy, and change our

12   CIA, "Review of the World Situation," 19 Jan. 1949, HSTP, PSF, box 250.
13   Memo by Acheson, 20 Dec. 1949, FRUS, 1949, 1: 615–16; see also, e.g., Acheson to Franks, 24 Dec. 1949, ibid., 7: 927; Acheson Testimony, 16 Feb. 1951, Senate, Armed Services and Foreign Relations, Assignment of Ground Forces, p. 81.
14   PPP:HST (1951), 8.

way of life so that we couldn't recognize it as American any longer." In other words, Soviet/Communist domination of the preponderant resources of Eurasia would force the United States to alter its political and economic system. The US government would have to restructure the nation's domestic economy, regiment its foreign trade, and monitor its domestic foes. "It would require," stressed Truman, "a stringent and comprehensive system of allocation and rationing in order to husband our smaller resources. It would require us to become a garrison state, and to impose upon ourselves a system of centralized regimentation unlike anything we have ever known."[15]

These possibilities were anathema to Truman and his advisers. Defending the nation's core values, its organizing ideology, and its free political and economic institutions was vital to national security.[16] The war resurrected faith in the capacity of the capitalist system to serve the welfare of the American people. For most Americans the record of total-itarian barbarity during the 1930s and 1940s discredited statist formulations of the good society. Instead of redistribution, Truman's supporters preferred productivity and abundance. Instead of planning, controls, and regulations, they preferred fiscal and monetary management. Instead of restructuring power in a capitalist society, they preferred to safeguard personal freedom and to focus attention on civil rights.[17] The good society was one that circumscribed the role of government in the nation's political economy; the good society was one that attributed primacy to the protection of civil liberties and individual rights. Yet that good society would be difficult to sustain either in a world divided by trade blocs or, worse yet, in a world dominated by the Kremlin's power.

These considerations inspired US officials to configure an external environment compatible with their domestic vision of a good society. They were driven less by a desire to help others than by an ideological conviction that their own political economy of freedom would be jeop-

15 *PPP:HST* (1952–3), 194–5, 189.
16 Barry Buzan, *People, States and Fear: The National Security Problem in International Relations*. Sussex, Eng.: Wheatsheaf, 1983, 44–53.
17 Otis L. Graham Jr., *Toward a Planned Society: From Roosevelt to Nixon*. New York: Oxford University Press, 1976, 91–114; Peter J. Katzenstein, ed., *Between Power and Plenty: Foreign Economic Policies of Advanced Industrial States*. Madison: University of Wisconsin Press, 1978, 23–5; Theodore Rosenof, "Freedom, Planning and Totalitarianism: The Reception of F. A. Hayek's *Road to Serfdom.*" *Canadian Review of American Studies* 5 (Fall 1974): 149–65; Alan Brinkley, "The New Deal and the Idea of the State." In *The Rise and Fall of the New Deal Order*. Ed. Steve Fraser and Gary Gerstle. Princeton, N.J.: Princeton University Press, 1989; Robert M. Collins, *The Business Response to Keynes, 1929–1964*. New York: Columbia University Press, 1981, 137–41, 204–9; Pells, *Liberal Mind in a Conservative Age*, 52–182; Alonzo Hamby, *Beyond the New Deal: Harry S. Truman and American Liberalism*. New York: Columbia University Press, 1973.

ardized if a totalitarian foe became too powerful. If additional critical resources and industrial infrastructure fell within the grasp of the Kremlin or were subject to autarkic practices, the United States would have to protect itself by increasing military spending or regimenting its domestic economy. And if such contingencies materialized, domestic freedoms would be imperiled because there was no way to separate the economic from the political realms of governmental activity.[18] Time and again, Acheson reiterated that his aim was "to foster an environment in which our national life and individual freedom can survive and prosper."[19]

Economic interests often reinforced geostrategic imperatives and ideological predilections. During the war there was a vast growth in the overall influence of large corporations and high-technology companies in the US economy. International bankers, corporate chief executives, and Wall Street and Washington lawyers like Robert Lovett, John J. McCloy, Ferdinand Eberstadt, Charles E. Wilson, Paul H. Nitze, James Forrestal, W. Averell Harriman, and Acheson assumed important positions in the State, War, Navy, and other departments. They were particularly aware of the relationships between foreign markets, American exports, and business profitability.[20] Their concerns about correlations of power, however, far exceeded their apprehensions about the well-being of the American economy. The latter surprised everyone by its durability and vigor. Tough choices between economic and strategic goals, however, rarely proved necessary. Because they defined power in terms of control over or access to resources, US officials could usually pursue economic and strategic objectives in tandem.[21]

18   Acheson. "Why a Loan to England?" 25 Jan. 1946, Acheson Papers (Yale University), series 1, box 46. The relationship between domestic and international economic freedom was a frequent theme of Acheson's. See, e.g., Testimony, 13 March 1946, Senate, Banking and Currency, *Anglo-American Financial Agreement*, 313–14; see also Statement by Clayton, 26 May 1947, *DSB* 16 (6 Apr. 1947): 628–9; Lloyd C. Gardner, *Architects of Illusion: Men and Ideas in American Foreign Policy, 1941–1949*. Chicago, Ill.: Quadrangle, 1970, 113–38, 202–31.
19   Dean G. Acheson, *This Vast External Realm*. New York: Norton, 1973, 19; Acheson Testimony, 14 Jan. 1952, Senate, Foreign Relations, *Executive Sessions*, 4: 2–3.
20   Allan M. Winkler, *Home Front U.S.A.: America During World War II*. Arlington Heights, Ill.: Harland Davidson, 1986, 10–23; Richard Polenberg, *War and Society: The United States, 1941–1945*. Philadelphia, Pa.: Lippincott, 1972, 236–7; Geoffrey Perrett, *Days of Sadness, Years of Triumph: The American People, 1939–1945*. Baltimore, Md.: Penguin, 1973, 299–309; Gabriel Kolko, *The Roots of American Foreign Policy*. Boston, Mass.: Beacon, 1969, 3–26; Thomas Ferguson, "From Normalcy to New Deal: Industrial Structure, Party Competition, and American Public Policy in the Great Depression." *International Organization* 38 (Winter 1984): 41–95.
21   See, e.g., President's Committee on Foreign Aid, *European Recovery*, esp. 19–22; Dept. of the Interior, *National Resources and Foreign Aid*, iii, 3.

Organizational imperatives, like economic interests, often buttressed geostrategic and ideological pressures but were not the mainspring behind national security policies. Service rivalries were intense. The Air Force and Navy had much to gain by exaggerating foreign threats and squeezing additional military expenditures out of an administration that initially believed it could pursue its national security objectives without engaging in extravagant defense spending.[22] But the basic outlook of military officers resembled that of civilians in the Pentagon and at Foggy Bottom. Controlling industrial infrastructure, natural resources, and skilled labor or denying them to a prospective adversary were keys to power relationships. So were the possession of strategic air power, atomic bombs, and overseas bases that could be used to strike the adversary's mobilization base or to retard his efforts to seize additional resources. Military officers, of course, wanted to modernize their equipment, augment their forces-in-being, and balance American commitments and military capabilities.[23] Yet they often defined interests more narrowly than did civilians and were usually less inclined to use force on the periphery than were their colleagues at the State Department. Indeed, once the Soviets acquired their own atomic capabilities and showed a greater willingness to take risks, State Department officials like Acheson and Nitze became far more vociferous advocates of military expenditures and of intervention in Third World areas than were military officers.[24]

Partisan politics hardened attitudes toward the Soviet Union, solidified anti-Communist sentiment, and influenced particular policies but did not shape the basic contours of national security thinking. During the war public attitudes toward the Soviet Union had become much more friendly. But even while Soviet armies were fighting the bulk of Nazi forces, even while millions of Soviet soldiers were dying on battlefields, and even while Roosevelt, Stalin, and Churchill were meeting at summit conferences and declaring their loyalty to one another, almost a third of all Americans still distrusted the Soviet Union. Most polls showed that fewer than half of all Americans expected cooperation to

22 Daniel Yergin, *Shattered Peace: The Origins of the Cold War and the National Security State.* Boston, Mass.: Houghton Mifflin, 1977, 337–65; Warner R. Schilling, Paul Y. Hammond, and Glenn H. Snyder. *Strategy, Politics, and Defense Budgets.* New York: Columbia University Press, 1962, 5–266.
23 See, e.g., NSC 35, "Existing International Commitments Involving the Possible Use of Armed Forces," 17 Nov. 1948, *FRUS, 1948,* 1: 656–62; JCS 800/14, Memo for the SecDef, 8 Nov. 1948, RG 218, CCS 370 (8-19-45), sec. 11.
24 These themes will become clear in the chapters that follow, but it might be mentioned here that DOS officials were the major proponents of the huge military buildup called for in NSC 68. See J. L. Gaddis, *Strategies of Containment: A Critical Appraisal of American National Security Policy.* New York: Oxford University Press, 1982, 92–5.

persist into the postwar period. In other words, the American people retained a strong residue of animosity and suspicion toward the Bolshevik motherland.[25]

Public attitudes may have been malleable, but after Roosevelt's death policymakers did little to cultivate friendly feelings among the American people toward the Soviet Union.[26] During 1945 and 1946 Truman and his advisers clearly feared that Republicans could exploit anti-Communism for their political advantage.[27] Democrats, however, distrusted the Soviets and the Communists as much as did their political opponents. Liberal anticommunism was as fierce as the conservative variety, although the former differentiated a little more carefully between Communists and other leftists.[28]

What distinguished the Democratic administration was its ability to translate its suspicions of the Soviet Union into action when circumstances demanded. Although Truman's style of leadership was to grant wide decisionmaking authority to his foreign policy advisers, the president and his aides all shared the conviction that, even while the United States faced grave dangers, it also possessed unprecedented strength. If it used that strength wisely to prevent a potential adversary from gaining leverage over additional power centers, the nation's preeminence would remain unchallenged. Republicans might argue that countries like China were as important as Western Europe, but they never posed an alternative vision of national security interests. So long as the president preached indiscriminate anti-Communism, he was politically vulnerable whenever and wherever the Communists seized or won power. Republican criticisms, in turn, reinforced the administration's determination to avoid future losses.[29]

At the end of the war, US officials did not think that they were engaged in a zero-sum game of power politics with the Soviet Union. They

25   Gary J. Buckley, "American Public Opinion and the Origins of the Cold War: A Speculative Reassessment." *Mid-America* 60 (Jan. 1978): 35–42; Lifka, *Totalitarianism*, 91–286.
26   Ralph Levering, *American Opinion and the Russian Alliance, 1939–1945*. Chapel Hill: University of North Carolina Press, 1976, 206–9; Thomas G. Paterson, *On Every Front: The Making of the Cold War*. New York: Norton, 1979, 113–37; Yonosuke Nagai and Akira Iriye, eds., *The Origins of the Cold War in Asia*. New York: Columbia University Press, 1977, 43–65.
27   J. L. Gaddis, *The United States and the Origins of the Cold War, 1941–1947*. New York: Columbia University Press, 1972.
28   Arthur Schlesinger, Jr., "The US Communist Party," *Life* (29 July 1946): 84–96; Steven Gillon, *Politics and Vision: The ADA and American Liberalism*. New York: Oxford University Press, 1987, 12; Pells, *Liberal Mind in a Conservative Age*, 52–116.
29   David R. Kepley, *The Collapse of the Middle Way: Senate Republicans and the Bipartisan Foreign Policy, 1948–52*. New York: Greenwood, 1988; Gary Reichard, *Politics as Usual: The Age of Truman and Eisenhower*. Arlington Heights, Ill.: Harland Davidson, 1988.

wanted to cooperate with the Kremlin. But they harbored a distrust sufficiently profound to require terms of cooperation compatible with vital American interests. Truman said it pointedly when he emphasized that the United States had to have its way 85 percent of the time. Senator Arthur H. Vandenberg, the Republican spokesman on foreign policy, was a little more categorical: "I think our two antipathetical systems can dwell in the world together – but only on a basis which establishes the fact that we mean what we say when we say it."[30]

Within a year, events transformed these suspicious attitudes into what became known as the containment policy. Did containment mean preponderance? Initially it meant preponderance only in a defensive sense: Soviet-directed world communism had to be thwarted lest the Kremlin gain control over the preponderant resources of Eurasia and seek to dominate the world.[31] At the end of the war, US officials certainly had no desire to retain substantial military forces overseas, to incur strategic commitments, or to supplant British, French, and Dutch political influence in large parts of the Third World (except perhaps in some oil-producing countries like Saudi Arabia).[32]

Policymakers in Washington preferred an economic approach. They sought to create an open world economy conducive to the free movement of goods, capital, and technology. They wanted to break down England's sterling bloc, create convertible currencies, and establish the conditions for nondiscriminatory trade. During 1994 and 1945, Roosevelt, Truman, and their advisers placed a great deal of stress on creating the International Monetary Fund and the World Bank. These instruments would foster world peace and international prosperity.[33]

30   Harry S. Truman, *Memoirs: 1945, Year of Decisions*. New York: Signet, 1955, 87; Arthur H. Vandenberg, *Private Papers of Senator Vandenberg*. Ed. Arthur H. Vandenberg, Jr. Boston, Mass.: Houghton Mifflin, 1952, 209.
31   This view is most clearly illustrated in the report written by Clark Clifford and George Elsey during the summer of 1946. See Arthur Krock, *Memoirs: Sixty Years on the Firing Line*. New York: Funk & Wagnalls, 1968, 422–82.
32   For an illuminating view of American attitudes toward the restoration of European influence in the Third World, see "Policy Paper Prepared in the Department of State," 22 June 1945. *FRUS, 1945*, 6: 556–80. Fraser Harbutt captures (and overstates) the American reluctance to intervene in European political-military affairs; see Fraser Harbutt, *The Iron Curtain: Churchill, America and the Origins of the Cold War*. New York: Oxford University Press, 1986; Hugh Thomas, *Armed Truce: The Beginnings of the Cold War, 1945–6*. New York: Atheneum, 1987, 572–3.
33   Richard N. Gardner, *Sterling-Dollar Diplomacy in Current Perspective: The Origins and Prospects of Our International Economic Order*. New York: Columbia University Press, 1980; Alfred E. Eckes Jr., *The Search for Solvency: Bretton Woods and the International Monetary System, 1941–1947*. Austin: University of Texas Press, 1975; Thomas G. Paterson, *Meeting the Communist Threat: America's Cold War History*. New York: Oxford University Press, 1988, 18–34; Gabriel Kolko, *Politics of War: The World and United States Foreign Policy 1943–1945*. New York: Random House, 1968, 242–66, 484–503.

US officials were ready to assume Britain's former role as financial hegemon. They recognized the connections between the economic and political spheres. If they stymied the diffusion of bilateral and autarkic practices, they would prevent artificial acquisitions of economic resources that could be used to build up military strength. Loans also might be used to extract political as well as economic concessions. In a world free of barriers to the movement of goods and capital, more-over, the private sector could serve as an instrument, albeit not a docile one, of state policy. Oil corporations, for example, while pursuing their own interests and generating growth in host countries, might help ensure American control over the most important raw material. If the United States managed an open world economy, it could be a more peaceful place and everyone would benefit. But the position of prepon-derance that the United States inherited as a result of the war would remain intact.[34]

Truman and his advisers were not naive. "We must face the fact," the president told Congress in one of his first postwar addresses, "that peace must be built upon power, as well as upon good will and good deeds." Truman wanted to inaugurate universal military training, establish an overseas base system, and maintain a monopoly over atomic weapons. "Until we are sure that our peace machinery is functioning adequately, we must relentlessly preserve our superiority on land and sea and in the air."[35] Strategic air power, financial hegemony, and economic predomi-nance were thought sufficient to thwart any prospective Soviet drive for preponderance.

Truman and his advisers miscalculated. Britain was weaker than they thought; European financial problems more intractable; German and Japanese economic woes more deep-seated; revolutionary nation-alism more virulent; Soviet actions more ominous; and American demobilization more rapid. In 1947 and 1948 US officials responded with new policies focusing on massive economic assistance and limited military aid. With equal effectiveness and more sophistication, the Truman administration used the private sector to fashion new sets of corporatist arrangements in Europe, arrangements that endeavored to mitigate social conflict, forestall Communist political victories, and foster economic growth. The overall purpose was to revive production in Western Europe, western Germany, and Japan and to integrate these

34   Katzenstein, *Between Power and Plenty*, 51–78; Gilpin, "Politics of Transnational Eco-nomic Relations"; Thomas G. Paterson, "The Abortive American Loan to Russia, and the Origins of the Cold War." *Journal of American History* 56 (June 1969): 70–92. For the inter-mingling of political and financial considerations in American loan-making, see also *FRUS, 1946* 1: 1410–36.
35   *PPP:HST* (1945), 411; see also 431–8, 546–60.

areas into an American-led orbit before they could gravitate to the East.[36]

US policymakers and intelligence analysts understood that the Kremlin might react negatively and take countermeasures. They believed, however, that Russian retaliatory measures would be limited. Soviet leaders would not go to war with the United States. The forces-in-being of the United States might be small but America's strategic superiority, atomic monopoly, and warmaking capabilities supported the risk-taking that inhered in the reconstruction of the industrial core of Eurasia. "As long as we can outproduce the world, can control the sea and can strike inland with the atomic bomb," James Forrestal noted in his diary in 1947, "we can assume certain risks otherwise unacceptable."[37]

By reviving the German and Japanese economies, the United States was restoring their latent military capabilities. America's former allies in World War II looked with great trepidation on the revitalization of their former enemies. There were no assurances that Germany and Japan would become peaceful democracies; past history suggested the contrary. Moreover, the specter of independent German and Japanese power might provoke the Kremlin to take preemptive military action. To allay Allied apprehensions about these different contingencies, the United States was willing to offer military guarantees. By joining alliances first in the Atlantic and then in the Pacific, and by endorsing French plans for a European coal and steel community and a European defense community, the Truman administration tried to mold multilateral political agreements and supranational institutions for the purpose of luring industrial core areas into an American-led community. Given Britain's determination to remain independent of a federated Europe, the North Atlantic Treaty Organization (NATO) served as a particularly useful mechanism to integrate Western Europe and England into an orbit amenable to American leadership. Neither an integrated Europe nor a united Germany nor an independent Japan must be permitted to memerge as a third force or a neutral bloc. Neutralism, said Acheson, "is a shortcut to suicide."[38]

36 Michael J. Hogan, *The Marshall Plan: America, Britain, and the Reconstruction of Western Europe, 1947–1952*. New York: Cambridge University Press, 1987; Howard B. Schonberger, "The Cold War and the American Empire in Asia." *Radical History Review* 33 (1985): 139–54.
37 James Forrestal, *The Forrestal Diaries*. Ed. Walter Millis. New York: Viking, 1951, 350–1; see also Dean G. Acheson, *Power and Diplomacy*. Cambridge, Mass.: Harvard University Press, 1959, 39, 86; PPS 33, "Factors Affecting the Nature of the US Defense Arrangements in the Light of Soviet Policies," 23 June 1948, in *PPS Papers*, 2: 281–92.
38 Acheson Testimony, 16 Feb. 1951, Senate, Armed Services and Foreign Relations, *Assignment of Ground Forces*, 78; see also Acheson, *Power and Diplomacy*, 83–5. For Acheson's views

In order to align Western Europe, West Germany, and Japan permanently with the United States, American officials were convinced that they had to narrow the dollar gap and help their industrial allies sell their goods, earn dollars, and purchase foodstuffs and raw materials in the underdeveloped periphery.[39] Linking core and periphery in the face of revolutionary nationalism was a daunting task. But American officials thought it could be managed. Eschewing responsibilities for the United States in the Third World, they tried to convince the British, French, and Dutch to co-opt nationalist movements by acknowledging the rights of colonial peoples to determine their own future and to establish their own governments. Policymakers in Washington insisted that decolonization could occur without endangering Western interests. Strategic requirements could be accommodated; bases obtained; investments and trade safeguarded. For American officials their own policies toward the Philippines set the model. Mutually beneficial relationships could be established by working with entrenched elites and even with emerging military modernizers. Metropolitan governments simply had to be wise enough to cede the formal levers of power and to make symbolic gestures before Communists wrapped themselves in the mantle of nationalism and monopolized it.[40]

As circumstances changed and threats mounted, US tactics shifted but the overall goal remained the same. The periphery had to be held or the Eurasian industrial core would be weakened. To simplify, Japan needed Southeast Asia; Western Europe needed the Middle East; and the American rearmament effort required raw materials from throughout the Third World. The Truman administration first offered limited amounts of technical and economic assistance and then larger and larger amounts of military aid. In Indochina, it came to finance a substantial part of the French struggle against Ho Chi Minh's Communist Viet Minh. But as French efforts in Indochina faltered and British

regarding Japan, see Acheson to Franks, 24 Dec. 1949, *FRUS, 1949*, 7: 928. For the use of NATO as an integrative mechanism, see, e.g., U.S. Delegation Minutes, 10 Sep. 1951, *FRUS, 1951*, 3: 1230. For the importance of integrating Germany with the West, see Acheson to John McCloy, 12 Apr. 1952, *FRUS, 1952–54*, 7: 206. For Harriman's antipathy to the third force idea, see Harriman Testimony, 9 Feb. 1949, House of Representatives, International Relations, *Executive Session Hearings*, 24–5.

39   See, e.g., Robert E. Wood, *From Marshall Plan to Debt Crisis: Foreign Aid and Development Choices in the World Economy*. Berkeley: University of California Press, 1986, 26–67; Michael Schaller, *The American Occupation of Japan: The Origins of the Cold War in Asia*. New York: Oxford University Press, 1985, 141–63.

40   See, e.g., Robert J. McMahon, *Colonialism and Cold War: The United States and the Struggle for Indonesian Independence, 1945–1949*. Ithaca, N.Y.: Cornell University Press, 1981. For the importance of the Philippines as a model, see Dean Rusk to H. Freeman Matthews, 31 Jan. 1951, *FRUS, 1951*, 6: 24–5. For the need to establish linkages with elites, see PPS, "The Position of the US with Respect to the General Area of the Eastern Mediterranean and the Middle East," 27 Dec. 1951, ibid., 5: 258–63.

policies in Iran and Egypt foundered, Truman, Acheson, and their advisers thought the United States should prepare mobile forces for intervention in Third World areas.[41]

The Korean War accelerated changes in American tactics. When Chinese troops crossed the Yalu River in the fall of 1950, US policy-makers did not retaliate for fear they might precipitate an escalatory cycle they could not control. The lesson was clear. The United States must be able to check enemy counteraction and, if deterrence failed, dominate the escalatory process. Hurriedly, the Truman administration proceeded to enlarge the atomic stockpile, develop the hydrogen bomb, rearm Germany, and strengthen NATO's conventional forces. Over-whelming strategic superiority was required to maintain the atomic umbrella under which the United States could support its friends, utilize covert actions, deploy its own mobile forces, and conduct conventional bombing raids in limited war situations. As the atomic monopoly had provided the psychological backdrop for the implementation of the Marshall Plan and the creation of the Federal Republic of Germany, strategic superiority still remained essential for inspiring American risk-taking on the periphery, deterring the adversary's countermeasures, and preserving Allied support and solidarity.[42]

All these tactics aimed to achieve a hierarchy of objectives: "strength at the center; strength at the periphery; the retraction of Soviet power and a change in the Soviet system." The United States, American offi-cials believed, should not risk war in order to break up the Soviet empire, or to drive a wedge between the Kremlin and its satellites, or to over-throw incumbent Communist regimes. But if the United States was suc-cessful at creating strength at the center and binding core and periphery, the West's attraction would be magnetic. The satellites would be pulled westward; German unification might occur on American terms; the Communist bloc could unravel. By containing Communist gains and Soviet expansion, American officials hoped to perpetuate American preponderance. The "United States and the Soviet Union," said Acheson's Policy Planning Staff, "are engaged in a struggle for prepon-derant power. . . . [T]o seek less than preponderant power would be to opt for defeat. Preponderant power must be the object of U.S. policy."[43]

41   See, e.g., US Minutes, 28 May 1952, *FRUS, 1952–54*, 13: 161–6; Summary of NSC Discussion, 25 Sep. 1952, ibid., 2: 136–8; Memo by Acheson, 24 Sep. 1952, ibid., 2: 140.
42   Memo, DOS-JCS Mtg., 16 Jan. 1952, *FRUS, 1952–54*, 12: 22–34; Memo by Nitze, 12 May 1952, ibid., 12: 89–91; Acheson, *Power and Diplomacy*, 50–4, 64–6, 80–1.
43   For the quotations, see Paper Drafted by the PPS, "Basic Issues Raised by Draft NSC 'Reap-praisal of U.S. Objectives and Strategy for National Security,'" ND, *FRUS, 1952–54*, 2: 64–5; see also NSC 68/1 and 68/2, "United States Objectives and Programs for the Cold War," 21 and 30 Sep. 1950, RG 273, NSC. For Germany, see Acheson to McCloy, 12 Apr. 1952, *FRUS, 1952–54*, 7: 206. For breaking up the Soviet bloc, see also PPS, "Future Policy Toward the USSR," 6 Jan. 1952, HSTP, PSF, box 116.

Preponderance did not mean domination. It meant creating a world environment hospitable to US interests and values; it meant developing the capabilities to overcome threats and challenges; it meant mobilizing the strength to reduce Soviet influence on its own periphery; it meant undermining the appeal of communism; it meant fashioning the institutional techniques and mechanisms to manage the free world; and it meant establishing a configuration of power and a military posture so that if war erupted, the United States would prevail. If adversaries saw the handwriting on the wall, they would defer to American wishes. The United States, said Paul Nitze in mid-1952, could "gain preponderant power."[44]

Images of the past cast their influence on American perceptions, tactics, and goals. Most of the civilians who were to make America's cold war policies – Acheson, Forrestal, Lovett, Draper, Harriman, McCloy, and Robert P. Patterson – were born in the 1880s and 1890s. As young men they watched Woodrow Wilson try to remake the world at Versailles and suffer repudiation at home. Many of them enjoyed lucrative careers in investment banking and law during the interwar years. From their comfortable affluence they observed the domestic travail of the Depression and the onslaught of Nazi aggression and Japanese militarism. The image of appeasement at Munich seared itself in their memories. In 1940 and 1941 they gravitated from the private sector to public service.[45]

When World War II approached its final stages, their intent was not to lose the peace as Wilson had done. They shared many Wilsonian goals. They regarded the United Nations as a symbol of great importance. Men like Acheson did not think that it would preserve the peace, but they did believe that membership in the United Nations would signal the end of the political isolation of the interwar years.[46] In 1919 the strife among the victorious allies had underscored their selfishness, triggered American revulsion, and culminated in the defeat of the

44 Nitze to Matthews, 14 July 1952, FRUS, 1952–54, 2: 58–9. Although the emphasis on military expenditures greatly increased after the acceptance of NSC 68 and the outbreak of the Korean War, there was a basic continuity of goals. This continuity was explicitly acknowledged in NSC papers. See NSC 135, "Reappraisal of United States Objectives and Strategy for National Security" [Summer 1952], ibid., 2: 144.
45 For illustrative background, see Walter Isaacson and Evan Thomas, The Wise Men: Six Friends and the World They Made. New York: Simon & Schuster, 1986. Isaacson and Thomas deal with Acheson, Harriman, McCloy, and Lovett as well as Kennan and Charles Bohlen. What they have to say about the backgrounds of the first four men is reflective of the career patterns of many other individuals who assumed important positions in the government during the war years and then rose to even greater prominence and power.
46 David S. McLellan, Dean Acheson: The State Department Years. New York: Dodd, Mead, 1976, 50–1.

League of Nations. Hence Truman, Roosevelt, and their advisers wished to avoid a premature rift with the Soviet Union in the spring of 1945. But they hoped that ratification of the UN charter would establish a pattern of international collaboration that could then be used to contain the Soviet Union should the Kremlin prove to be a destructive force in the postwar world.[47]

To avert isolationism, the Democrats had learned that bipartisanship was essential. Wilson had underestimated his political foes and had treated Congress contemptuously. His heirs were determined to see that these errors did not recur. Republicans and senators would be consulted; they would be asked to attend the key conferences; they would have the chance to contribute to agreements and treaties.[48]

Wisened by the experiences of the 1920s and 1930s, Truman administration officials also desired to play a more constructive role in international economic affairs. During the war years, for example, Acheson testified frequently on the lend-lease agreements. He never failed to emphasize the importance of lower tariffs, increased trade, and nondiscrimination. When peace returned, the United States would have to play a more responsible role as a creditor nation. It would have to exert leadership in the formation of the International Monetary Fund and the World Bank; it would have to enlarge the lending powers of the Export–Import Bank; it would have to avoid a new wrangle over war debts; and it would have to mobilize the private sector in behalf of international stabilization.[49]

According to Harley Notter, the State Department official in charge of planning, these commercial and financial initiatives also were "indispensable to postwar security."[50] The bilateralism and autarky of the 1930s contracted trade, intensified commercial rivalries, and allowed totalitarian governments to acquire the materiel and resources to wage war.[51] In his testimony on the Bretton Woods agreements in June 1945, Acheson vividly described how Germany had organized a system that

47   Robert Dallek, *Franklin D. Roosevelt and American Foreign Policy*. New York: Oxford University Press, 1979, 502–29; James MacGregor Burns, *Roosevelt: The Soldier of Freedom*. New York: Harcourt Brace Jovano-vich, 1979, 564–79; Gaddis, *United States and the Origins of the Cold War*, 23–31.

48   Gaddis, United States and the Origins of the Cold War, 29–30; Kepley, *Collapse of the Middle Way*.

49   Acheson Testimony, 3 Feb. 1943. House of Representatives, Foreign Affairs, *Extension of the Lend-Lease Act*, 86–9; Address by Sumner Welles, in NFTC, *Report of the Twenty-Ninth National Foreign Trade Convention*, 360–2; Dept. of Commerce, *The United States in the World Economy*.

50   Harley A. Notter, *Postwar Foreign Policy Preparation, 1939–1945*. Washington, D.C.: GPO, 1950, 128.

51   Henry Grady, "Taking Stock of Our Foreign Trade Position," in NFTC, *Report of the Twenty-Seventh National Foreign Trade Convention*, 450.

turned Europe inward upon itself "and with perfectly amazing skill had made that system work and work so effectively that the Germans were able to fight all the rest of the world and support reasonably well the peoples of Europe." Acheson feared that the deplorable conditions that beset postwar Europe might again force that continent to turn inward, with incalculable consequences for the peace of the world and for American safety.[52] Multilateral trade was a mechanism to stymie trade alliances that not only could erode American prosperity but could also foster configurations of power that endangered American security. The unrestricted flow of capital and goods would tend to bind other nations to the United States. If necessary, their resources might then be used to bolster the military strength of the free world.[53]

Many of the top civilian officials who molded the Truman administration's foreign policies had been intimately familiar with American financial diplomacy and international economic developments in the interwar years.[54] Their knowledge of events in Weimar Germany profoundly influenced their policies. As after World War I, they believed that European stability depended on German reconstruction. But they had learned that the raw materials and industrial resources of the Ruhr and Rhine must not remain in German hands alone, where they had been used to support the German war machine. German coal and steel had to be co-opted for the benefit of all Western Europe through the imposition of international controls or the development of supranational mechanisms.[55] Moreover, prompt action was imperative because Acheson, McCloy, and their associates always sensed the precariousness of the democratic experiment in postwar Germany. If concessions were not made to democratic leaders like Konrad Adenauer, if German autonomy were not restored to moderates, Germany would fall once again into the hands of virulent nationalists. Whether they be on the right or the left, they would insist on even more extreme concessions and would be willing to turn toward the Kremlin for help. The

52   Acheson Testimony, 12 June 1945, Senate, Banking and Currency, *Bretton Woods Agreements Act*, 2: 20–2, 33, 49.
53   Stephen D. Krasner, *Defending the National Interest: Raw Materials Investments and U.S. Foreign Policy*. Princeton, N.J.: Princeton University Press, 1978, 317–43; Robert Gilpin, *War and Change in World Politics*. New York: Cambridge University Press, 1981, 138–46; Thomas G. Paterson, *Soviet–American Confrontation: Postwar Reconstruction and the Origins of the Cold War*. Baltimore, Md.: Johns Hopkins University Press, 1973, 1–29; Joseph Coppock to Winthrop G. Brown, 30 Dec. 1947, *FRUS, 1947*, 1: 825–6.
54   Issacson and Thomas, *Wise Men*, 119–30; Ronald W. Pruessen, *John Foster Dulles: The Road to Power*. New York: Free Press, 1982.
55   Ferdinand Eberstadt to Forrestal, 9 and 16 Sep. 1946 and 2 Nov. 1946, Eberstadt Papers, box 28; Forrestal to Eberstadt, 13 Sep. 1946, ibid.; Memo by John Foster Dulles, 26 Feb. 1947, Dulles Papers, box 31; Dulles, "The Problem of Germany and the Problem of Europe," 17 Jan. 1947, ibid., box 32.

Rapallo and Molotov–Ribbentrop agreements resonated in the memories of US officials, who were aware that both Weimar and Nazi Germany had been willing to play a Russian card when it served German interests.[56]

Whereas concessions to German democrats made sense, appeasement of a totalitarian foe must never be contemplated. So long as they hoped to secure favorable agreements, Truman and his advisers were willing to deal with Stalin.[57] But when the Soviet government refused to accept free elections in Poland, Bulgaria, and Romania, rebuffed the Baruch Plan for the control of atomic energy, rejected American blueprints for postwar Germany, probed for weak spots in the Eastern Mediterranean and the Near East, and appeared ready to capitalize on prospective Communist successes in Greece, Italy, and France, US officials concluded that they had to take unilateral actions to build situations of strength. Appeasing an adversary who might be intent on world domination made no sense. The lessons of Munich and of the recent war were fresh in their minds. Free men had allowed the Nazis to militarize the Rhineland, annex Austria, and seize Czechoslovakia, had acquiesced to the Japanese conquest of Manchuria and the invasion of China, and had permitted Axis domination of much of Eurasia. Truman would not make the same mistakes again.[58]

The men who advised Truman were the same people who had gathered around Roosevelt to prepare the United States for conflict. For Acheson, Forrestal, Lovett, Patterson, McCloy, Harriman, Nitze, and many other officials, the events of 1940 altered their careers and shaped their thinking. Their wartime work in the government on mobilization, procurement, lend-lease, and commercial warfare underscored the relationships between economic resources and military capabilities.[59] They saw how industrial strength bestowed military power, how geo-

56 See, e.g., Acheson to David Bruce, 30 Oct. 1949, *FRUS, 1949*, 3: 623; McCloy to Henry Byroade, 25 Apr. 1950, ibid., 4: 633–5; McCloy to Acheson, 25 Apr. 1950, ibid., 4: 682–3; Geoffrey W. Lewis and Theodore Achilles to Byroade, 2 May 1950, ibid., 3: 913–14.
57 Harry S. Truman, *Off the Record: The Private Papers of Harry S. Truman*. Ed. Robert H. Ferrell. New York: Harper & Row, 1980, 57; Harry S. Truman, *Dear Bess: Letters from Harry to Bess Truman*. Ed. Robert H. Ferrell. New York: Norton, 1983, 522.
58 See Truman's eloquent summary of developments in his farewell address to Congress, 15 Jan. 1953, *PPP:HST* (1952–3), 1199–202; Paterson, Meeting the Communist Threat, 3–17; Ernest R. May, *"Lessons" of the Past: The Use and Misuse of History in American Foreign Policy*. New York: Oxford University Press, 1973, 19–51; Robert Jervis, *Perception and Misperception in International Politics*. Princeton, N.J.: Princeton University Press, 1976, 266–70. For the logic that inhered in this perspective, see William Taubman, *Stalin's American Policy: From Entente to Detente to Cold War*. New York: Norton, 1982.
59 For Forrestal, see James W. Doig, and Erwin C. Hargrove, eds., *Leadership and Innovation: A Biographical Perspective on Entrepreneurs in Government*. Baltimore, Md.: Johns Hopkins University Press, 1987; For Patterson, see Elberton R. Smith, *The Army and Economic Mobilization*. Washington, D.C.: GPO, 1959; for Lovett, see Jonathan Foster Fanton, "Robert A. Lovett: The

graphical conquest enhanced aggressive purposes. According to Acheson, the Nazi "New Order" and the Japanese "Co-Prosperity Sphere" "meant that the resources and the population of neighboring countries have been turned entirely to the ends of the enemy and have been spent with utter ruthlessness."[60] . . .

For US officials, the most decisive and lasting legacy of the wartime experience was that potential adversaries must never again be allowed to gain control of the resources of Eurasia through autarkical economic practices, political subversion, and/or military aggression. The acquisition of such resources allowed potential foes to augment their military capabilities, encouraged them to penetrate the Western Hemisphere, tempted them to attack the United States, and enabled them to wage a protracted struggle. Postwar peace and stability had to be constructed on the foundation of nonaggression, self-determination, equal access to raw materials, and nondiscriminatory trade.[61] When these principles were violated, nations used military power and autarkical practices to accrue strength disproportionate to their size and stature, dysfunctional to the international system, and dangerous to the physical security of the United States. Faced with such realities, American officials had to contemplate substantial changes in the political economy of the United States, including huge defense expenditures, increments in the powers of the federal government, infringements on free-market mechanisms, and curtailment of individual liberties.

Axis aggression and military successes in 1940 and 1941 demonstrated that the traditional principles of self-determination and the open door principles that heretofore had been geared to American economic needs and ideological inclinations, now had profound implications for the national security, physical safety, and political economy of the United States. Once this fusion of geopolitical, economic, ideological, and strategic considerations occurred, traditional foreign policy goals were transformed into national security imperatives. The self-imposed restraints on political commitments, military guarantees, and the use of force eroded. The economic costs of global embroilments, which had

War Years." Ph.D. diss., Yale University, 1978; for Acheson, see McLellan, Acheson, 44–56; for Harriman, see Averell W. Harriman and Elie Abel. *Special Envoy to Churchill and Stalin, 1941–1946*. New York: Random House, 1975, 56–192; see also Bruce Catton, *The War Lords of Washington*. New York: Harcourt, Brace, 1948; Samuel P. Huntington. *The Soldier and the State: The Theory and Politics of Civil-Military Relations*. Cambridge, Mass.: Harvard University Press, 1957.

60   Acheson, "The War, Rehabilitation, and Lasting Peace," 18 Dec. 1943, *DSB* 9 (18 Dec. 1943): 421.

61   For a similar argument, see the essay by Detlef Junker, in Frank Trommler and Joseph McVeigh, *America and the Germans: An Assessment of a Three Hundred Year History*. Vol. 2, *The Relationship in the Twentieth Century*. Philadelphia: University of Pennsylvania Press, 1985, 30–43.

heretofore constrained American strategic obligations abroad, now became less salient than their alleged geopolitical and military benefits. Roosevelt's advisers were prepared to use their acquired wisdom to help Truman mobilize US power to overcome the threats and dangers of the postwar world.

3

Dividing the World

John Lewis Gaddis

Originally appeared in John Lewis Gaddis, *We Now Know: Rethinking Cold War History*. Oxford University Press, © John Lewis Gaddis 1997.

There were important parallels, but equally important differences, in the careers of Hitler and Stalin. Both had risen from being outsiders in their respective societies to positions of unchallenged authority over them; both had been underestimated by potential rivals; both were prepared to use whatever methods were available – including terror – to achieve their purposes. Both exploited the fact that a harsh peace and the onset of a global economic crisis had stalled the advance of democracy in Europe, but not the technological means of controlling large populations; both made full use of the opportunities for propaganda, surveillance, and swift action provided by such innovations as the telephone, radio, motion pictures, automobiles, and airplanes. Both benefited, as a consequence, from the conviction of many Europeans that authoritarianism was the wave of the future. Both merged personal with national interests; both dedicated themselves to implementing internationalist ideologies.

But where Stalin looked toward an eventual world proletarian revolution, Hitler sought immediate racial purification. Where Stalin was cautiously flexible, Hitler stuck to his perverse principles through thick and thin: he never placed the security of his state or even himself above the task of achieving literally, and at whatever cost, his goals of Aryan supremacy and Jewish annihilation. Where Stalin was patient, prepared to take as long as necessary to achieve his ambitions, Hitler was frenetic, determined to meet deadlines he himself had imposed. Where Stalin sought desperately to stay out of war, Hitler set out quite deliberately to provoke it.[1]

Both authoritarians wanted to dominate Europe, a fact that placed them at odds with the traditional American interest in maintaining a balance of power there. But only Hitler was in a position to attempt domination: he therefore created, for the United States, the European democracies, and even the Soviet Union itself, a threat whose urgency, one might have thought, would have transcended whatever differences divided his potential victims.

It certainly did so in Washington and London. Franklin D. Roosevelt had long regarded Nazi Germany as the primary danger to American security and had sought, ever since extending diplomatic recognition to the Soviet Union in 1933, to leave the way open for cooperation with Moscow.[2] Winston Churchill loathed Marxism–Leninism at least as much as his predecessor Neville Chamberlain, but he shared Roosevelt's view that geopolitics was more important that ideology.[3] Both leaders foresaw the fragility of the Nazi–Soviet alliance and were prepared to accept Soviet help in containing Hitler whenever that became possible. They also repeatedly warned Stalin of the impending German attack in the winter and spring of 1941.[4] Only the Soviet dictator's misplaced faith in a fellow authoritarian – a kind of brutal romanticism, to which his own temperament and style of governing would allow no challenge – prevented the necessary defensive measures and made Hitler's invasion in June of that year such a devastating surprise.[5] "My people and I, Iosif Vissarionovich, firmly remember your wise prediction," NKVD chief Lavrentii Beria wrote to Stalin on the day before the invasion: "Hitler will not attack us in 1941!"[6]

1   These comparisons are based primarily upon Alan Bullock, *Hitler and Stalin: Parallel Lives*, New York, 1992; but see also Robert C. Tucker, *Stalin in Power: The Revolution from above, 1928–1941*, New York, 1990, pp. 591–2; and Norman Rich, *Hitler's War Aims: Ideology, the Nazi State, and the Course of Expansion* (New York: Norton, 1973). On Hitler's personal responsibility for World War II, see John Mueller, *Retreat from Doomsday: The Obsolescence of Major War* (New York: Basic Books, 1989), pp. 64–8. R. C. Raack, *Stalin's Drive to the West, 1938–1945: The Origins of the Cold War* (Stanford: Stanford University Press, 1995) makes the important point, though, that Stalin did see a war between Nazi Germany and the Western democracies as likely to advance Soviet interests.
2   John L. Gaddis, *Russia, the Soviet Union, and the United States: An Interpretive History*, 2nd ed., New York, 1990, pp. 132–43.
3   See e.g. Martin Gilbert, *Winston S. Churchill: Finest Hour, 1939–1941* (Boston: Houghton Mifflin, 1983), pp. 101–2.
4   A favor he chose not to reciprocate later in the year when he received information from his spy, Richard Sorge, in Tokyo, that the Japanese were planning to attack Pearl Harbor. See Valentin M. Berezhkov, *At Stalin's Side: His Interpreter's Memoirs from the October Revolution to the Fall of the Dictator's Empire*, trans. Sergei V. Mikheyev (New York: Birch Lane Press, 1994), p. 261.
5   Dimitri Volkogonov, *Stalin: Triumph and Tragedy*, New York, 1991, pp. 394–6.
6   Quoted in Amy Knight, *Beria: Stalin's First Lieutenant* (Princeton: Princeton University Press, 1993), p. 109.

The German Führer had no comparable illusions about his Soviet counterpart, but he too subordinated geopolitical logic to authoritarian romanticism. He struck because he had always believed German racial interests required *Lebensraum* in the east; but he paid little attention to what Napoleon's precedent suggested about the imprudence of invading Russia while Great Britain remained undefeated. It is even more difficult to account for Hitler's declaration of war on the United States the following December, four days after the Japanese bombed Pearl Harbor. Had he not acted, Roosevelt would have found himself under immense pressure to divert American resources – including the Lend Lease aid already flowing to Great Britain and even by then to the Soviet Union – to the Pacific. The best explanation of Hitler's behavior appears to be that excitement over Japan's entry into the war impaired his ability to think clearly, and in an autocratic system no mechanisms existed to repair the damage.[7]

Both Stalin and Hitler made foolish mistakes in 1941, and for much the same reason: their systems of government reflected and reinforced their own romanticism, providing few safeguards against incompetence at the top.[8] The effect turned out to be a fortunate one, because it eliminated any possibility of an authoritarian coalition directed against the United States and its democratic allies; instead, the democracies now aligned themselves, however uneasily, with one authoritarian state against the other. German statecraft had once again drawn Americans and Russians into Europe, but this time in such a way as to throw them, despite deep ideological differences, into positions of desperate dependence upon one another. For without the Soviet Union's immense expenditure of manpower against the Germans, it is difficult to see how the Americans and British could ever have launched a successful second front. But without the United States' material assistance in the form of Lend-Lease, together with its role in holding the Japanese at bay in the Pacific, the Red Army might never have repelled the Nazi invasion in the first place.[9]

---

7   See Bullock, *Hitler and Stalin*, pp. 766–7; also Eric Hobsbawm, *The Age of Extremes: A History of the World, 1914–1991*, New York, 1994, p. 392, and Norman Rich, *Hitler's War Aims: Ideology, the Nazistate, and the Course of Expansion*, New York, 1973, pp. 224–46.
8   A point George Orwell made in 1946, noted in Michael Shelden, *Orwell: The Authorized Biography* (New York: HarperCollins, 1991), pp. 435–6. Richard Pipes has recently re-emphasized the common authoritarian roots of communism and fascism in *Russia Under the Bolshevik Regime*, New York, 1994, pp. 240–81; but see also the classics on this subject, Hannah Arendt, *The Origins of Totalitarianism* (New York: Harcourt, 1951), and Carl J. Friedrich and Zbigniew Brzezinski, *Totalitarian Dictatorship and Autocracy* (Cambridge, Mass.: Harvard University Press, 1956), as well as Abbott Gleason, *Totalitarianism: The Inner History of the Cold War* (New York: Oxford University Press, 1995).
9   See, on the importance of Lend-Lease, *Khrushchev Remembers: The Glasnost Tapes*, p. 84; also Robert Conquest, *Stalin: Breaker of Nations* (New York: Viking Penguin, 1991), p. 247.

Tocqueville had long ago foreseen that the United States and Russia, if ever moved to do so, would command human and material resources on an enormous scale: their *potential* power exceeded that of any European state he could envisage. What neither Tocqueville nor anyone else could have anticipated were the circumstances that might cause Americans and Russians to apply this strength, simultaneously, beyond their borders, and in a common cause. Hitler's twin declarations of war accomplished that, giving the Soviet Union and the United States compelling reasons to re-enter the European arena with, quite literally, a shared sense of vengeance. Through these unexpectedly unwise acts, therefore, this most improbable of historical agents at last brought Tocqueville's old prophecy within sight of fulfillment.

When a power vacuum separates great powers, as one did the United States and the Soviet Union at the end of World War II, they are unlikely to fill it without bumping up against and bruising each other's interests. This would have happened if the two postwar hegemons had been constitutional democracies: historians of the wartime Anglo-American relationship have long since exposed the bumping and bruising that did take place, even among these closest of allies.[10] Victory would require more difficult adjustments for Russians and Americans because so many legacies of distrust now divided them: the distinction between authoritarian and democratic traditions; the challenge communism and capitalism posed to one another; Soviet memories of allied intervention in Russia after World War I; more recent American memories of Stalin's purges and his opportunistic pact with Hitler. It was too much to expect a few years of wartime cooperation to sweep all of this away.

At the same time, though, these legacies need not have produced almost half a century of Soviet–American confrontation. The leaders of great nations are never entirely bound by the past: new situations continually arise, and they are free to reject old methods in attempting to deal with them. Alliance in a common cause was as new a situation as one can imagine in the Russian–American relationship. Much would depend, therefore, upon the extent to which Roosevelt and Stalin could – in effect – *liberate* their nations' futures from a difficult past.

The American President and his key advisers were determined to secure the United States against whatever dangers might confront it after victory, but they lacked a clear sense of what those might be or

10   Randall Bennett Woods, *A Changing of the Guard: Anglo-American Relations, 1941–1946* (Chapel Hill: University of North Carolina Press, 1990) provides the most recent account of Anglo-American disagreements over the nature of the postwar world.

where they might arise.[11] Their thinking about postwar security was, as a consequence, more general than specific. They certainly saw a vital interest in preventing any hostile power from again attempting to dominate the European continent. They were not prepared to see military capabilities reduced to anything like the inadequate levels of the interwar era, nor would they resist opportunities to reshape the international economy in ways that would benefit American capitalism. They resolved to resist any return to isolationism, and they optimistically embraced the "second chance" the war had provided to build a global security organization in which the United States would play the leading role.[12]

But these priorities reflected no unilateral conception of vital interests. A quarter century earlier, Wilson had linked American war aims to reform of the international system as a whole; and although his ideas had not then taken hold, the coming of a second world war revived a widespread and even guilt-ridden interest in them as a means of avoiding a third such conflict.[13] Roosevelt persuaded a skeptical Churchill to endorse Wilson's thinking in August, 1941, when they jointly proclaimed, in the Atlantic Charter, three postwar objectives: self-determination – the idea here was that people who could choose their own forms of government would not want to overthrow them, hence they would achieve, to use a Rooseveltian term, freedom from fear; open markets – the assumption was that an unrestricted flow of commodities and capital would ensure economic prosperity, hence freedom from want; and collective security – the conviction that nations had to act together rather than separately if they were ever to achieve safety.[14] To put it in language Mikhail Gorbachev would employ decades later, security would have to be a condition *common to all*, not one granted to some and withheld from others.[15]

Despite this public commitment to Wilsonian principles, neither Roosevelt nor Churchill ruled out more realistic practices. Had postwar planning been left to them alone, as in democracies it could not be, they

11   John Lewis Gaddis, *The Long Peace: Inquiries into the History of the Cold War* (New York: Oxford University Press, 1987), pp. 21–9.
12   Melvyn P. Leffler, *A Preponderance of Power: National Security, the Truman Administration, and the Cold War* (Stanford: Stanford University Press, 1992), pp. 19–24. See also Robert A. Divine, *Second Chance: The Triumph of Internationalism in America During World War II* (New York: Atheneum, 1967); and John Lewis Gaddis, *The United States and the Origins of the Cold War, 1941–1947* (New York: Columbia University Press, 1972), pp. 1–31.
13   Divine, *Second Chance*, pp. 168–74. See also Akira Iriye, *The Globalizing of America, 1913–1945* (New York: Cambridge University Press, 1993), pp. 199–200.
14   Theodore A. Wilson, *The First Summit: Roosevelt and Churchill at Placentia Bay 1941* (Boston: Houghton Mifflin, 1969).
15   See e.g. Mikhail Gorbachev, *Perestroika: New Thinking for Our Country and the World* (New York: Harper & Row, 1987), p. 142.

might well have come up with something like what Roosevelt occasionally talked about: the idea of four great powers – the United States, Great Britain, the Soviet Union, and Nationalist China – operating as world policemen, using force or the prospect of it to keep smaller states in line.[16] But even this cold-blooded approach, like the Wilsonian constraints that kept the politically sensitive Roosevelt from insisting on it, implied a sense of *collective* security among the four: it would not have worked if any one of them had sought to maximize security for itself, while attempting to deny it to others.[17] There was, thus, little unilateralism in F.D.R.'s thinking, whether he was operating in his idealistic or his realistic mode.

The United States would seek power in the postwar world, not shy away from it as it had done after world War I. It would do so in the belief that only it had the strength to build a peace based on Wilsonian principles of self-determination, open markets, and collective security. It would administer that peace neither for its exclusive advantage nor in such a way as to provide equal benefits to all: many as yet ill-defined possibilities lay in between these extremes. Nor would Roosevelt assume, as Wilson had, public and Congressional approval; rather, the administration would make careful efforts to ensure domestic support for the postwar settlement at every step of the way.[18] There would be another attempt at a Wilsonian peace, but this time by the un-Wilsonian method of offering each of the great powers as well as the American people a vested interest in making it work. It was within this framework of pragmatism mixed with principle that Roosevelt hoped to deal with Stalin.

The Soviet leader, too, sought security after World War II: his country lost at least 27 million of its citizens in that conflict;[19] he could hardly have done otherwise. But no tradition of *common* or *collective* security shaped postwar priorities as viewed from Moscow, for the very good reason that it was no longer permitted there to distinguish between state interests, party interests, and those of Stalin himself. National security had come to mean personal security, and the Kremlin boss saw so many threats to it that he had already resorted to murder on a mass scale in order to remove all conceivable challengers to his regime. It would be hard to imagine a more *unilateral* approach to security than the inter-

---

16 Warren F. Kimball, *The Juggler: Franklin Roosevelt as Wartime Statesman* (Princeton: Princeton University Press, 1991), pp. 95–9.

17 See Lloyd C. Gardner, *Spheres of Influence: The Great Powers Partition Europe from Munich to Yalta* (Chicago: Ivan R. Dee, 1993), pp. 149–50.

18 Divine, *Second Chance* provides the most thorough account.

19 Volkogonov, *Stalin: Triumph and Tragedy*, p. 505. See also Viacheslav Chubarov, "The War After the War," *Soviet Studies in History* 30 (Summer 1991), 44–6.

nal practices Stalin had set in motion during the 1930s. Cooperation with external allies was obviously to his advantage when the Germans were within sight of his capital, but whether that cooperation would extend beyond Hitler's defeat was another matter. It would depend upon the ability of an aging and authoritarian ruler to shift his own thinking about security to a multilateral basis, and to restructure the government he had made into a reflection of himself.[20]

It is sometimes said of Stalin that he had long since given up the Lenin–Trotsky goal of world revolution in favor of "socialism in one country," a doctrine that seemed to imply peaceful coexistence with states of differing social systems. But that is a misunderstanding of Stalin's position. What he really did in the late 1920s was to drop Lenin's prediction that revolutions would arise spontaneously in other advanced industrial countries; instead he came to see the Soviet Union itself as the center from which socialism would spread and eventually defeat capitalism.[21] The effect was to switch the principal instrument for advancing revolution from Marx's idea of a historically determined class struggle to a process of territorial acquisition Stalin could control. "The idea of propagating world Communist revolution was an ideological screen to hide our desire for world domination," one of his secret agents recalled decades later.[22] "This war is not as in the past," Stalin himself explained to the Yugoslav communist Milovan Djilas in 1945: "whoever occupies a territory also imposes his own social system. . . . It cannot be otherwise."[23]

Stalin was fully prepared to use unconventional means to promote Soviet interests beyond the territories he ruled. He kept Lenin's Com-

20   For the centrality of Stalin to all aspects of Soviet policy during this period, see Vladislav Zubok and Constantine Pleshakov, "The Soviet Union," in David Reynolds, ed., *The Origins of the Cold War in Europe: International Perspectives* (New Haven: Yale University Press, 1994), esp. pp. 57, 63, 68; David Holloway, *Stalin and the Bomb: The Soviet Union and Atomic Energy, 1939–1954* (New Haven: Yale University Press, 1994), p. 370; and Lydia V. Pozdeeva, "The Soviet Union: Territorial Diplomacy," in David Reynolds, Warren F. Kimball, and A. O. Chubarian, eds., *Allies at War: the Soviet, American, and British Experience, 1939–1945* (New York: St. Martin's Press, 1994), pp. 378–9.

21   My analysis here follows Tucker, *Stalin in Power*, pp. 45–50. But see also Raack, *Stalin's Drive to the West*, pp. 12–15, 20, 103; Vlasdislav Zubok and Constantine Pleshakov, *Inside the Kremlin's Cold War: From Stalin to Krushchev*, Cambridge, Mass., 1996, p. 13; William Taubman, *Stalin's American Policy: From Entente to Detente to Cold War* (New York: Norton, 1982), pp. 10–30; Bernard S. Morris, *Communism, Revolution, and American Policy* (Durham: Duke University Press, 1987), pp. 7–10, 30–1; Gabriel Gorodetsky, "The Formulation of Soviet Foreign Policy: Ideology and *Realpolitik*," in Gorodetsky, ed., *Soviet Foreign Policy 1917–1991: A Retrospective* (London: Frank Cass, 1994), pp. 30–44; and Lars H. Lih's "Introduction" in Lih, Oleg V. Naumov, and Oleg V. Khlevniuk, eds., *Stalin's Letters to Molotov, 1925–1936* (New Haven: Yale University Press, 1995), pp. 5–6.

22   Pavel and Anatoli, Sudoplatov, *Special Tasks: The Memoirs of an Unwanted Witness – A Soviet Spymaster*, Boston, 1994, p. 102.

23   Milovan Djilas, *Conversations with Stalin*, trans. Michael B. Petrovich (New York: Harcourt, Brace & World, 1962), p. 114.

intern in place but turned it to his own purposes: this became clear during the Spanish Civil War, when Stalin used Comintern agents as much to wipe out Trotskyists as to fight fascists.[24] One of his most far-sighted initiatives involved the recruitment of an elaborate network of youthful spies in Great Britain and the United States during the 1930s – most of them anti-fascist intellectuals – years before they could have risen to positions that would have given them anything significant to spy upon.[25] Nor did Stalin rule out war itself as a means of advancing the revolutionary cause. He would not, like Hitler, risk military conflict to meet some predetermined timetable. But he did see wars *among capitalists* as likely to weaken them and therefore speed "socialist encirclement:" that may be one reason why he failed to foresee the German attack in 1941.[26] And he by no means excluded the possibility of an eventual war with capitalism involving the Soviet Union itself. "Stalin looked at it this way," his foreign minister, Viacheslav Molotov recalled: "World War I has wrested one country from capitalist slavery; World War II has created a socialist system; and the third will finish off imperialism forever."[27]

It would be easy to make too much of Stalin's words, for reality always separates what people say from what they are able to do. What is striking about Stalin, though, is how small that separation was. To a degree we are only now coming to realize, Stalin *literally* imposed his rhetoric upon the country he ran: this was a dictator whose subordinates scrutinized his every comment, indeed his every gesture, and attempted to implement policies – even the most implausible scientific doctrines – on the basis of them.[28] Not even Hitler ran so auto-

24 Hugh Thomas, *The Spanish Civil War* (New York: Harper, 1961), pp. 214–17, 452–5. See also George Orwell's classic account, *Homage to Catalonia* (New York: Harcourt, 1952); and, for new information on Stalin's purges within the Comintern, Kevin McDermott, "Stalinist Terror in the Comintern: New Perspectives," *Journal of Contemporary History* 30 (1995), 111–30.

25 Christopher Andrew and Oleg Gordievsky, *KGB: The Inside Story of its Foreign Operations from Lenin to Gorbachev* (New York: HarperCollins, 1990), pp. 184–232; Genrikh Borovik, *The Philby Files: The Secret Life of Master Spy Kim Philby*, ed. Philip Knightley (Boston: Little, Brown, 1994), pp. 23–168; Allen Weinstein, *Perjury: The Hiss–Chambers Case* (New York: Knopf, 1978), pp. 112–57. See also, for the activities of the American Communist Party, Harvey Klehr, John Earl Haynes, and Fridrikh Igorevich Firsov, *The Secret World of American Communism* (New Haven: Yale University Press, 1995).

26 Raack, *Stalin's Drive to the West*, pp. 11–36; also Zubok and Pleshakov, *Inside the Kremlin's Cold War*, p. 37. For a more general discussion of Stalin's views on the relationship between war and revolution, see William Curti Wohlforth, *The Elusive Balance: Power and Perceptions during the Cold War* (Ithaca: Cornell University Press, 1993), pp. 40–6.

27 *Molotov Remembers: Inside Kremlin Politics: Conversations with Felix Chuev*, ed. Albert Resis (Chicago: Ivan R. Dee, 1993), p. 63. See also Wohlforth, *The Elusive Balance*, pp. 43–4, 76; and Holloway, *Stalin and the Bomb*, pp. 151–2.

28 Tucker, *Stalin in Power*, pp. 551–77; Volkogonov, *Stalin*, pp. 501, 550–1.

cratic a system.[29] The result was a kind of self-similarity across scale,[30] in which the tyrant at the top spawned smaller tyrants at each level throughout the party and state bureaucracy: their activities extended down to the level of scrutinizing stamp collections for evidence that their owners might value the images of foreign potentates more than those of Lenin and Stalin.[31] It was typical of the Kremlin boss, the most consummate of narcissists,[32] that he thought very far ahead indeed about security. But it was always and only his own security that he was thinking about.

Here, then, was the difficulty. The Western democracies sought a form of security that would reject violence or the threat of it: security was to be a *collective* good, not a benefit denied to some in order to provide it to others. Stalin saw things very differently: security came only by intimidating or eliminating potential challengers. World politics was an extension of Soviet politics, which was in turn an extension of Stalin's preferred personal environment:[33] a zero-sum game, in which achieving security for one meant depriving everyone else of it. The contrast, or so it would seem, made conflict unavoidable.

But is this not putting things too starkly? The United States and its democratic allies found ways to cooperate with the Soviet Union, after all, in fighting Germany and Japan. Could they not have managed their postwar relationship similarly, so that the safety Stalin demanded could have been made to correspond with the security the West required? Could there not have been a division of Europe into spheres of influence which, while they would hardly have pleased everybody, might have prevented an ensuing four and a half decades of superpower rivalry?

Stalin appears to have relished his role, along with Roosevelt and Churchill, as one of the wartime Big Three.[34] Such evidence as has surfaced from Soviet archives suggests that he received reassuring reports about Washington's intentions: "Roosevelt is more friendly to us than any other prominent American," Ambassador Litvinov commented in June 1943, "and it is quite obvious that he wishes to cooperate with us." Whoever was in the White House, Litvinov's successor Andrei Gromyko

29   Wohlforth, *The Elusive Balance*, p. 61. For the relative looseness with which Nazi Germany was run, see Bullock, *Hitler and Stalin*, pp. 424–8, 434–5.
30   For a scientific analogue, see James Gleick, *Chaos: Making a New Science*, New York, 1987, pp. 83–118.
31   Tucker, *Stalin in Power*, p. 469.
32   Bullock, *Hitler and Stalin*, pp. 464–5.
33   Taubman, *Stalin's American Policy*, p. 16.
34   Zubok and Pleshakov, *Inside the Kremlin's cold War*, p. 25; Berezhkov, *At Stalin's Side*, pp. 236–8.

predicted a year later, the Soviet Union and the United States would "manage to find common issues for the solution of . . . problems emerging in the future and of interest to both countries."[35] Even if Stalin's long-range thinking about security did clash with that of his Anglo-American allies, common military purposes provided the strongest possible inducements to smooth over such differences. It is worth asking why this *practice* of wartime cooperation did not become a *habit* that would extend into the postwar era.

The principal reason, it now appears, was Stalin's insistence on equating security with territory. Western diplomats had been surprised, upon arriving in Moscow soon after the German attack in the summer of 1941, to find the Soviet leader already demanding a postwar settlement that would retain what his pact with Hitler had yielded: the Baltic states, together with portions of Finland, Poland, and Romania. Stalin showed no sense of shame or even embarrassment about this, no awareness that the *methods* by which he had obtained these concessions could conceivably render them illegitimate in the eyes of anyone else. When it came to territorial aspirations, he made no distinction between adversaries and allies:[36] what one had provided the other was expected to endorse.

Stalin coupled his claims with repeated requests for a second front, quite without regard to the fact that his own policies had left the British to fight Germany alone for a year, so that they were hardly in a position to comply. He reiterated his military and territorial demands after the Americans entered the war in December, despite the fact that they were desperately trying to hang on in the Pacific against a Japanese adversary against whom the Soviet Union – admittedly for good strategic reasons – had elected not to fight. This linkage of postwar requirements with wartime assistance was, as the Russians used to like to say, "no accident." A second front in Europe in 1942 would have been "a completely impossible operation for them," Molotov later acknowledged. "But our demand was politically necessary, and we had to press them for everything."[37]

On the surface, this strategy succeeded. After strong initial objections, Roosevelt and Churchill did eventually acknowledge the Soviet Union's

35 Litvinov to Molotov, 2 June 1943, and Gromyko dispatch, 14 July 1944, both printed in Amos Perlmutter, *FDR & Stalin: A Not So Grand Alliance, 1943–1945* (Columbia: University of Missouri Press, 1993), pp. 243, 268. See also Zubok and Pleshakov, *Inside the Kremlin's Cold War*, pp. 28–31; and Vladimir O. Pechatnov, "The Big Three After World War II: New Documents on Soviet Thinking about Post War Relations with the United States and Great Britain," Cold War International History Project [hereafter CWIHP] Working Paper 13 (July 1995).
36 Steven Merritt Miner, *Between Churchill and Stalin: The Soviet Union, Great Britain, and the Origins of the Grand Alliance* (Chapel Hill: University of North Carolina Press, 1988), pp. 252–7.
37 *Molotov Remembers*, p. 45.

right to the expanded borders it claimed; they also made it clear
that they would not oppose the installation of "friendly" governments
in adjoining states. This meant accepting a Soviet sphere of influence
from the Baltic to the Adriatic, a concession not easily reconciled
with the Atlantic Charter. But the authors of that document
saw no feasible way to avoid that outcome: military necessity required
continued Soviet cooperation against the Germans. Nor were they
themselves prepared to relinquish spheres of influence in Western
Europe and the Mediterranean, the Middle East, Latin America, and
East Asia.[38] Self-determination was a sufficiently malleable concept that
each of the Big Three could have endorsed, without sleepless nights,
what the Soviet government had said about the Atlantic Charter:
"practical application of these principles will necessarily adapt itself
to the circumstances, needs, and historic peculiarities of particular
countries."[39]

That, though, was precisely the problem. For unlike Stalin, Roosevelt
and Churchill would have to defend their decisions before domestic
constituencies. The *manner* in which Soviet influence expanded was
therefore, for them, of no small significance.[40] Stalin showed little
understanding of this. Having no experience himself with democratic
procedures, he dismissed requests that he respect democratic propri-
eties. "[S]ome propaganda work should be done," he advised Roosevelt
at the Tehran conference after the president had hinted that the
American public would welcome a plebiscite in the Baltic States.[41] "It is
all nonsense!" Stalin complained to Molotov. "[Roosevelt] is their military leader and commander in chief. Who would dare object to him?"[42]
When at Yalta F.D.R. stressed the need for the first Polish election to be
as pure as "Caesar's wife," Stalin responded with a joke: "They said that
about her, but in fact she had her sins."[43] Molotov warned his boss, on
that occasion, that the Americans' insistence on free elections elsewhere
in Eastern Europe was "going too far." "Don't worry," he recalls Stalin

---

38   David Reynolds, et al., "Legacies: Allies, Enemies, and Posterity," in Reynolds et al., *Allies at War*, pp. 422–3.
39   Quoted in Gardner, *Spheres of Influence*, p. 103.
40   Ibid. 215–25; Gaddis, *The United States and the Origins of the Cold War*, pp. 133–73. See also Warren I. Cohen, *America in the Age of Soviet Power, 1945–91* (New York: Cambridge University Press, 1993), pp. 9, 249; and William Larsh, "W. Averell Harriman and the Polish Question, December 1943–August 1944," *East European Politics and Societies 7* (Fall 1993), 513–54.
41   Bohlen notes, Roosevelt–Stalin conversation, 1 Dec. 1943, *Foreign Relations of the United States* [hereafter *FRUS*]: *The Conferences at Cairo and Tehran, 1943* (Washington: Government Printing Office, 1961), pp. 594–5.
42   Berezhkov, *At Stalin's Side*, p. 240.
43   Bohlen notes, 6th plenary meeting, 9 Feb. 1945, *FRUS: The Conferences at Malta and Yalta, 1945* (Washington: Government Printing Office, 1955), p. 854.

as replying, "work it out. We can deal with it in our own way later. The point is the correlation of forces."[44]

The Soviet leader was, in one sense, right. Military strength would determine what happened in that part of the world, not the enunciation of lofty principles. But unilateral methods carried long-term costs Stalin did not foresee: the most significant of these was to ruin whatever prospects existed for a Soviet sphere of influence the East Europeans themselves might have accepted. This possibility was not as far-fetched as it would later seem. The Czechoslovak president, Eduard Beneš, spoke openly of a "Czech solution" that would exchange internal autonomy for Soviet control over foreign and military policy. W. Averell Harriman, one of Roosevelt's closest advisers and his ambassador to the Soviet Union after 1943, was keenly interested in such an arrangement and hoped to persuade the Poles of its merits.[45] F.D.R. and Churchill – concerned with finding a way to respect both Soviet security interests and democratic procedures in Eastern Europe – would almost certainly have gone along.

Nor was the idea out of the question from Stalin's point of view. He would, after all, approve such a compromise as the basis for a permanent settlement with Finland.[46] He would initially allow free elections in Hungary, Czechoslovakia, and the Soviet occupation zone in Germany. He may even have *anticipated an enthusiastic response* as he took over Eastern Europe. "He was, I think, surprised and hurt," Harriman recalled, "when the Red Army was not welcomed in all the neighboring countries as an army of liberation."[47] "We still had our hopes," Khrushchev remembered, that "after the catastrophe of World War II, Europe too might become Soviet. Everyone would take the path from

44   *Molotov Remembers*, p. 51. See also Pozdeeva, "The Soviet Union: Territorial Diplomacy," p. 362.
45   Larsh, "W. Averell Harriman and the Polish Question," pp. 514–16. See also Vojtech Mastny, *Russia's Road to the Cold War: Diplomacy, Warfare, and the Politics of Communism, 1941–1945* (New York: Columbia University Press, 1979), pp. 58–9, 133–44; and Karel Kaplan, *The Short March: The Communist Takeover in Czechoslovakia: 1945–1948* (New York: St. Martin's Press, 1987), pp. 3–5.
46   Zubok and Pleshakov, *Inside the Kremlin's Cold War*, pp. 117–19. See also Tuomo Polvinen, *Between East and West: Finland in International Politics, 1944–1947*, ed. and trans. D. G. Kirby and Peter Herring (Minneapolis: University of Minnesota Press, 1986), esp. pp. 280–1; and Jussi Hanhimäki, "'Containment' in a Borderland: The United States and Finland, 1948–49," *Diplomatic History* 18 (Summer 1994), 353–74.
47   W. Averell Harriman and Elie Abel, *Special Envoy to Churchill and Stalin, 1941–1946* (New York: Random House, 1975), p. 405. See also Zubok and Pleshakov, "The Soviet Union," pp. 64–9; and Wohlforth, *The Elusive Balance*, pp. 51–3. An implicit confirmation of the view that Polish Communists expected to be welcomed in Poland occurs in an interview with Jakub Berman in Teresa Toranska, *"Them:" Stalin's Polish Puppets*, trans. Agnieska Kolakowska (New York: Harper & Row, 1987), p. 257.

capitalism to socialism."[48] It could be that there was another form of romanticism at work here, quite apart from Stalin's affinity for fellow authoritarians: that he was unrealistic enough to expect ideological solidarity and gratitude for liberation to override old fears of Russian expansionism as well as remaining manifestations of nationalism among the Soviet Union's neighbors, perhaps as easily as he himself had overridden the latter – or so it then appeared – within the multinational empire that was the Soviet Union itself.[49]

If the Red Army could have welcomed in Poland and the rest of the countries it liberated with the same enthusiasm American, British, and Free French forces encountered when they landed in Italy and France in 1943 and 1944, then some kind of Czech–Finnish compromise might have been feasible. Whatever Stalin's expectations, though, this did not happen. That non-event, in turn, removed any possibility of a division of Europe all members of the Grand Alliance could have endorsed. It ensured that an American sphere of influence would arise there largely by consent, but that its Soviet counterpart could sustain itself only by coercion. The resulting asymmetry would account, more than anything else, for the origins, escalation, and ultimate outcome of the Cold War.

The question is worth asking, then: *why* did the Czech–Finnish solution work only in Finland and nowhere else? Why did Hitler's victims not welcome the Russians – who had done more than anyone else to defeat him – as warmly as they did the Americans and their British and French allies? The answer, at its simplest level, has to do with how much one can expect from human nature.

Stalin as well as Roosevelt and Churchill miscalculated when they assumed that there could be *friendly* states along an *expanded* Soviet periphery. For how could the USSR absorb the Baltic States entirely and carve off great portions of Germany, Poland, Romania, and Czechoslovakia,[50] while still expecting the citizens of those countries to maintain cordial attitudes toward the state that had done the carving?[51] It is of course true that the Finns, who were also carved upon, did somehow manage it. But not everyone else was like the Finns: if allowed free

48   *Khrushchev Remembers: The Glasnost Tapes*, p. 100. See also Kaplan, *The Short March*, pp. 1–2; and Djilas, *Conversations with Stalin*, p. 154.
49   [For more on this, see Chapter II.]
50   The Carpatho-Ukraine, formerly part of Czechoslovakia, had been annexed by Hungary with Hitler's approval in 1939; in 1943 Stalin demanded and received agreement from the Czech government-in-exile to its postwar incorporation into the Soviet Union.
51   Zubok and Pleshakov, "The Soviet Union," p. 60.

elections, it was by no means certain that Poles and Romanians would show the same remarkable qualities of self-control for which their northern neighbor would become famous. Nor was it obvious, even where the Russians permitted other Eastern Europeans to make a choice, that Moscow would follow its own Finnish example and stay out of their internal affairs: these states did have Germany, not Sweden, on the other side of them, and that surely made a difference.

But there was more to the matter than just geography: compounding it was a growing awareness of the particular system Stalin had imposed upon his own people and might well export elsewhere. The war was ending with the defeat of fascism, but not authoritarianism. The price of relying upon one authoritarian to conquer another had been that both would not simultaneously disappear. However vast the moral capital the Soviet Union – and the European communist parties – had accumulated in fighting the Germans, it could not obscure the fact that Stalin's government was, and showed every sign of continuing to be, as repressive as Hitler's had ever been.[52] A movement that had set out, a century earlier, to free the workers of the world from their chains was now seeking to convince its own workers and everyone else that the condition of being in chains was one of perfect freedom. People were not blind, though, and victory over German authoritarianism brought fears of Soviet authoritarianism out into the open.[53]

Worried that this might happen, Roosevelt and Churchill had hoped to persuade the Europeans that Stalin himself had changed: that he meant what he said when he denied any desire to extend his own system beyond its borders; that they could therefore safely accept the boundary changes he demanded and the sphere of influence within which he proposed to include so many of them. But this strategy required Stalin's cooperation, for it could hardly succeed if the Soviet leader failed to match his deeds with the Atlantic Charter's words. Unless the Soviet Union could show that it had shifted from a unilateral to a multilateral approach to security, there could be little basis for consent from Europeans certain to fall under its control. That situation, in turn, would place the Americans and the British in the painful position of being able to cooperate with Moscow only by publicly abandoning principles they themselves had proclaimed, and that Stalin himself appeared to have endorsed.

Authoritarians tend to see ends as justifying means, and are generally free to act accordingly. Democracies rarely allow that luxury, even

---

52   See, on this important point, Raack, *Stalin's Drive to the West*, pp. 67–71.
53   The point is best confirmed by reading George Orwell's classic novels *Animal Farm* (New York: Harcourt, 1946) and *1984* (New York: Harcourt, 1949); but see also Shelden, *Orwell: The Authorized Biography*, pp. 369–70.

if their leaders might, in their darker moments, wish for it. What people think does make a difference, and yet nothing in Stalin's experience had prepared him for this reality. Thus it was that although the objective he sought *appeared* to correspond with what his allies wanted – a secure postwar world – the *methods* by which he pursued that goal proved profoundly corruptive of it. Poland best illustrates the pattern.[54]

Presumably Stalin had security in mind when he authorized the murder, at Katyn and elsewhere in the spring of 1940, of at least 15,000 Polish officers captured during the invasion that followed the Nazi–Soviet Pact. He apparently hoped to avoid disturbances that might endanger his relationship with Hitler, to clear out overcrowded camps, and perhaps also to eliminate potential leaders of a future Poland who might be unsympathetic to Soviet interests. He cannot have given the matter much thought, for he was only meting out to the Poles the kind of treatment he had already accorded several million Soviet citizens, and would extend to many others in the future.[55]

What Stalin did not anticipate was that he would need to repair his relations with the Poles after Hitler attacked the Soviet Union in 1941, that he would find it necessary to recognize the Polish government-in-exile in London and reconstitute a Polish army on Soviet soil to fight the Germans, and that the Nazis, in 1943, would reveal the Katyn atrocity to the world. Rather than admit responsibility, Stalin chose to break off relations with the London Poles, who had called for an international investigation. He then created a puppet regime of his own in Lublin and begin treating it as the legitimate government of Poland, a maneuver he backed with force as the Red Army moved into that country in 1944. Stalin subsequently failed to support, or even to allow the Americans and the British to supply by air, an uprising of the Polish resistance in Warsaw, with the result that the Germans wound up completing, on a far more massive scale, the purge of Polish anti-communists he himself had started at Katyn four years earlier. This tragic sequence of events reflected Stalin's tendency, when confronting the prospect of insecurity, to try to redesign the future rather than admit that his own past behavior might have contributed to the problem in the first place.

Stalin in the end got the acquiescent Polish government he wanted, but only at enormous cost. The brutality and cynicism with which he handled these matters did more than anything else to exhaust the good-

54   I have borrowed this example from Conquest, *Stalin*, pp. 229–30, 256–8. But see also, for new information, Raack, *Stalin's Drive to the West*, pp. 73–101; and Knight, *Beria*, pp. 103–4.
55   Amy Knight provides chilling examples of the casualness with which Stalin could authorize the punishment of whole classes of individuals. See ibid. 126–7.

will the soviet war effort had accumulated in the West, to raise doubts about future cooperation in London and Washington,[56] and to create deep and abiding fears throughout the rest of Europe. He also earned the enduring hostility of the Poles, thereby making their country a constant source of *insecurity* for him and for all of his successors.[57] The most effective resistance to Soviet authority would eventually arise in Poland – effective in the sense that the Kremlin never found a way to suppress it.[58] And in an entirely appropriate aftermath, the belated official acknowledgement of Stalin's responsibility for Katyn, which came only in 1990, turned out to be one of the ways in which the last Soviet government acknowledged, not only the illegitimacy of the sphere of influence Stalin had constructed half a century before, but its own illegitimacy as well.[59]

It used to be thought that authoritarian leaders, unfettered by moral scruples, had powerful advantages over their democratic counterparts: it was supposed to be a source of strength to be able to use all means in the pursuit of selected ends. Today this looks much less certain. For the great disadvantage of such systems is the absence of checks and balances: who is to tell the authoritarian in charge that he is about to do something stupid? The killings Stalin authorized, the states he seized, the boundary concessions he insisted upon, and the sphere of influence he imposed provided no lasting security for the Soviet Union: just the opposite. His actions laid the foundations for a resistance in Europe that would grow and not fade with time, so that when a Soviet leader appeared on the scene who was not prepared to sustain with force the system Stalin had constructed, the Soviet empire, and ultimately the Soviet Union itself, would not survive the experience.

Social psychologists make a useful distinction between what they call "dispositional" and "situational" behavior in interpreting the actions of individuals. Dispositional behavior reflects deeply rooted personal characteristics which remain much the same regardless of the circumstances in which people find themselves. One responds inflexibly – and

56   George F. Kennan, *Memoirs: 1925–1950* (Boston: Atlantic Little, Brown, 1967), pp. 199–215, describes the reaction in Washington; but see also Larsh, "Harriman and the Polish Question," pp. 550–1, which emphasizes how the events in Warsaw eroded Harriman's earlier sympathy for the Soviet position on Poland.
57   Krystyna Kersten, *The Establishment of Communist Rule in Poland, 1943–1948*, trans. John Micgiel and Michael H. Bernhard (Berkeley: University of California Press, 1991), provides a fine account, based on Polish sources, of how Soviet authority was imposed against the wishes of the majority of Poles.
58   See Timothy Garton Ash, *The Polish Revolution: Solidarity* (London: Penguin Books, 1983).
59   David Remnick, *Lenin's Tomb: The Last Days of the Soviet Empire* (New York: Random House, 1993), pp. 3–9. Sudoplatov, *Special Tasks*, pp. 276–8, provides an interesting account of the Katyn cover-up.

therefore predictably – to whatever happens. Situational behavior, conversely, shifts with circumstances; personal traits are less important in determining what one does. Historians need to be careful in applying this insight, though, because psychologists know how tempting it can be to excuse one's own actions by invoking situations, while attributing what others do to their dispositions.[60] It would be all too easy, in dealing with so controversial a matter as responsibility for the Cold War, to confuse considered judgment with that most satisfying of sensations: the confirmation of one's own prejudices.[61]

By the end of 1945 most American and British leaders had come around – some reluctantly, others eagerly – to a dispositional explanation of Stalin's behavior. Further efforts to negotiate or compromise with him were likely to fail, or so it seemed, because success would require that he cease to be what he was. One could only resolve henceforth to hold the line, remain true to one's own principles, and wait for the passage of time to bring a better world. Such at least was the view of a new George Kennan, whose top secret "long telegram" from Moscow of 22 February 1946, would shape American policy over the next half century more profoundly than his distant relative's denunciations of tsarist authoritarianism had influenced it during the preceding one. Nor was "containment" just an American strategy: Frank Roberts, the British *chargé d'affaires* in the Soviet capital, was dispatching similar arguments to London even as former prime minister Winston Churchill, speaking at Fulton, Missouri, was introducing the term "iron curtain" to the world.[62] It was left to Kennan, though, to make the dispositional case most explicitly in a lesser-known telegram sent from Moscow on 20 March: "Nothing short of complete disarmament, delivery of our air and naval forces to Russia and resigning of powers of government to American Communists" would come close to alleviating Stalin's distrust, and even then the old dictator would

60   Deborah Welch Larson, *Origins of Containment: A Psychological Explanation* (Princeton: Princeton University Press, 1985), p. 37. See also Alexander L. George, "Ideology and International Relations: A Conceptual Analysis," *Jerusalem Journal of International Relations* 9 (1987), 6.
61   Among those who have suggested that such a thing can happen are Michael J. Hogan, "The Vice Men of Foreign Affairs," *Reviews in American History* 21 (1993), esp. p. 327; and Bruce Cumings, " 'Revising Postrevisionism,' or, The Poverty of Theory in Diplomatic History," *Diplomatic History* 17 (Fall 1993), especially 549–56.
62   Kenneth M. Jensen, ed., *Origins of the Cold War: The Novikov, Kennan, and Roberts "Long Telegrams" of 1946* (Washington: United States Institute of Peace, 1991) conveniently reprints the Kennan and Roberts dispatches. See also Kennan, *Memoirs: 1925–1950*, pp. 290–7; and Frank Roberts, *Dealing with Dictators: The Destruction and Revival of Europe, 1930–70* (London: Weidenfeld & Nicolson, 1991), pp. 107–10. For Churchill's speech and its background, see Fraser Harbutt, *The Iron Curtain: Churchill, America, and the Origins of the Cold War* (New York: Oxford University Press, 1986).

probably "smell a trap and would continue to harbor the most baleful misgivings."[63]

If Kennan was right, we need look no further in seeking the causes of the Cold War: Stalin was primarily responsible. But how can we be sure that this perspective and the policies that resulted from it did not reflect the all too human tendency to attribute behavior one dislikes to the *nature* of those who indulge in it, and to neglect the *circumstances* – including one's own behavior – that might have brought it about? Is there a test historians can apply to avoid this trap?

One might be to check for evidence of consistency or inconsistency, within a particular relationship, in each side's view of the other. Attitudes that show little change over the years, especially when circumstances have changed, suggest deep roots and hence dispositional behavior. Trees may bend slightly before the wind, but they stay in place, for better or for worse, until they die. Viewpoints that evolve with circumstances, however, reflect situational behavior. Vines, after all, can creep, climb, adhere, entwine, and if necessary retreat, all in response to the environment that surrounds them. Roosevelt's vine-like personality is universally acknowledged, and needs no further elaboration here: there could hardly have been a *less* dispositional leader than the always adaptable, ever-elusive F.D.R. But what about Stalin? Was he capable of abandoning, in world politics, the paranoia that defined his domestic politics? Could he respond to conciliatory gestures, or was containment the only realistic course?

Stalin's behavior toward fellow-authoritarians did twist and turn. He gave Hitler the benefit of the doubt at several points, but viewed him as an arch-enemy at others. His attitudes toward Josef Broz Tito in Yugoslavia and Mao Zedong in China would evolve over the years, albeit in opposite directions.[64] But Stalin's thinking about democratic capitalists remained rooted to the spot: he always suspected their motives. "Remember, we are waging a struggle (negotiation with enemies is also struggle) . . . with the whole capitalist world," he admonished Molotov as early as 1929.[65] He dismissed Roosevelt's and Churchill's warnings of an impending German attack in 1941 as provocations designed to hasten that event.[66] He authorized penetration, by his spies, of the Anglo-American atomic bomb project as early as June 1942, long before his allies made the formal but by then futile decision to withhold such information from him.[67] He placed repeated obstacles in the path of

63   Kennan to James F. Byrnes, 20 Mar. 1946, *FRUS: 1946*, vi. 723.
64   [See Chapters II and III.]
65   Stalin to Molotov, 9 Sept. 1929, in Lih et al., *Stalin's Letters to Molotov*, p. 178.
66   Volkogonov, *Stalin*, p. 391.
67   Knight, *Beria*, p. 133. See also Robert Chadwell Williams, *Klaus Fuchs: Atom Spy* (Cambridge, Mass.: Harvard University Press, 1987).

direct military cooperation with the Americans and the British during the war.[68] He not only arranged to have Roosevelt's and Churchill's living quarters at the Tehran Conference bugged; he also had Beria's son, a precocious linguist, translate the tapes daily and report to him on what was said.[69] "Churchill is the kind who, if you don't watch him, will slip a kopeck out of your pocket," Stalin famously warned on the eve of the landings in Normandy in June 1944, surely the highpoint of allied cooperation against the Axis. "Roosevelt is not like that. He dips in his hand only for bigger coins."[70]

A compliment? Perhaps, in Stalin's grudging way, but hardly an expression of trust. The Soviet leader is on record as having expressed compassion – once, at Yalta – for the president's physical infirmity: "Why did nature have to punish him so? Is he any worse than other people?" But the very novelty of the remark impressed Gromyko, who heard it: his boss "rarely bestowed his sympathy on anybody from another social system."[71] Only a few weeks later the same Stalin astounded and infuriated the dying Roosevelt by charging that secret Anglo-American negotiations for the surrender of Hitler's forces in Italy were really a plot to keep the Red Army out of Germany.[72] Many years later a Soviet interviewer would suggest to Molotov that "to be paralyzed and yet to become president of the United States, and for three terms, what a rascal you had to be!" "Well said," the old Bolshevik heartily agreed.[73]

If anyone knew Stalin's mind it was Molotov, the ever-faithful *apparatchik* who came to be known, for the best of reasons, as "his master's voice."[74] Even into his nineties, Molotov's recollections of F.D.R. were clear, unrepentant, and unvarnished. A Roosevelt request for the use of Siberian air bases to bomb Japanese targets had been an excuse "to occupy certain parts of the Soviet Union instead of fighting. Afterward it wouldn't have been easy to get them out of there." The President's larger intentions were transparent:

> Roosevelt believed in dollars. Not that he believed in nothing else, but he considered America to be so rich, and we so poor and worn out, that we would surely come begging. "Then we'll kick their ass, but for now we

68   Gaddis, *The United States and the Origins of the Cold War*, pp. 80–92.
69   Knight, *Beria*, pp. 130–1.
70   Djilas, *Conversations with Stalin*, pp. 66, 73.
71   Andrei Gromyko, *Memoirs*, trans. Harold Shukman (New York: Doubleday, 1989), p. 98.
72   Peter Grose, *Gentleman Spy: The Life of Allen Dulles* (Boston: Houghton Mifflin, 1994), pp. 224–45, provides the most recent assessment of this once-controversial episode.
73   *Molotov Remembers*, p. 51.
74   See Steven Merritt Miner, "His Master's Voice: Viacheslav Mikhailovich Molotov as Stalin's Foreign Commissar," in Gordon A. Craig and Francis L. Loewenheim, eds., *The Diplomats: 1939–1979* (Princeton: Princeton University Press, 1994), pp. 65–100.

have to keep them going." That's where they miscalculated. They weren't Marxists and we were. They woke up only when half of Europe had passed from them.

"Roosevelt knew how to conceal his attitude toward us," Molotov recalled, "but Truman – he didn't know how to do that at all." Charm, though, could not hide facts: "Roosevelt was an imperialist who would grab anyone by the throat."[75]

If Stalin's wartime attitude toward Roosevelt was half as distrustful as Molotov's in retirement, then a significant pattern emerges: neither American nor British sources reveal anything approaching such deep and abiding suspicion on the Anglo-American side. Churchill subsequently credited himself, to be sure, with having warned of Soviet postwar intentions; but the archives have long since revealed a more complex pattern in which his hopes alternated with his fears well into 1945.[76] In the case of Roosevelt, it is difficult to find *any* expressions of distrust toward Stalin, public or private, until shortly before his death. If he had doubts – surely he had some – he kept them so carefully hidden that historians have had to strain to find traces of them.[77] Kennan first put forward his dispositional explanation of Stalin's actions in the summer of 1944.[78] But in contrast to Molotov, he found no sympathy at the top, nor would he for some time to come.

From this perspective, then, one has to wonder whether the Cold War really began in 1945. For it was Stalin's disposition to wage cold wars: he had done so in one form or another throughout his life, against members of his own family, against his closest advisers and their families, against old revolutionary comrades, against foreign communists, even against returning Red Army war veterans who, for whatever reason, had contacts of any kind with the West in the course of defeating Nazi Germany.[79] "A man who had subjected all activities in his own country to his views and to his personality, Stalin could not behave

75 *Molotov Remembers*, pp. 45–6, 51.
76 David Reynolds, "Great Britain," in Reynolds, ed., *The Origins of the Cold War in Europe*, p. 80.
77 See e.g. Gaddis, *Strategies of Containment*, pp. 3–13.
78 Kennan, *Memoirs: 1925–1950*, pp. 224–34.
79 The details are well documented in Tucker, *Stalin in Power*, Bullock, *Hitler and Stalin*, Volkogonov, *Stalin*, Robert Conquest, *The Great Terror: A Reassessment*, New York, 1990, and of course in Alexander Solzhenitsyn's influential trilogy, *The Gulag Archipelago* (New York: Harper & Row, 1974–8). But see also Molotov's simultaneously poignant and chilling account of Stalin's ordering the arrest of his own wife, in *Molotov Remembers*, pp. 322–5. James M. Goldgeier has recently argued that Stalin's approach to diplomatic bargaining drew upon his methods for consolidating power internally – not a reassuring conclusion (*Leadership Style and Soviet Foreign Policy: Stalin, Khrushchev, Brezhnev, Gorbachev* (Baltimore: Johns Hopkins University Press, 1994), pp. 17–21, 34–51).

differently outside," Djilas recalled. "He became himself the slave of the despotism, the bureaucracy, the narrowness, and the servility that he imposed on his country."[80] Khrushchev put it more bluntly: "No one inside the Soviet Union or out had Stalin's trust."[81]

Roosevelt's death in April 1945, then, is not likely to have altered the long-term course of Soviet–American relations: if Stalin had never trusted him, why should he have trusted that "noisy shopkeeper" Harry S. Truman, or the harder-line advisers the new president came to rely upon?[82] The Labour Party's subsequent victory in the British general election produced no improvement in Anglo–Soviet relations either: Stalin was entirely ecumenical in the range of his suspicions, and if anything detested European socialists more than he did European conservatives. Khrushchev describes him going out of his way at the December 1945 Moscow Foreign Ministers' Conference to insult both Truman – who fortunately was not present – and British Foreign Secretary Ernest Bevin: "What caused Stalin to behave that way? This is difficult to explain. I think he believed he could run the policy of the whole world. That's why he behaved in such an unrestrained way toward representatives of countries that were our partners."[83]

If doubts remained about Stalin's disposition, he thoroughly dispelled them in his first major postwar address, made on the eve of his own "election" to the Supreme Soviet in February 1946. The speech was not, as some Americans regarded it, a "declaration of World War III."[84] It was, though, like Molotov's reminiscences, a revealing window into Stalin's mind. World War II, the Kremlin leader explained, had resulted *solely* from the internal contradictions of capitalism, and *only* the entry of the Soviet Union had transformed that conflict into a war of liberation. Perhaps it might be possible to avoid future wars if raw materials and markets could be "periodically redistributed among the various countries in accordance with their economic importance, by agreement and peaceful settlement." But, he added, "that is impossible to do under present capitalist conditions of the development of world economy."[85]

80   Djilas, *Conversations with Stalin*, pp. 132–3.
81   *Khrushchev Remembers: The Glasnost Tapes*, p. 132.
82   See Holloway, *Stalin and the Bomb*, p. 247; also Zubok and Pleshakov, *Inside the Kremlin's Cold War*, pp. 39–40. For an excellent description of Stalin's first meeting with the new American president, see David McCullough, *Truman* (New York: Simon & Schuster, 1992), pp. 416–20.
83   *Khrushchev Remembers: The Glasnost Tapes*, p. 67. The text refers to Aneurin Bevan, but this is obviously an error.
84   The phrase was that of Justice William O. Douglas, carefully noted in Secretary of the Navy James V. Forrestal's diary. See Walter Millis, ed., *The Forrestal Diaries* (New York: Viking, 1951), p. 134.
85   Stalin speech of 9 Feb. 1946, in Robert V. Daniels, ed., *A Documentary History of Communism*, rev. edn. (Hanover, NH: University Press of New England, 1984), p. 138 (emphases

What all of this meant, Stalin's most perceptive biographer has argued, was nothing less than that "the postwar period would have to be transformed, in idea if not in actual fact, into *a new prewar period.*"[86]

"There has been a return in Russia to the outmoded concept of security in terms of territory – the more you've got the safer you are." The speaker was former Soviet foreign minister and ambassador to the United States Maxim Litvinov, who had personally negotiated the establishment of Soviet–American diplomatic relations with Franklin D. Roosevelt. The occasion was an interview, given in Moscow to CBS correspondent Richard C. Hottelet a few months after Stalin's speech. The cause, Litvinov explained, was "the ideological conception prevailing here that conflict between Communist and capitalist worlds is inevitable." What would happen, Hottelet wanted to know, if the West should suddenly grant all of the Soviet Union's territorial demands? "It would lead to the West's being faced, after a more or less short time, with the next series of demands."[87]

Litvinov managed, remarkably enough, to die in bed.[88] His views on the breakdown of wartime cooperation, though, had hardly been a secret: his colleagues regularly listened to recordings of his conversations acquired, as Molotov put it, "in the usual way." Why was the old diplomat not arrested, charged with treason, and shot? Perhaps his public advocacy of collective security and cooperation with the West, paradoxically, shielded him: Stalin did, from time to time, worry about how his regime looked to the outside world. Perhaps his boss kept Litvinov alive in case the Soviet Union ever again needed the West's assistance. Perhaps he was just lucky, an explanation his successor as foreign minister favored. "Litvinov remained among the living," Molotov recalled with his usual grim clarity, "only by chance."[89]

added). For more on the circumstances and implications of this speech, see Hugh Thomas, *Armed Truce: The Beginnings of the Cold War, 1945–46* (London: Hamish Hamilton, 1986), pp. 3–17; and Albert Resis, "Stalin, the Politburo, and the Onset of the Cold War, 1945–1946," *The Carl Beck Papers in Russian and East European Studies* #701 (Apr. 1988), pp. 13–17.

86   Robert C. Tucker, *The Soviet Political Mind: Stalinism and Post-Stalinist Change*, rev. edn. (New York: Norton, 1971), p. 91 (emphasis in original). See also Wohlforth, *The Elusive Balance*, pp. 62–5.

87   Hottelet's account of this conversation is summarized in *FRUS: 1946*, vi, 763–5, and was first published in the *Washington Post*, 21–5 Jan. 1952, shortly after Litvinov's death. See also Phillips, *Between the Revolution and the West*, pp. 172–3; and Jonathan Haslam, "Litvinov, Stalin, and the Road Not Taken," in Gorodetsky, ed., *Soviet Foreign Policy 1917–1991*, pp. 59–60.

88   Remnick, *Lenin's Tomb*, p. 15; also Zinovy Sheinis, *Maxim Litvinov* (Moscow: Progress Publishers, 1990), p. 350; and Haslam, "Litvinov, Stalin, and the Road Not Taken," p. 61. On the basis of a conversation with Anastas Mikoyan, though, Valentin Berezhkov claims that Stalin had Litvinov killed in an automobile accident (*At Stalin's Side*, pp. 316–19).

89   *Molotov Remembers*, p. 69. See also Berezhkov, *At Stalin's Side*, p. 319.

Only a few months after Litvinov's death Stalin too died in bed, probably as a result of medical neglect stemming from the fact that he had come, by 1953, to see even his own doctors as mortal enemies.[90] That terminal but characteristic event provides a useful vantage-point from which to look back to see how the Cold War had come to pass, and to speculate on whether it might have been avoided.

One hundred and eighteen years earlier, Tocqueville had predicted bipolarity but not necessarily hostility. He was a careful enough historian to understand that the trends visible to him in 1835 would only *frame* future history. Individuals as yet invisible would *determine* it by what they did with the conditions they encountered. "Men make their own history," another keen long-term observer, Karl Marx, would later note, "but they do not make it just as they please; they do not make it under circumstances chosen by themselves, but under circumstances directly found, given and transmitted from the past."[91]

The role of the historian is, or ought to be, to focus exclusively neither on individuals nor on the circumstances they inherit, but on how they intersect. One way to do that is to think of history as an experiment we can rerun[92] – if only in our minds – keeping Tocqueville-like trends constant but allowing for Marx-like variations in the individuals who have to deal with them. If the result replicates what actually happened, then it seems safe to assume that, on balance, circumstances and not men determined the outcome. But if it appears that different individuals might have altered the course of events – if rerunning the experiment does not always produce the same result – then we should question deterministic explanations, for what kind of determinism empowers unique personalities at distinctive moments?

Certain aspects of the Russian–American relationship would change very little in an experiment rerun with 1835 as a starting point: geographical position, demographic potential, contrasting traditions of social and political organization. It is difficult to conceive how the Americans might have evolved an autocratic form of government, or the Russians a democratic one. Neither country was likely to remain inactive on the international scene; each would surely have found cause, sooner or later, to intervene in European and East Asian affairs.

But could it have been foreseen that both would transform their respective traditions of democracy and authoritarianism into globalist ideologies at precisely the same moment, as Wilson and Lenin did? Could

90   Volkogonov, *Stalin*, pp. 567–76.
91   "The Eighteenth Brumaire of Louis Bonaparte," originally published in 1852, quoted in Robert C. Tucker, ed., *The Marx–Engels Reader*, 2nd edn. (New York: Norton, 1978), p. 595.
92   See, for another example of this technique, Stephen Jay Gould, *Wonderful Life: The Burgess Shale and the Nature of History* (New York: Norton, 1989).

it have been anticipated that Stalin would then shift the internationalism of the Bolshevik revolution, not simply back to a form of Russian nationalism resembling that of the tsars, but to a brutal variety of narcissism matched only by the contemporaneous leader of an antipathetic ideology? Could it have been expected that Hitler would then forge a coalition of communism and capitalism directed against himself, culminating with the fraternal embraces of victorious Soviet and American troops in the center of Germany? Could it have been predicted that this alliance would then fall apart, within a matter of months, leaving in its wake almost half a century of cold war?

Geography, demography, and tradition contributed to this outcome but did not determine it. It took men, responding unpredictably to circumstances, to forge the chain of causation; and it took one man in particular, responding predictably to his own authoritarian, paranoid, and narcissistic predisposition, to lock it into place.[93] Would there have been a Cold War without Stalin? Perhaps. Nobody in history is indispensable.

But Stalin had certain characteristics that set him off from all others in authority at the time the Cold War began. He alone pursued personal security by depriving everyone else of it: no Western leader relied on terror to the extent that he did. He alone had transformed his country into an extension of himself: no Western leader could have succeeded at such a feat, and none attempted it. He alone saw war and revolution as acceptable means with which to pursue ultimate ends: no Western leader associated violence with progress to the extent that he did.

Did Stalin therefore seek a Cold War? The question is a little like asking: "does a fish seek water?" Suspicion, distrust, and an abiding cynicism were not only his preferred but his necessary environment; he could not function apart from it. "Conciliation struck Stalin as trickery or naiveté," William Taubman has concluded, "and toughness only confirmed the Soviets' image of America as an unreconstructed enemy."[94] The Americans would in time develop a similar view of Stalin and his successors; some of their leaders would hold onto it long after the reasons for it had begun to disappear. But that was not the prevailing attitude in Washington, or in other Western capitals, in 1945. It was, consistently had been, and would remain Stalin's, until the day of his own medically under-attended demise.

93   Wilfried Loth, *The Division of the World: 1941–1945* (New York: St. Martin's Press, 1988), pp. 304–11, makes a good case for the Cold War not having been predetermined; but I think he underestimates Stalin's role in bringing it about.
94   Taubman, *Stalin's America Policy*, p. 9; see also p. 74.

Part II

First Attempts at Conflict Management

Introduction to Part II

During the 1950s Cold War policies in East and West were mainly concerned with the search for a solution to the complicated German question including the development of a more closely integrated European continent. For the Soviet Union the question of how to separate the Federal Republic from the West and establish a reunited and neutral Germany was paramount. Stalin did not believe that it would be possible to turn the whole of Germany into a communist state. For the West the dominant question was how best to irreversibly integrate West Germany with the western world and bring about a rapprochement between Bonn and Paris. The latter was attempted by means of European integration and, because of Moscow's overwhelming conventional military strength, through the rearmament of West Germany. Yet, this policy was controversial even within the West and threatened to undermine the coherence of the western alliance as it had been established in April 1949 with the founding of the North Atlantic Treaty Organisation (NATO). Moreover, this kind of solution to the German question demanded skilful management to avoid creating the impression in the Kremlin that German militarism was on the rise again and posed a serious security risk to the Soviet Union. Such a perception might well lead Moscow to resort to a preventative attack on the West across the Elbe river; the line dividing East and West from each other in the middle of Germany. The German problem thus threatened to undermine the preservation of global peace if not handled carefully.

The other main task facing politicians during the early Cold War years, therefore, was the attempt to prevent the escalation of the East–West conflict in Europe into a hot war. Since Hiroshima and Nagasaki the threat of a nuclear holocaust hung over the world. The "policy of strength" as it was emerging in both East and West needed to be contained and carefully managed. After all, in March 1950 it had been announced that the Soviet Union had already exploded its first atomic bomb in August 1949; the Soviet Union's rapid technological progress was entirely unexpected and took the West very much by surprise. This progress, as was later revealed, was partially based on Soviet atomic espionage activities. Moreover, the invasion of the American protected South Korea by North Korean forces in June 1950 led to widespread fear in the West that the Soviet Red Army and East German police forces might well be inclined to invade the Federal Republic of Germany to bring about German unification on Stalin's terms and incorporate Germany into the Soviet orbit. Under the impact of these developments the huge rearmament programme called for in the American document NSC-68 was signed into law by President Truman. Rapid progress with the integration of the Federal Republic of Germany into the western world and French–German rapprochement by means of the gradually unfolding process of European integration was regarded as utterly necessary to fortify the coherence of the western world. Above all, West German rearmament was seen as vital to improving the conventional military capability of the West. Yet, due to French opposition in 1952 it was eventually decided to set up a European Army within a European Defence Community (EDC) on the model of the European Coal and Steel Community (ECSS). It was believed that this would avoid the necessity of creating an independent West German army and general staff while still providing German soldiers for the western defence effort. Whilst Washington had been able to overcome its initial preference for West German integration into NATO, the British government remained greatly opposed to a "federalist" solution to the German question, both in its military and political/economic dimension.

In both East and West very few of the major politicians of the time pondered ways and means of overcoming the early Cold War and finding a negotiated East–West settlement. The contribution by Klaus Larres discusses how one of the few imaginative proposals to reconsider fundamentally the entire Cold War framework was put forward by British Prime Minister Winston Churchill in 1953–4. The Prime Minister's policy exemplified the complexities and contradictions contained in the western world's approach to the Cold War. While strongly in favour of the establishment of Franco-German friendship and the reintegration of Germany into the international community, Churchill very much disliked the American tendency to persuade Britain to become part of the European integration process. Instead, he wished to re-establish the close Anglo-American "special relationship" of the Second World War years, re-emphasize the importance of Britain in world affairs and arrive at an early termination of the Cold War. This would enable his country to focus on replenishing its economic resources. Churchill contemplated the possibility of embarking on personal summit negotiations to offer Moscow the neutrality of a reunified Germany. The British Prime Minister's proposal was not very different from the suggestions contained in the Stalin note of March 1952. However, Churchill emphasized that a new contractual relationship had to be established between Moscow and Germany which was to be guaranteed by Britain. Churchill believed that such a deal would be necessary to overcome the Cold War and thus preserve global peace and enable his country to maintain its great power status in the post-war world. He feared that the continued division of both Europe and Germany would be a recipe for disaster as German and European nationalism could not be expected to tolerate this state of affairs for any length of time. The 1953 uprising in East Germany seemed to confirm this. Yet, Churchill's attempt at post-war "Big Three" (or on occasion "Big Four") summit diplomacy to overcome the Cold War did not succeed. While the new collective leadership in Moscow, which had come to power following Stalin's death in March 1953, was lukewarm about the Prime Minister's plans, almost the entire western alliance was strongly opposed to and deeply concerned about Churchill's plan to change the western world's Cold War strategy.

When Churchill's successor managed successfully to convene the Geneva Four Power conference in mid-1955, the first East–West heads of government meeting since the Potsdam conference of 1945, only a brief "thaw" but no lasting détente was achieved. The time was not ripe to overcome the Cold War; mutual suspicions and East–West distrust were still much too great. At this stage of the Cold War it did not seem feasible to embark on more than a cautious if not superficial policy of conflict management to contain the Cold War without attempting to terminate it. As argued in the chapter by Vladislav Zubok and Constantine Pleshakov, it would need a severe crisis and the threat of the extinction of humanity to catapult the superpowers into developing a more constructive frame of mind for the de-escalation of the Cold War.

Yet, between 1958 and 1961 during the second Berlin crisis, merely the old conflict management techniques were utilized to prevent the outbreak of open East–West hostilities. Khrushchev's attempt to obtain recognition of the GDR and turn Berlin into an independent and de-militarized Free City appeared to bring the world to the brink of war. British Prime Minister Harold Macmillan employed the Churchillian policy of personal summit diplomacy to overcome East–West tension. However, like Churchill, Macmillan found himself confronted with bitter criticism and the accusation of "appeasement" of the Soviet Union from his western allies. Moreover, due to the crisis of the shooting down of the American U-2 spy plane over Soviet territory, the Paris four power conference in 1960 to stabilize the Cold War failed before it had really commenced. Instead of stabilizing the Cold War the abortive Paris meeting and the verbal clashes between Eisenhower and Khrushchev heightened Cold War tension. Macmillan's hectic crisis diplomacy during the conference could not avoid its failure. After the 1956 Suez crisis this was further symbolic confirmation that by the early 1960s the Cold War appeared to have largely become a superpower affair with the former European great powers Britain and France playing a mere supporting role to the USA. Britain's first application to join the EEC in 1962 also indicated this. Not a negotiated East–West agreement but only the building of the Berlin War in August 1961 resulted in the enforced uneasy stabilization of the partition of Europe under the respective security umbrellas of the two superpowers.

The management of the Cold War rather than the attempt to terminate it for good remained the order of the day when John F. Kennedy became American president in January 1961. Early on in his presidency, and in particular in the aftermath of the disastrous American supported invasion of Fidel Castro's Cuba by Cuban exiles (the Bay of Pigs adventure), the new American President intended to embark on de-escalating the Cold War and considering disengagement zones in the middle of Europe despite the opposition of West Germany, one of America's most loyal Cold War allies. However, for Kennedy the achievement of a real and lasting détente between East and West rather than a solution to the German question was paramount. Yet, his April 1961 meeting with Khrushchev in Vienna was unsuccessful and the Soviet leader may well have received the wrong impression of Kennedy's personality and political stamina. The subdued American reaction to the erection of the Berlin Wall in August 1961 may have reinforced this impression.

It was thus not so much the prolonged second Berlin crisis and the building of the Wall but, above all, the immeasurably more dangerous Cuban Missile Crisis of late 1962 which persuaded the two superpowers to embark on a much more active and systematic joint approach to international crisis management to contain the Cold War. After having only just managed to retreat from the verge of nuclear war both Kennedy and Khrushchev realised that Washington and Moscow had to co-operate if they wished to be successful in taming the Cold War and embarking on the road towards a more lasting East–West détente. By 1963 not the termination of the Cold War as envisaged by Churchill in 1953/4 but merely the careful containment and management of the East–West appeared to be the only feasible and practicable policy available to Kennedy and Khrushchev.

4

Integrating Europe or Ending the Cold War? Churchill's Post-war Foreign Policy

Klaus Larres

Originally appeared in the *Journal of European Integration History*, vol. 2, no. 1 (1996), © Klaus Larres.

[B]y the end of the war and the beginning of the post-war period Churchill regarded a solution to the following political issues as particularly urgent for the development of a peaceful world: Franco-German reconciliation and the re-integration of Germany into the European family of nations; the settlement of conflicts and peaceful co-operation with Stalin in the post-war world; and last but not least, the development of the Anglo-American 'special relationship'. Ultimately, Churchill hoped that the successful pursuit of all these closely interlinked aims would serve to rebuild and maintain Britain's role as a world power. He did not hesitate to announce that the "main aim" of his policy was "to restore the greatness of Britain".[1] Churchill had not worked out any concrete plans for building a united Europe. He was much more obsessed with ensuring Britain's survival as a great power in the post-war world. To him Britain's elevated international status as well as its many global commitments ruled out any British participation in an integrated Europe, which would have meant joining the weak and devastated European states who, unlike the UK, had not been able to withstand Hitler's onslaught. He merely hoped that Britain would be able to develop its "new association with Europe without in the slightest degree weakening the sacred ties which unite Britain

---

1 Speech addressed to the crowd assembled in the football stadium of Wolverhampton, 22 July 1949. Quoted in *Keesing's Contemporary Archive*, vol. 7: 1948–50, London, 1950, p. 10129.

with her daughter States across the oceans".[2] Churchill held the widely shared illusion that the Empire and Commonwealth and not some kind of western European bloc would serve as a power base for Britain's influence in the post-war world. After all, Britain needed, in Denis Healey's words, "new sources of power, not new sources of responsibility".[3]

Leader of the Opposition (1945–51)

Defeated in the general election of July 1945, Churchill began the post-war era by concentrating on writing his memoirs and enjoying his enormous reputation as the world's most famous person.[4] Churchill's political importance in the years 1945–51 did not lie in the development of any convincing alternative strategies with which he attempted to challenge Prime Minister Attlee's policies. Neither did he contribute much to drawing up new Conservative policies for the future. He left those important but tiresome occupations largely to Rab Butler, Lord Woolton and Anthony Eden, his heir apparent.[5] The new leader of the opposition concentrated instead on addressing matters of global concern. Those he found much more interesting and stimulating. Above all, his references to the East–West conflict and to the unity of Europe received great attention. As far as the latter issue was concerned, Churchill largely followed the ideas which he had developed during the Second World War.

Churchill's original contribution to addressing the many problems of the post-war world, therefore, did not consist of his vague and ambiguous calls for European unity. His unique contribution can be found in his repeated calls for negotiations with the Soviet Union to overcome the post-war differences among the Big Three. Although the observed that an "iron curtain" had descended across the European continent and that Moscow could only be impressed by a show of force, he did not believe that Stalin sought to provoke the outbreak of yet another war. Therefore, he made it his business to call upon the nations of the world to arrive at a peaceful settlement of the conflicts which had led to the

2   Speech to the Council of the European Movement, Brussels, 26 Feb. 1949, in R. S. Churchill (ed.), *In the Balance: Speeches 1949 and 1950*, London 1951, p. 29.
3   D. Healey, *When Shrimps Learn to Whistle: Signposts for the Nineties*, London 1990, pp. 68–9 (quote: p. 68).
4   See N. Rose, *Churchill: An Unruly Life*, London 1994, p. 328.
5   See K. Larres, *Politik der Illusionen: Churchill, Eisenhower und die deutsche Frage*, Göttingen 1995, pp. 40–41; P. Addison, *Churchill on the Home Front, 1900–55*, London 1993, pp. 386 ff.; also J. Ramsden, *The Age of Churchill and Eden, 1940–1957*, London 1955; F. A. Mayer, *The Opposition Years: Winston S. Churchill and the Conservative Party, 1945–51*, New York 1992.

East–West divide. He explained his ambition in full during a speech in the House of Commons in late January 1948 by pointing out that he wanted "to arrive at a lasting settlement" with the help of "formal diplomatic processes". Otherwise there seemed to be a "very real danger in going on drifting too long".[6]

However, Churchill had not suddenly "gone soft" on Communism. He pursued a twin-track approach.[7] He argued that the Soviet Union first had to be impressed by western unity of purpose, military preparedness and political, economic and military strength. Only then would negotiations with Moscow be viable in order to settle the Cold War amicably and without either side losing face. He had already expressed the view in August 1945, with reference to the atomic bomb, that there were "three and perhaps four years before the concrete progress made in the United States can be overtaken". During this period it was all-important to re-organize international relations in a peaceful way and establish an international atomic control agency, if a nuclear war between East and West was to be avoided. . . .[8]

[T]o Churchill his twin-track strategy of western unity and rearmament and the more or less simultaneous pursuit of genuine negotiations was still the only feasible policy which would prevent another world war.

Churchill's repeated calls for European unity, and even for the creation of a United States of Europe between 1945 and 1951 as leader of the opposition, must be seen as part of his strategy to impress upon Stalin the coherence, strength and resolution of the western world led by the Anglo-American "fraternal association".[9] Other factors like a Franco-German rapprochement, German re-integration into the civilized world, the development of economic stability in Europe, and a certain willingness to bow to American pressure in the European question were also important considerations which led to his calls for a united Europe.[10] However, Churchill's grand design for the post-war world consisted of arriving at an amicable settlement with the Soviet Union by means of "negotiations from strength". His calls for European unity were part and parcel of that scenario; they ought not to be

6   House of Commons Debates (hereafter: H.C. Deb.), 5th series, vol. 446, 23 Jan. 1948, cols. 560, 561.
7   S. J. Lambakis speaks of a "carrot and stick approach". See his *Winston Churchill: Architect of Peace: A study of Statesmanship and the Cold War*, Westport, Ct. 1993, p. 111.
8   "There is not an hour to be wasted; there is not a day to be lost". Churchill, "Debate on the Address", H.C. Deb., 5th series, vol. 413, 16 Aug. 1945, col. 80.
9   See Larres, *Politik der Illusionen*, pp. 40–62; also Churchill's speech at the Albert Hall, London, 14 May 1947, when he attended a "United Europe Meeting", in R. S. Churchill (ed.), *Europe Unite: Speeches 1947 and 1948*, London 1950, pp. 83–5: "The whole purpose of a united democratic Europe is to give decisive guarantees against aggression" (p. 83).
10   See for example Churchill's speech to the Congress of Europe in The Hague, 7 May 1948, in R. S. Churchill (ed.), ibid., pp. 310–17.

regarded as separate from that design. It is clear that European integration for its own sake was not one of his prime objectives. His "ultimate
aim" was the end of the Cold War and with it "the unity and freedom of
the whole of Europe".[11]

The issues which appeared to be most pressing to him (good relations
with Moscow; Anglo-American relations; European unity without full
British participation), all made an appearance in one of his most famous
speeches ever – his address at Westminster College in Fulton, Missouri,
on 5 March 1946. The Fulton speech in fact outlined Churchill's grand
strategy for the post-war world by calling for both an international settlement and a policy of strength while emphasizing the enduring importance of the British Empire and Commonwealth.

This speech attracted particular attention because of its at first sight
violent anti-Russian tone, which elevated Churchill almost overnight to
the Cold Warrior *par excellence*. Churchill used the address to warn the
world with his forceful rhetoric of Stalin's aggressive intentions and the
ever encroaching expansionist ambitions of the Soviet Empire. According to British Ambassador Lord Halifax, the persuasive language of the
speech gave "the sharpest jolt to American thinking of any utterance
since the end of the war".[12] Above all, it convinced President Truman
that American public opinion was gradually accepting the seemingly
unbridgeable post-war differences with Stalin's Soviet Union and was
warming up to fighting the Cold War.[13]

However, it can be seen clearly that Churchill did not just employ the
Fulton speech, officially entitled "The Sinews of Peace", to address the
threat from the East. He also pointed to the possibilities for a peaceful
settlement with Moscow. Churchill declared that he did not believe that
a new war was "inevitable" or "imminent" or that "Soviet Russia desires
war". Instead of "closing our eyes" to Stalin's expansionist policy or
embarking on "a policy of appeasement", he recommended a different
strategy by emphasizing that "what is needed is a settlement [with
Stalin], and the longer this is delayed, the more difficult it will be and
the greater our dangers will be".[14] At Fulton Churchill first publicly pro-

11   Churchill, speech to the Council of the European Movement, Brussels, 26 Feb. 1949, in
R. S. Churchill (ed.), *In the Balance*, p. 29.
12   Halifax to Foreign Office, 10 March 1946, quoted in P. Boyle, "The British Foreign Office
View of Soviet-American Relations, 1945–46", *Diplomatic History*, vol. 3 (1979), p. 314.
13   See F. Harbutt, "American Challenge, Soviet Response: The Beginning of the Cold War,
February–May 1946", in: *Political Science Quarterly*, vol. 96 (1981–82), p. 633; idem., *The Iron
Curtain: Churchill, America, and the Origins of the Cold War*, New York 1986, pp. 183 ff., esp.
197–208; H. B. Ryan, "A New Look at Churchill's 'Iron Curtain' Speech", Historical Journal,
vol. 22 (1979), pp. 895–920; M. P. Leffler, *A Preponderance of Power: National Security, The
Truman Administration, and the Cold War*, Stanford, Ca. 1992, pp. 107–10.
14   R. S. Churchill (ed.), *The Sinews of Peace: Postwar Speeches*, London 1948, pp. 93–105
(quotes: pp. 100–3).

posed his twin-track approach of how to deal with the Soviet Union without provoking a war.

As far as Europe was concerned, he declared that "the world requires a new unity in Europe from which no nation should be permanently outcast". Thus, he hinted at the necessity of integrating Germany into such a scheme. He resurrected his Second World War ideas on the future of Europe by emphasizing that "we should work with conscious purpose for a grand pacification of Europe, within the structure of the United Nations (. . .) one cannot imagine a regenerated Europe without a strong France." It was, however, obvious to Churchill that a united Europe led by France would hardly be able to deal with the world's post-war problems. Therefore, he emphasized the importance of the Anglo-American special relationship. After all, he believed that "a good understanding with Russia" and its maintenance "through many peaceful years" could only be reached with the help of "the general authority of the United Nations Organization" and above all with the support of "the whole strength of the English-speaking world and all its connections". In particular, he emphasized that nobody should "underrate the abiding power of the British Empire and Commonwealth".

> If the population of the English-speaking Commonwealth be added to that of the United States with all that such co-operation implies in the air, on the sea, all over the globe and in science and in industry, and in moral force, there will be no quivering, precarious balance of power to offer its temptation to ambition or adventure. On the contrary, there will be an overwhelming assurance of security.[15]

It was obvious that Churchill was not thinking of Britain as part of a united Europe. Instead, together the USA and the UK would safeguard the security as well as the democratic spirit of the world.[16] Churchill's speech at the University of Zurich on 19 September 1946 elaborated on his vision for a united Europe. He called for building "a kind of United States of Europe" to restore the material and spiritual wealth and happiness of the people on the continent. He did not think that a "regional organization of Europe" would conflict with the United Nations. Quite the opposite. He was convinced that "the larger synthesis will only survive if it is founded upon coherent natural groupings": After all, there was already such a "natural grouping". "We British have our own

15   Ibid., pp. 98–104.
16   See also Churchill's similar but much briefer speech at the reception of the Lord Mayor and civic authorities of New York at the Waldorf Astoria, New York, on 15 March 1946, in ibid., pp. 115–20.

Commonwealth of Nations. These do not weaken, on the contrary, they strengthen, the world organization. They are in fact its main support". Above all, Churchill believed that in order to save Europe from "infinite misery" and "final doom", an "act of faith in the European family and an act of oblivion against all the crimes and follies of the past" were required. He then outlined his vision of a strong and energetic Europe by calling for Franco-German co-operation. "France and Germany must take the lead together":

> The first step in the re-creation of the European family must be a partnership between France and Germany. In this way only can France recover the moral leadership of Europe. There can be no revival of Europe without a spiritually great France and a spiritually great Germany. The structure of the United States of Europe, if well and truly built, will be such as to make the material strength of a single state less important. Small nations will count as much as large ones and gain their honour by their contribution to the common cause.[17]

A few months prior to this speech Churchill had outlined in the House of Commons that the main threat to post-war European stability did not rest in the devastated Germany but would result from "the confusion and degeneration into which all Europe (. . .) is rapidly sinking". This situation, he feared, could easily be exploited by the forces of international communism.[18] Despite his ambition to achieve a settlement with Stalin, Churchill was realistic enough to come to the conclusion, as early as June 1946, that the long-term division of both Germany and the European continent had to be expected:

> We have to face the fact that, as we are going on at present, two Germanys are coming into being (. . .) I say it with much regret, but without any hesitancy – that, when all has been tried and tried in vain (. . .) it is better to have a world united than a world divided; but it is also better to have a world divided than a world destroyed.[19]

Churchill's approach for dealing with the defeated German nation consisted of his hope that the western world would succeed "over a period of years to redeem and reincorporate" the Germans into the free world. Above all, the Germans had to be fully integrated into a united western Europe.[20] In his Zurich speech he even mentioned that he envisaged the United States of Europe as a "federal system" and the forma-

---

17 Ibid., pp. 198–202.
18 "Foreign Affairs" speech, H.C. Deb., 5th series, vol. 427, 5 June 1946, col. 2030.
19 "Foreign Affairs" speech, ibid., vol. 428, 5 June 1946, cols. 2028, 2031.
20 "Foreign Affairs" speech, ibid., vol. 427, 5 June 1946, col. 2029; "Foreign Affairs" speech, ibid., vol. 459, 10 Dec. 1948, col. 711. See also G. A. Craig, "Churchill and Germany", in R. Blake and Wm. B. Louis (eds.), *Churchill*, Oxford 1993, pp. 37–40.

tion of a "Council of Europe" – even if not all European states were prepared to immediately join this system. Moreover, in the course of the speech he seemed to hint at the possibility that Britain might be part of this scheme when saying that time was running out as the protective shield of the atomic bomb would in a few years also have been acquired by the enemy. "If we are to form the United States of Europe or whatever name or form it may take, we must begin now." But then, at the very end of the speech, Churchill made it clear that Britain would remain outside:

> Great Britain, the British Commonwealth of Nations, mighty America, and I trust Soviet Russia – for then indeed all would be well – must be the friends and sponsors of the new Europe and must champion its right to live and shine.[21]

Thus, Churchill had not entirely given up his idealistic vision of a united Europe closely associated with the Big Three: As the leaders of the United Nations, they would guide and oversee European developments in a peaceful and co-operative way from the outside. To Churchill Britain was still "with" Europe but not "of" it.

Since his speech at Zurich University, Churchill's strong support for the European unity movement was taken for granted. His audiences either entirely misunderstood his words which distanced Britain from participation, preferred not to listen too carefully to such statements or they hoped that Churchill did not really mean what he said. Some of his speeches were indeed quite ambiguous. Churchill often employed his high profile statements on European unity to embarrass the Labour government, enhance his own profile and score political points for the Conservatives.[22] Moreover, the leader of the opposition seemed to display more pro-European activities than the Labour government with its very cautious and reserved attitude to the increasingly popular European unity movements.[23] Churchill, for example, presided at the

21   R. S. Churchill (ed.), *Sinews of Peace*, pp. 197–202.
22   See for example his speech at the Albert Hall, London, 14 May 1947, when he attended a "United Europe Meeting", in R. S. Churchill (ed.), *Europe Unite*, p. 84; his "United Europe Exhibition" speech, Dorland Hall, London, 17 November 1948, in ibid., p. 466; and above all his speech on the Schuman Plan to the House of Commons, 27 June 1950, in Churchill, *In the Balance*, pp. 287 ff. G. Warner is convinced that Churchill's and the Conservatives' strategy "was not only irresponsible but also hypocritical, since they were no more willing than their Labour opponents to surrender British sovereignty to the kind of federalist authority advocated at The Hague" ("The Labour Governments and the Unity of Western Europe, 1945–51", in R. Ovendale (ed.), *The Foreign Policy of the British Labour Governments, 1945–51*, Leicester 1984, pp. 67–8). For a similar view see M. Camps, *Britain and the European Community, 1955–63*, London 1964, pp. 11–12.
23   See the brief overviews in D. W. Urwin, *The Community of Europe: A History of European Integration since 1945*, 2nd ed., London 1995, pp. 1 ff.; D. Dinan, *Ever Closer Union? An Introduction to the European Community*, Basingstoke 1994, pp. 9 ff.

first Congress of Europe in The Hague in May 1948 while the Labour government and the Labour party had initially called for a boycott of the event. He used the opportunity to call upon the participants to "resolve that in one form or another a European Assembly shall be constituted". He was also in favour of admitting the Germans to this Assembly.[24] Ultimately, Churchill's strong support led to the establishment of the Council of Europe in May 1949. In the House of Commons on 27 June 1950 Churchill strongly criticized the Labour government for not participating in the talks about a European Coal and Steel Community (ECSC), the Schuman Plan. He even declared that "the whole movement of the world is towards an inter-dependence of nations" and "national sovereignty is not inviolable" and may be "resolutely diminished" for the sake of the nations concerned.[25] A few months later, on 11 August 1950, during a speech to the Consultative Assembly of the Council of Europe in Strasbourg, it was again Churchill who made the very controversial proposal to begin with the "immediate creation of a unified European Army", including a German contingent.[26] This encouraged Jean Monnet and the French Defence Minister René Pleven to work out a scheme for a supranational European Defence Community (EDC), in late 1950, based on the ECSC model. In the wake of the outbreak of the Korean War, the European Army proposal allowed France to give in to strong American pressure for German rearmament while avoiding the creation of an independent German army and a German general staff. Despite strong American and French pressure, the British did not feel that they could join such a European defence organization.[27]

Yet, despite all the activities on behalf of a united Europe, Churchill continued to remain convinced that Britain was a special case. The United Kingdom was at the center of three concentric circles consisting of the British Empire and Commonwealth, the English speaking world, and a united Europe. Politicians of all major parties in Britain and also the vast majority of the general public genuinely believed that as a respected and highly influential member in all of Churchill's three circles, Britain had a unique and ultimately beneficial global role to

24   R. S. Churchill (ed.), *Europe Unite*, pp. 310–17 (quote: p. 317).
25   Idem., *In the Balance*, pp. 287–303 (quotes: pp. 302–03). See also R. Bullen, "The British Government and the Schuman Plan, May 1950–March 1951", in K. Schwabe (ed.), *The Beginnings of the Schuman Plan 1950/51*, Baden-Baden 1988, pp. 199–210; E. Dell, *The Schuman Plan and the British abdication of leadership in Europe*, London 1995.
26   R. S. Churchill, ibid., pp. 347–52 (quote: p. 352). See also A. Ch. Azzola, *Die Diskussion um die Aufrüstung der BRD im Unterhaus und in der Presse Großbritanniens November 1949–Juli 1952*, Meisenheim 1971.
27   See above all E. Furdson, *The European Defence Community*, London 1980; S. Dockrill, *Britain's Policy for West German Rearmament, 1950–55*, Cambridge 1991; H.-E. Volkmann and W. Schwengler (eds.), *Die Europäische Verteidigungsgemeinschaft. Stand und Probleme der Forschung*, Boppard 1985. L. Köllner et al. (eds.), *Die EVG-Phase*, Boppard 1990.

perform. It could, therefore, not simply join the continental European nations in a federation. Together with the United States, Britain was the leader of the free world with the additional task of guiding Washington towards a responsible policy.[28] In fact, as far as Europe was concerned and despite all party political rhetoric Churchill's views hardly differed from the perspective of Prime Minister Attlee and Foreign Secretary Ernest Bevin. "Cooperation with Europe was desirable; integration with Europe was not".[29]

Post-war British leaders were "prepared to work for a united Europe, seeing that as the only way in which Western Europe could survive in the long run as a narrow fringe on the west of the great Communist empire of Eurasia" – but did not intend to participate in that venture themselves. Politicians from all major parties had a "nasty feeling" that if Britain "went off into Europe and left the Americans outside, they would reduce their own commitment". And committing the Americans to Western Europe was the "prime concern" which united the vast majority of politicians in Westminster.[30] Thus, Churchill's war-time objections to the creation of a purely western European bloc under British leadership were still widely shared.

The Labour government's early interest in close co-operation with the European continental states in the years between 1945 and 1948 ought to be regarded as mere contingency planning. Part of this policy were the creation of an Anglo-French military alliance (the Dunkirk Treaty) in March 1946, Foreign Secretary Ernest Bevin's initial enthusiasm for a customs union with some of the continental states, and the formation of a Western European Union, as expressed in Bevin's speech to parliament in January 1948 and realized by means of the Brussels Treaty Organization three months later. Although almost all of these schemes avoided any supranational elements and concentrated on intergovernmental co-operation, they largely represented attempts to develop a British led third force in world affairs based on co-operation with the

---

28   On 9 October 1948 Churchill declared with reference to the three circles: "(. . .) we have the opportunity of joining them all together. If we rise to the occasion in the years that are to come it may be found that once again we hold the key to opening a safe and happy future to humanity, and will gain for ourselves gratitude and fame". "Perils Abroad and At Home", speech to the Annual Conservative Party Conference, Llandudno, Wales, in R. R. James (ed.), *Winston S. Churchill: His Complete Speeches, 1897–1963*, vol. 7: 1940–49, London 1974, p. 7712. See also for similar remarks in 1949, ibid., pp. 7870–71; also *Keesing's Contemporary Archive*, vol. 7, 1948–50, p. 10288.

29   Quote: Camps, *Britain*, p. 4. For the view of the Labour governments see for example K. O. Morgan, *Labour in Power, 1945–51*, Oxford 1984, pp. 66ff., 271ff., 389–98, 417–21; G. Warner, "Labour Governments", pp. 61ff.; S. Croft, "British Policy towards Western Europe, 1945–51", in P. M. R. Stirk and D. Willis (eds.), *Shaping Postwar Europe: European Unity and Disunity, 1945–57*, London 1991, pp. 77ff.

30   Quotes: Healey, *When Shrimps Learn to Whistle*, p. 76.

European continent.[31] After all, until the beginning of the successful implementation of the Marshall Plan with the help of the OEEC in early 1948 and the negotiations from mid-1948 which led to the creation of NATO, Britain could not be sure whether or not there would be an active and benevolent American involvement in Western Europe. However, this policy of co-operation which included quite naturally a certain dependence on and involvement with Western Europe had always been regarded as a compromise solution, as a mere alternative to an American commitment to Europe.[32] For both Attlee's Labour government and Churchill's Conservative opposition, American involvement in European affairs was their ultimate aim. Thus Britain's bipartisan European policy strategy after the war largely consisted of attempting merely to oversee developments on the continent, in close consultation and co-operation with the United States.[33]

This chasm between the attitude prevalent in London and the view of the "federalists" on the continent only became clear to the French and others in the course of 1948–9 when the government in Paris began supporting supranational solutions by proposing the creation of a genuine "European parliament". While Bevin was merely thinking in terms of a pragmatic and evolutionary "step-by-step" approach to European co-operation, France, Italy, the Benelux countries and soon also the newly created West German state favoured a speedy formal federation to further the continent's economic reconstruction. European unity was also seen partially as a way to neutralize Europe in the Cold War; some talked of the development of a European third force between the two superpowers, though this idea soon petered out.[34]

Moreover, by 1948–9 (beginning in 1947 with the announcement of Marshall Plan aid) the United States strongly favoured the creation of a supranational Europe where majority decision-making would apply.[35]

31 See K. Larres, "A Search for Order: Britain and the Origins of a Western European Union, 1944–55", in B. Brivati and H. Jones (eds), *From Reconstruction to Integration: Britain and Europe since 1945*, Leicester 1993, pp. 71–2, 85–6. See also Warner, "Labour Governments", pp. 61–82.
32 Ibid. See also M. Hogan, *The Marshall Plan: America, Britain, and the reconstruction of Western Europe, 1947–52*, Cambridge 1987, pp. 46–8.
33 As Young has persuasively shown, this also applied to the "pro-Europeans" within the Conservative party like Macmillan, Maxwell Fyfe, Eccles, etc. who were somewhat more prepared than Churchill and Eden to associate Britain with the European continent. However they did not think in terms of integration with a federal supranational Europe either. See J. W. Young, "Churchill's 'No' to Europe: The 'rejection' of European Union by Churchill's post-war government, 1951–52", *Historical Journal* 28 (1985), pp. 923 ff.
34 See Hogan, *Marshall Plan*, pp. 47–8; Warner "Labour Governments", pp. 61 ff.; Croft, "British Policy", pp. 77 ff.; Camps, *Britain*, p. 3.
35 See Warner, ibid., pp. 65 ff. For Acheson's views see for example: Foreign Relations of the United States (hereafter: FRUS) 1949, vol. 4 p. 472 (telegram to US Embassy in Paris, 19 Oct. 1949).

Several reasons existed for American pressure for the speedy creation of such an integrated Europe: the perception of an ever increasing threat from the Soviet Union; an American Congress which seemed to be inclined to make further Marshall aid dependent on progress with European integration; a worsening of the general psychological atmosphere in Europe; and last, but not least, a lack of identity and a feeling of inferiority within the new Federal Republic of Germany. It was hoped in Washington that a return to nationalism and international unreliability could be prevented by integrating the West Germans firmly and irreversibly into Western Europe.[36]

Churchill and above all Prime Minister Attlee, however, were highly suspicious of Washington's increasingly impatient demands that Britain should shoulder the responsibility for leading Western Europe into a supranational federation and, much to their mutual dislike, even participate in such a union. President Roosevelt's declaration at the end of the war that the United States would withdraw from Europe within two to three years was still fresh in the minds of politicians. The differences in approach between Britain and the continental Europeans as well as the Americans became clear, for example, over disputes regarding the form the OEEC should take for the administration of Marshall Plan aid.[37] It also led to the fact that the Council of Europe set up in May 1949 soon proved to be a bad compromise as it represented the combination of a "federal" with a "functional" solution. Although the Council included a Consultative Parliamentary Assembly, it was not a proper European parliament with legislative powers. Instead, it represented merely a debating chamber ("an irresponsible talking-shop") which was largely controlled by the Committee of Ministers – an organ based on traditional intergovernmental co-operation.[38] Indeed, Churchill found himself in full agreement with the Labour government and traditional British policy when he came out strongly in favour of not attempting to turn the Council into a supranational body by changing "the powers which belong to the duly constituted national parliaments'. He believed that "such a course would be premature (. . .) [and] detrimental to our long-term interests". The most positive feature of the Council of Europe was perhaps its very existence as a symbol of some kind of western European co-operation and West Germany's member-

36   See K. Schwabe. "'Ein Akt konstruktiver Staatskunst' – die USA und die Anfänge des SchumanPlans", in Schwabe (ed.), *Beginnings of the Schuman Plan*, pp. 214–15.
37   See J. Gillingham, *Coal, Steel, and the Rebirth of Europe, 1945–55: The Germans and the French form Ruhr Conflict to Economic Community*, Cambridge 1991, pp. 120–33; Camps, *Britain*, pp. 6–8.
38   See Churchill's "United Europe Exhibition" speech, Dorland Hall, London, 17 Nov. 1948, in R. S. Churchill, *Europe Unite*, p. 466 (quote: ibid.). See also Warner, "Labour Governments", pp. 68–70.

ship which, it was hoped, would be useful in facilitating a Franco-German rapprochement.[39]

When Churchill returned to No. 10 Downing Street in late 1951, he was widely associated with his calls for a "united Europe" in Zurich, the Hague and elsewhere, and that despite his anti-supranational statement quoted above. That clear misperception of Churchill's views led to some unfounded expectation among continental politicians that Britain's European policy was about to change. That was mere wishful thinking. As Churchill no longer needed European matters as a tool with which to embarrass the Labour party or as an instrument to obtain global attention, he lost almost all his remaining interest in the question of European unity. Most of his last years as Prime Minister were characterized by intensive advocacy of "summit diplomacy" to end the Cold War rather than by an European integration policy. In his final speech during the election campaign of 1951 Churchill made it unambiguously clear what he intended to achieve. He hoped that Stalin would be willing to participate in "a friendly talk with the leaders of the free world [to] see if something could not be arranged which enabled us all to live together quietly."

> If I remain in public life at this juncture it is because, rightly or wrongly, but sincerely, I believe that I may be able to make an important contribution to the prevention of a third world war and to bring nearer that lasting peace settlement which the masses of the people (. . .) fervently desire. I pray indeed that I may have this opportunity. It is the last prize I seek to win."[40]

Prime Minister again (1951–55)

Churchill received the opportunity to convince the world of his summit diplomacy when the British people gave him a majority of 17 seats on 25 October 1951 to form his last government. The new Prime Minister was already 77 years old and his health had been in a precarious state for some years. His government was "too much characterized by its chief's stubborn battle for [political and physical] survival to be a splendid affair".[41] Churchill's peacetime premiership largely was a very

39 See Churchill's speech before the Consultative Assembly of the Council of Europe, Strasbourg, 17 Aug. 1949, in R. S. Churchill, ibid., pp. 81–2 (quotes: p. 80); also his speech to the same forum on 11 Aug. 1950, in ibid., pp. 347 ff.
40 Speech in Plymouth, Home Park Football Ground, 23 Oct. 1951, in James (ed.), *Complete Speeches*, vol. 8: 1950–63, London 1974, p. 8282.
41 R. Jenkins, "Churchill: The Government of 1951–1955", in Blake and Louis (eds.), *Churchill*, p. 497; for an overview of this administration see A. Seldon, *Churchill's Indian Summer: The Conservative Government, 1951–55*, London 1981.

consensual affair aiming at consolidation rather than radical change. Indeed, he reversed only very few of the Labour government's legislation (e.g. the nationalization of iron and steel).[42]

Churchill also continued Attlee's policy towards European integration. Despite occasional hints to the contrary while in opposition, he left the Labour government's decision not to participate in the Schuman Plan unaltered. By means of the Eden Plan of 1952 his government merely attempted to re-design the High Authority of the ECSC as well as the supranational EDC organs yet to be established into a non-supranational body by proposing that both the ESCS and the EDC would be closely linked to the Council of Europe. This was, however, eventually rejected by most European states.[43] Churchill had taken no active interest in the ill-fated Eden Plan. His age no longer allowed him to give equal consideration to all the many different areas of government. With the exception of Egypt and the attempt to maintain Britain's imperial position in the Near East, Churchill concentrated entirely on his summit diplomacy and related issues. He neglected almost all other external (and domestic) matters.[44] European issues would only attract his attention when they were directly connected to his policy as a global peacemaker. In late November 1951, when referring to his Zurich speech of 1946 in a cabinet paper entitled "United Europe", Churchill made it unambiguously clear that he had "never thought that Britain (. . .) should become an integral part of a European Federation".[45]

His government's attitude towards the European Defence Community, signed in 1952, was therefore never more than lukewarm though the EDC was the domineering issue during his peace-time government as far as European integration was concerned. The EDC was not only the instrument to achieve western European rearmament on a supranational basis but also the means to integrate West Germany irreversibly into the West while giving the Federal Republic its sovereignty in return. Thus, the linkage between West German sovereignty (the so-called contractual agreements were also signed in May 1952) and the ratification of the EDC meant in fact that the further development of the

42   In a parliamentary speech in November 1951 Churchill explained the remedy for "deeply and painfully divided' Britain: "What the nation needs is several years of quiet, steady administration, if only to allow Socialist legislation to reach its full fruition. What the House needs is a period of tolerant and constructive debating (. . .)", H.C. Deb., 5th series, vol. 493, 6 Nov. 1951, cols. 68–9.
43   See Young, "Churchill's 'No' ", pp. 927, 932–6; A. Nutting, *Europe will not wait: A warning and a way out*, London 1960, pp. 42–6; D. Spierenburg and R. Poidevin, *The History of the High Authority of the ECSC*, London 1994, pp. 202–4.
44   See for example E. Shuckburgh, *Descent to Suez, Diaries, 1951–56*, London 1986, pp. 24 ff.
45   PRO: CAB 129/48, C(51)32nd conclusions (29 Nov. 1951); see also A. Montague Browne, *Long Sunset, Memoirs*, London 1995, pp. 271–2.

western alliance as well as the attachment of the Bonn Republic to the West were at stake. Everything seemed to depend on the ratification of the EDC by its six member states (France, West Germany, Italy, Benelux).[46] However, these ratification problems did not impress Churchill too much. European matters were largely left to the competent though not very sympathetic Anthony Eden. Churchill was not so much concerned with the successful integration of the Federal Republic with the West by means of the EDC as with the creation of an international détente and an end to the Cold War thus rendering the EDC unnecessary and terminating the division of Germany. It was Churchill's main goal to end the Cold War by means of an informal Anglo-American summit conference with the Soviet Union. He hoped to be able to negotiate away the division of Germany. As will be outlined below in detail, throughout 1953 and to some extent also in 1954 the British Prime Minister was quite prepared to sacrifice the Federal Republic's integration with the West. He believed that the creation of a neutral and united Germany (in the Yalta and Potsdam borders) would be the expedient to overcome the Cold War and to ensure a more peaceful and – as was generally assumed – infinitely more stable world.[47]

However, during Stalin's lifetime he was always torn between his wish to negotiate a compromise peace with the Kremlin and the terrible realities of Soviet power politics in Eastern Europe which seemed to make any rapprochement with Moscow impossible.[48] Thus, when Stalin proposed in his Note of March 10, 1952 the reunification of Germany on a neutral basis, Churchill hardly became involved in the heated debate in the western world over the question of whether or not Stalin's suggestion was meant seriously.[49] In 1951–52 Churchill was rather pessimistic. He was deeply shocked by the purges and show trials in the CSSR and soon concluded that "the chances of achieving anything with Stalin were almost nil".[50] Moreover, Eden's strategy of arriving at a

---

46   See note 80 above; also K. Adenauer, *Erinnerungen 1945–53*, Stuttgart 1965, pp. 169 ff.; H.-J. Rupieper, *Der besetzte Verbündete. Die amerikanische Deutschlandpolitik 1949–55*, Opladen 1991.

47   See Larres, *Politik der Illusionen*, pp. 127 ff. In the 1950s hardly anyone was able to imagine that three decades later the Cold War would be seen as a source of stability creating a "long peace". For the latter J. L. Gaddis, "The Long Peace: Elements of Stability in the Postwar International System", *International Security*, vol. 10, no. 4 (1986), pp. 99–142.

48   PRO: FO 371/106 537, 1044/2/53 G, letter from Christopher Steel, UK Embassy Washington, to Paul Mason, FO, 16 Jan. 1953. See also J. Colville, *The Fringes of Power: 10 Downing Street Diaries, 1939–1955*, New York 1985, p. 660: diary entry, 5 Jan. 1953.

49   PRO: PREM 11/168, minute Churchill to Eden, M. 235/52, 13/4/1952. For the attitude of the British government, see PRO: PREM 11/168; FO 800/793; FO 800/777. See also particularly R. Steininger, *The German Question: The Stalin Note of 1952 and the problem of reunification*, New York 1990.

50   See note 48.

rapprochement with Moscow by initiating secret and informal talks between November 1951 and January 1952 with Soviet Foreign Minister Vyshinsky had come to nothing.[51] During Churchill's visit to the USA in early 1952, President Truman told the Prime Minister that "the time was not ripe" for East–West negotiations. Churchill was forced to admit "that in present circumstances he would not be in favour of proposing a meeting with the leaders of the Soviet Union".[52] However, by June 1952 Churchill had regained some of his old optimism. He was confident that if Eisenhower were elected President, the USA might be interested in a "joint approach" to Moscow. This would eventually lead "perhaps to a congress in Vienna where the Potsdam Conference would be reopened and concluded".[53]

With the death of Stalin on 5 March 1953, Churchill energetically began with the realization of this policy in spite of the strong doubts of most of his closest advisers.[54] After all, in the immediate aftermath of the dictator's death the new Soviet leadership consisting of Malenkov, Beria and Molotov had begun to embark on a peace campaign. It included proposals designed to limit the escalation of the Cold War.[55] It appeared that the new leaders in Moscow needed a calmer international atmosphere in order to settle in internally and solve the serious economic problems of their country if they wished to remain in power for any length of time. Moreover, a fierce struggle for power seemed to have erupted in Moscow. There were even rumours that the new leadership (particularly Beria) was considering to sacrifice the GDR and give its agreement to German unification on the basis of its neutrality.[56] However, this information frightened most western politicians and

---

51 PRO: FO 800/820, conversation Eden-Soviet ambassador in London, 28 Dec. 1952 (draft); FO 800/694, letter Eden to Minister of State Selwyn Lloyd, 24 Jan. 1952.
52 PRO: CAB 21/3057, Folder 9/102, 8 Feb. 1952; also FRUS 1952–54, vol. 6, pp. 693 ff.; Shuckburgh, *Descent to Suez*, p. 32.
53 Colville, *Fringes of Power*, pp. 653–4: diary entry, 13–15 June 1952; see also Colville's essay in J. Wheeler-Bennett (ed.), *Action this Day: Working with Churchill*, London 1984, p. 129.
54 For the following see above all Larres, *Politik der Illusionen*, pp. 72 ff.; M. S. Fish, "After Stalin's Death: The Anglo-American Debate Over a New Cold War", in: *Diplomatic History*, vol. 10 (1986), pp. 333–55; and some of the articles in J. W. Young (ed.), *The Foreign Policy of Churchill's Peacetime Administration, 1951–55*, Leicester 1988.
55 See FRUS 1952–54, Vol. 8, p. 1132: Beam to State Department, 18.3.1953. For a good overview see PRO: FO 371/106 510/NS 1015/39: "Chronology of Principal Events in Soviet Affairs, Jan.–June, 1953", dated 16 July 1953 (draft paper); and "Soviet Policy. Calendar of events since Stalin's death", memorandum by Lord Salisbury, dated 3 July 1953; *Eisenhower Library*, Abilene, Ks. (hereafter: EL): Jackson Papers, Record 1953–54, "Soviet Lures and Pressures Since Stalin's Death, March 5 to 25, 1953" & March 26 to April 13, annex, 26 March & 15 April 1953; and H. Salisbury, *Moscow Journal*, Chicago 1962, pp. 364–6, 369–71.
56 Up to the present day it is very controversial whether or not Moscow would have been prepared to enter into negotiations regarding German unification between March and June 1953 (after Stalin's death and before the uprising in the GDR), if the West had indicated that

diplomats, including West German Chancellor Adenauer and the British Foreign Office. They feared Moscow might be about to repeat and perhaps improve upon Stalin's reunification offer of March 1952.[57] Any such suggestion could well endanger German rearmament and the establishment of the increasingly unpopular EDC.[58] Therefore, none of the western statesmen involved, except Churchill, wished to believe that the Soviet Union was seriously considering giving up the GDR in order to obtain the unification and neutralization of Germany.[59] Above all, it was generally thought that a neutral Germany would in the long run be a country dominated by the Soviet Union. Western statesmen, including Adenauer, agreed that they only would consider German unification if it meant unity on western terms – a united and democratic Germany fully integrated with the West. As long as this was not possible, at least the western part of the country had to be irreversibly anchored in the western alliance.[60] Before this had happened, most western politicians did not entertain any notion of entering into negotiations with the Soviet Union.[61]

Accordingly, the new American President Eisenhower was not very keen on Churchill's letters containing his summit proposals, which reached him in March and April 1953.[62] He replied in a rather vague

genuine prospects for an agreement existed. For a brief overview of the relevant literature see K. Larres, "Preserving Law and Order: Britain, the United States and the East German Uprising of 1953', *Twentieth Century British History*, vol. 5 (1995), pp. 333–4; also Ch. F. Ostermann, "The United States, the East German Uprising of 1953 and the Limits of Rollback", *Cold War International History Project*, Working Paper No. 11 (1994).

57 See EL: John Foster Dulles Papers, Drafts of Presidential Correspondence, Box 1, memorandum Nitze to Dulles, "Peace Plan Speech. Consideration relating to the redraft of March 19, 1953", 20.3.1953; *National Archives*, Washington, DC (hereafter: NA): lot 64D563, PPS Records, 1947–53, Box 16, Folder Germany 1950–53, memorandum Fuller, "Possible Four-Power Talks on Germany", 17 April 1953; PRO: FO 371/106 532/NS 10345/9, minute Roberts to Strang about his conversation with Bohlen in London, 9.4.1953; FO 371/103 660/C 1016/23, 28 March 1953; FO 371/103 659/C 1916/16, 13 April 1953; FO 371/106 532/NS 10345/9, 9 April 1953; FRUS, 1952–54, Vol. 8, p. 1138. See also H. Blankenhorn, *Verständnis und Verständigung: Blätter eines politischen Tagebuchs 1949 bis 1979*, Frankfurt/Main 1980, pp. 144–5.

58 PRO: FO 371/103 659/C 1016/16, comment Roberts, 21 April 1953, on telegram Hayter, Paris, to Dixon, FO, 13 April 1953.

59 For example, Dulles' deputy Bedell Smith explained, "[that] (. . .) he did not believe that the Soviets were ready to give up their zone at this time. Although it was entirely possible and even likely that the Russians would make another offer to reunite Germany before the EDC enters into force, such a bid would not be sincere and would be nothing but an attempt to prevent or delay the establishment of a European Army". FRUS, 1952–54, Vol. 7, 30 March 1953, pp. 410–11.

60 See for example PRO: FO 371/103 660/C 1016/32, memorandum Roberts to Strang, "A unified, neutralized Germany", 19 May 1953.

61 PRO: FO 800/778, Makins, Washington, to FO, No. 726, about a conversation with Bedell Smith, 6 April 1953.

62 See P. G. Boyle (ed.), *The Churchill-Eisenhower Correspondence, 1953–55*, Chapel Hill 1990, pp. 31 ff.

and hesitant way. This, however, encouraged the Prime Minister to believe that he might still be able to change the President's mind.[63] But Churchill was entirely mistaken. While he wanted to exploit the unstable situation in the Soviet Union to initiate Big Three negotiations,[64] Eisenhower was intent on destabilizing the Soviet Government even further with a new psychological warfare offensive. Part of this was the "Chance for Peace" speech with which Eisenhower and his close adviser C. D. Jackson intended to counter the increasingly successful peace campaign waged by the Kremlin. Even anti-Communist hawk Foreign Secretary John Foster Dulles advised Eisenhower against the dangerous consequences of exploiting the fluid situation in Moscow, warning that the new leaders might overreact.[65]

On May 11, 1953 Churchill took the initiative. In a speech in the House of Commons, he revived his plan to arrange for a World War II-style summit between the United States, the Soviet Union and Britain.[66] Churchill wished to enter negotiations to solve all outstanding East–West problems at a meeting unfettered by a formal agenda. In several secret conversations and memoranda Churchill subsequently expressed the notion that a reunited and neutral Germany and the sacrifice of the Federal Republic's rearmament and integration with the West might prove a suitable price for a global détente. At one point he told his advisers confidentially "that he had not closed his mind to the possibility of a unified and neutralized Germany (. . .) as part of a settlement with the Russians".[67] Churchill envisaged the signing of a security pact between the Soviet Union and a reunited Germany, rather like the Locarno pact of 1925, which would be guaranteed by Great Britain.[68]

The dominant factor in Churchill's consideration was the realization that only a global détente would allow Britain to catch up with the two superpowers in the economic and military field, maintain its Empire and Commonwealth and remain one of the great powers of the world.

63   See for example Eisenhower's letters to Churchill on 25 April and 5 May 1953, in: Boyle (ed.), *Correspondence*, pp. 47, 49–50.
64   See Churchill's "Foreign Affairs" speech in parliament on 11 May 1953, H.C. Deb., 5th series, Vol. 515, cols. 883–98.
65   See K. Larres, "Eisenhower and the First Forty Days after Stalin's Death: The Incompatibility of Détente and Political Warfare", *Diplomacy & Statecraft*, Vol. 6 (1995), pp. 431–69.
66   See note 64.
67   PRO: FO 371/103 660/C 1016/32 (19/5/53), minute Dixon to Strang and Roberts about his conversation with Churchill on 16 May 1953.
68   PRO: FO 371/103 660/C 1016/32, minute Dixon to Strang and Roberts, 19 May 1953, about his conversation with Churchill on 16 May 1953; ibid., minute Strang to Dixon, 19 May 1953, about his conversations with Churchill on 18.5.1953; ibid., PREM 11/449 (also in FO 800/794), Churchill to Strang, M 178/53, 31.5.1953. See also H.C. Deb., 5th series, Vol. 515, 11 May 1953, cols. 896–7.

Churchill was aware that, if no détente with the Soviet Union was achieved and the armaments race and Cold War competition between the two blocs continued, Britain would lose out, and be forever dependent on the generosity of the United States. If détente could be realized, his country would be able to reduce its world-wide military commitments and concentrate on its economic and technological development, including the manufacturing of a British H-bomb and the necessary methods of delivery. A West German newspaper commented that after Britain had lost a quarter of her wealth in the war, Churchill's "purpose now was to secure a long period of peace and recovery" for his country.[69]

However, Churchill's notion that London could bring about a global détente with Britain as the guarantor of peace and security between the Soviet Union and a united but neutral Germany, much exaggerated Britain's importance and its military capabilities in the post-war world. The Prime Minister's own Foreign Office, including Foreign Secretary Eden,[70] the majority of the cabinet, as well as the American administration and Chancellor Adenauer were therefore very much opposed to Churchill's ideas. At a time when the EDC treaty was about to be ratified, Churchill's ideas were endangering the whole western concept of how to tackle the German question. If a summit seemed to be in the pipeline, French, German and other parliamentarians could be expected to wait and see whether or not German unification on a neutral basis materialized as this would make the rearmament of the Federal Republic unnecessary. Furthermore, there was considerable concern that his plans in their superficial simplicity would find the support of western public opinion.[71] Under these circumstances, it seemed ever more unlikely that the French parliament would consider giving up France's military sovereignty by agreeing to merge French forces with German and other forces into a supranational European army. After all, the creation of the EDC represented an almost revolutionary re-structuring of the national defence policies of its member states. The European nations were asked to give up a considerable part of their sovereignty – a

---

69   PRO: FO 371/103 704/C 1073/4, Frankfurter Allgemeine Zeitung (FAZ), 14 May 1953; also C 1073/3, FAZ, 12 May 1953; D. C. Watt, "Churchill und der Kalte Krieg', Schweizer Monatshefte, Sonderbeilage, Vol. 61 (1981), p. 18.

70   Under the influence of his senior Foreign Office advisers, Eden had changed his mind. Despite his own attempts at détente in 1951–52, a year later he came out in opposition to Churchill's policy. As "heir apparent" Eden had become convinced that the retirement of the increasingly difficult if not senile Prime Minister would only be postponed by Churchill's policy of initiating a global détente. See for example the numerous diary entries for the years from 1953 by Colville, Fringes of Power; Shuckburgh, Descent to Suez; Lord Moran, Winston Churchill: The Struggle for Survival, 1940–1965, London 1966.

71   Birmingham University Archive, UK: Avon Papers, AP 20/16/127, letter Nutting to Eden, 25.6.1953; AP 20/1/30, diary entry Eden, 27.11.1954. See also R. R. James, Anthony Eden, London 1986, p. 365.

sacrifice London and Washington strictly declined to consider. The American diplomat Leon W. Fuller concluded in early 1953:

> An important aspect of EDC which Americans, perhaps, fail to perceive with sufficient clarity, is that it is basically a permanent, organic reform of a revolutionary nature but proposed as an emergency device to meet an urgent and critically dangerous situation. It is obvious, for one thing, that we are pressing Europeans to do something that it is inconceivable we would do ourselves. The British stand aloof for much the same reason – for them, as for us, merger of national sovereignty respecting defense in a supra-national federation is unthinkable.[72]

Churchill's speech expedited top secret efforts to work out alternatives to the EDC as well as plans regarding demilitarized zones in Central Europe – just in case it would prove impossible to persuade the French to ratify the EDC treaty.[73]

British experts, both in the Foreign Office and in the military, viewed the EDC with great scepticism. They – like the Labour government in 1950 – became much more interested in the integration of the Federal Republic into NATO. This seemed to be the militarily best and least complicated way to achieve German rearmament.[74] This explains why Churchill's trusted friend Field Marshall Montgomery and the Chiefs of Staff, above all the Air Force Chief of Staff Sir John Slessor, who had however retired in January 1953, encouraged the Prime Minister to go ahead with his plans.[75] In all likelihood this was connected with their deep-seated suspicion of schemes advocating a united Europe and their unanimous rejection of the EDC. Like Churchill they regarded an army fighting for an unidentified lofty European ideal and consisting of nationalities of six or more European nations as militarily inefficient and lacking

72   NA: lot 64D563, PPS Records, 1947–53, Box 16, Folder: Germany 1950–53, memorandum Fuller, State Department, "An Alternative U.S. Course of Actions Respecting EDC and a German Settlement" (17 March 1953). See also H.-H. Jansen, *Grossbritannien, das Scheitern der EVG und der NATO-Beitritt der Bundesrepublik Deutschland*, Bochum 1992, pp. 40 ff.
73   See PRO: FO 371/103 704/C 1073/10, minute Colville to Shuckburgh, 27 July 1953; FO 371/103 665/C 1071/60/G, memorandum Roberts to Strang, 17 June 1953, about his conversation with Con O'Neill, who reported on a conversation with Blankenhorn during the latter's visit to London on 15 June; FO 371/103 704/C 1073/10, minute Colville to Shuckburgh, 27 July 1953. See also Adenauer, *Erinnerungen*, pp. 225–6; Blankenhorn, *Verständnis*, pp. 158–62.
74   See PRO: FO 371/105 989/M 2813/3, FO memorandum, "U.K. Relationship with European supranational institutions and particularly the EDC" (16 Feb. 1953); see also M. Charlton, *The Price of Victory*, London 1983, pp. 124 ff.
75   See Montgomery's memoranda to Churchill dated 26 June 1953 and 2 July 1953, in *Liddell-Hart-Archive*: Ismay Papers III/12/5 and 6/1; and Ismay's letter dated 6 July 1953, in ibid., III/12/7a. On Slessor see also E. Hinterhoff, *Disengagement*, London 1959), pp. 145, 174–5. However, later J. Slessor was quite critical of Churchill's policy. See his *What Price Coexistence? A Policy for the Western Alliance*, London 1962, pp. 37–40.

in motivation.[76] During a cabinet meeting in December 1952, Eden stated, that West Germany's membership of NATO, "might well be preferable militarily". Churchill also explained, that "he would not be unduly disturbed if the present plans for a European Defence Community were not carried into effect."[77] He was in favour of a coalition army like NATO and regarded the idea of a supranational European army as unworkable; he called it a "sludgy amalgam".[78] In May 1953 the Prime Minister declared that France was not really that important for the western alliance. If Paris refused to ratify the EDC treaty, West Germany would simply become a member of NATO.[79] However, due to continued French opposition to West Germany's membership of NATO and despite their own doubts about the EDC, until the scheme's ultimate failure in August 1954, Churchill and Eden continued advocating the EDC solution in public as the only realistic possibility to obtain German rearmament.[80] Still, despite various step-by-step agreements to associate Britain with the EDC, London steadfastly refused to join the Community as a full member.[81]

Therefore, the ratification prospects of the EDC were rather gloomy. Between December 1952 and January 1953 this led even Adenauer to express his hope in a conversation with British High Commissioner Kirkpatrick and his acting American counterpart Reber, that London and Washington "would publicly support Germany's membership of NATO and the United Nations".[82] Kirkpatrick believed that the time had not yet come for a public declaration of a change of policy: "this is a dangerous suggestion at the moment."[83] However, again in early March 1953, the Chancellor's line of thinking was made clear. In view of the bad ratification prospects in Paris, his confidant Blankenhorn secretly conveyed to him that Adenauer believed that "for the first time one would have to consider the possibility of a national German army as an alternative".[84] In mid-March Adenauer even asked Blankenhorn to

76 See Charlton, *Price of Victory*, pp. 124 ff.
77 PRO: CAB 128/25, C.C.(52)102nd conclusions (4 Dec. 1952).
78 Charlton, *Price of Victory*, p. 124.
79 PRO: FO 800/821, SU/53/33, memorandum Strang about a conversation with Churchill on 4 May 1953.
80 See PRO: CAB 128/25, C.C.(52)102nd conclusions, 4 Dec. 1952; FRUS 1952–54, vol. 7, pp. 416–19: memorandum for Dulles, 29 March 1953.
81 See J. W. Young, "German Rearmament and the European Defence Community", in Young (ed.), *Foreign Policy*, pp. 81–108; also the list of British association engagements in H. J. Heiser, *British Policy with regard to the unification efforts on the European continent*, Leyden 1959, pp. 65–6.
82 PRO: FO 371/103 918/CW 1016/1, minute Roberts to Strang, 2 Jan. 1953. The quoted sentence was crossed out with red ink by Eden.
83 Ibid., letter from Kirkpatrick to Roberts, 23 Dec. 1952.
84 PRO: FO 371/103 925/CW 1013/17, letter from M. Thomas to D. Malcolm about his conversation with Blankenhorn, 3 March 1953. See also CW 1013/20, letter from Johnston to W. D. Allen, 14 March 1953; and for Adenauer's thoughts see FO 371/103 664/C 1071/32, minute Roberts to Strang, 4 June 1953.

submit highly secret plans to the American government. The Chancellor suggested to give up the linkage between the EDC treaty and the contractual agreement, to begin with the training of German troops and the re-enforcement of the German border police. Adenauer basically proposed that the treaties of May 1952 should enter into force immediately once ratification by the West German parliament had been secured. German rearmament and sovereignty, then, would not have to await ratification of the EDC by the other member states. Once again he also contemplated West German membership of NATO as this seemed to be the only realistic alternative to the EDC. The Chancellor was aware that the realization of German rearmament without Bonn's membership in a western defence pact was impossible.[85]

However, Adenauer's suggestions were heavily criticized, in particular by American Secretary of State John Foster Dulles who insisted on West Germany adhering to the EDC. After all, one of the (many) reasons why Churchill's attempt to enter into summit talks with the Soviet Union was firmly condemned by the Eisenhower administration consisted in its belief that such a development would make the ratification of the EDC and decisive progress towards a united Europe much more difficult. Despite the development of contingency plans, on the whole Washington and Bonn continued to regard the EDC as the only realistic possibility for achieving German rearmament and integration with the West. Eisenhower, for example, warned that any alternatives to the EDC were "too alarming to contemplate" as the American people were always ready to turn towards "complete isolationism".[86]

During the second half of June 1953 Churchill arrived at the conclusion that either the EDC or some other solution to German rearmament and western integration had to be realized before the West would permit him to convene a summit conference with the Soviet Union. Even if such an event would then not be able to bring about German unification, Churchill believed that a summit meeting could contribute to instigating a global détente. It would therefore still be a worthwhile enterprise to pursue. As the Prime Minister had never been in favour of the EDC and did not believe that the French parliament would ever ratify

85   See NA: 762A.13/3-1753, Conant, Bonn, to Dulles No. 4259, 17 March 1953 (see also FRUS 1952–54, vol. 7, pp. 405–8); /3-2953, "Agenda for Adenauer Visit", two memoranda with the same title by James Riddleberger for Dulles, dated 29 March 1953; NA: 740.5/3-2353, "Blankenhorn Visit to McCloy", memorandum MacArthur II for Dulles, 23 March 1953; see also FRUS 1952–54, vol. 7, pp. 416–19; EL: John Foster Dulles Papers, Subject Series, Folder: Germany, 1953–54 (2), memorandum of the conversation between Blankenhorn and McCloy in Washington, 15 March 1953.
86   Boyle (ed.), Correspondence, p. 85: Eisenhower to Churchill, 6 July 1953. Dulles had a similar opinion. See for example, PRO: PREM 11/373 (WU 1197/489 G), 10 July 1953. See also D. Felken, Dulles und Deutschland. Die amerikanische Deutschlandpolitik 1953–59, Bonn 1993, pp. 222 ff., esp. 230–5.

the treaty, he pushed increasingly hard to obtain West German membership of NATO as soon as possible. For example in a memorandum dated July 9, 1953, Churchill suggested that it might be a good idea to confront the French with an ultimatum. Britain and the United States should ask the French parliament to ratify the EDC by the end of October 1953.[87] If they did not do so, a new NATO treaty would have to be concluded possibly without French participation. This strategy was soon referred to as the policy of the "empty chair". According to Churchill this new NATO pact would have the advantage of not giving any of the member states a veto about the inclusion of the Federal Republic.[88] The Prime Minister had of course in mind that once West Germany had become a member he would be able to immediately continue with his summit diplomacy. On July 6, 1953 he stated:

> With either EDC or a reformed NATO (with or without France's formal adhesion) we should be in a far better position to talk to Russia than if the present indefinite delay continued. (. . .) Let us therefore, as our first aim, persuade the French to ratify EDC in October. This could and should be coupled with a declaration of willingness for a four-Power Conference before the end of the year.[89]

Although eventually the NATO alternative to the EDC was realized in 1954/55, this came much too late to be of any help to Churchill's summit policy. The opposition to his plans from Washington, Bonn and from within his own Foreign Office had not abated. Moreover, the elderly Prime Minister had already suffered a severe stroke in June 1953.[90] In collusion, Adenauer and Dulles used this opportunity to undermine Churchill's policy. At a western Foreign Ministers' Conference in Washington in July 1953, Dulles, with the help of Blankenhorn, and a letter submitted by the Chancellor, persuaded his British and French colleagues to invite the Soviet Union to a conference. It seemed necessary to show German public opinion that the West was prepared to discuss the German question with the USSR.[91] Adenauer was scared,

87   PRO: CAB 129/61, C.(53)194, memorandum Churchill to Salisbury and Strang, 6 July 1953. See also Moran, *Churchill*, p. 425: diary entry, 6 July 1953.
88   See Dockrill, *Britain's Policy*, pp. 131, 140, 149.
89   PRO: CAB 129/61, C.(53)194, memorandum Churchill to Salisbury und Strang, 6 July 1953.
90   See Colville, *Fringes of Power*, pp. 668–70; Moran, *Churchill*, pp. 408–74; M. Gilbert, *Winston S. Churchill, Vol. 8: Never Despair, 1945–1965*, London 1988 pp. 846–92.
91   See NA: 762A.00/6-2653, Conant, Bonn, to Dulles, No. 5485, 26 June 1953; ibid., PPS 64D563, Box 20029, Folder "Germany, 1953", memorandum Beam to Bowie: "Tactics in Presenting a Western Plan for a United Germany", 30 June 1953; ibid., 396.1-WA/7-1753, personal letter Conant to Dulles, 17 July 1953. For Adenauer's letter see his *Erinnerungen*, pp. 224–6; PRO: PREM 11/419, UK Embassy Washington to FO, No. 1461, 11 July 1953. See also FRUS 1952–54, Vol. 5, pp. 1606–7: memorandum of the conversation between Riddleberger

however, that a summit meeting before the general election in the Federal Republic to be held in September would only weaken the appeal of his pro-EDC position, and strengthen the attraction of the opposition SPD's clamouring for neutrality and reunification.[92] Moreover, Adenauer objected to any Big Three or four-power conference on Germany in principle. He feared that the great powers would decided Germany's fate behind his back, and might even renege on the Federal Republic's integration with the West.[93] Therefore, Dulles did not suggest a heads of government meeting as Churchill wished, but a conference of foreign ministers, which would exclude the participation of the British Prime Minister. Moreover, Dulles and Bidault, the French Foreign Minister, were agreed that the conference should end in failure as usual, for which Soviet intransigence should be blamed.[94] Although Lord Salisbury, who was standing in for the convalescent Eden who was recuperating, showed some hesitation over this strategy, he did not support Churchill's vision and in the end weakly agreed with his colleagues. There could be no compromise solution on the lines of something like a neutral and reunified Germany.[95] Moscow eventually accepted the invitation, and suggested a four-power Foreign Ministers' Conference in Berlin in January and February 1954.[96]

Before this conference was convened, Churchill, who had made a comparatively quick recovery from his stroke, began resurrecting his summit diplomacy. He succeeded in persuading Eisenhower and the French Prime Minister Pinay to attend a western top-level conference in Bermuda. The Prime Minister hoped that he would be able to convince the President to agree to a three-power (without the French) heads of governments' conference with the Soviet Union.[97] However, in the

---

and Blankenhorn, 10 July 1953; NA: 396.1-WA/7-1053, Conant, Bonn, to Dulles and Riddleberger, No. 169, 10 July 1953. For the whole rather complicated episode see in detail Larres, *Politik der Illusionen*, pp. 185 ff.

92 See PRO: PREM 11/449, memorandum of conversation between Roberts and Crouy-Chanel, minister at the French embassy in London, 12 June 1953.

93 For Adenauer's so-called "Potsdam complex" see H.-P. Schwarz, *Adenauer. Der Aufstieg, 1876–1952*, Stuttgart 1986, pp. 827ff.

94 See the discussions during the Washington meeting of western foreign ministers in June 1953: FRUS 1952–54, Vol. 5, pp. 1608ff. A bound volume of the British minutes, telegrams and reports sent to London can be found in: PRO: PREM 11/425; PREM 11/419; FO 371/125 033/ZP 3/34/G. See also Larres, *Politik der Illusionen*, pp. 197–207.

95 Ibid.

96 The Soviet Note accepting a conference (dated 26 Nov. 1953) is published in FRUS 1952–54, Vol. 7, pp. 673–7.

97 Boyle (ed.), *Correspondence*, p. 93: Churchill to Eisenhower, 5 Nov. 1953; p. 93–4: Eisenhower to Churchill, 6 Nov. 1953; p. 95: Churchill to Eisenhower, 7 Nov. 1953. See also PRO: PREM 11/418, C.C.(53) 64th conclusions, minute 2, 9 Nov. 1953; NA: 611.41/11-1053, anonymous memorandum, "United States Objectives at Bermuda", 10 Nov. 1953; EL: John Foster Dulles Papers, Subject Series, Box 8, Folder: Germany, 1953–54 (2), letter Dulles to Conant, 20 Nov. 1953.

course of the conference in early December, and much to Eden's and the British Foreign Office's relief, Eisenhower remained steadfast. The President preferred the foreign ministers' conference as arranged by Dulles and Adenauer in the course of the Washington meeting in July. A deeply disappointed and embittered Churchill returned to London. He had also finally realized that the American decision to let the projected conference with Moscow end in failure could not be prevented.[98]

Indeed, apart from an agreement to convene a conference on Indochina and Korea in the summer, the Berlin Conference of January and February 1954 achieved no tangible results. Both sides seemed to be content with the European status quo.[99] Western politicians now intensified their efforts to get the EDC treaty ratified by the French Parliament which despite American pressure still showed no inclination of voting on the Treaty.[100] In the following months, particularly in Britain but also in the United States and in the Federal Republic, alternative schemes were once again secretly worked out in case the EDC should fail.[101]

Although Churchill had realized after the conferences at Bermuda and Berlin that the US was not prepared to alter its position on the German question, he did not want to give up his plans for a summit

98   See FRUS, 1952–54, Vol. 5, pp. 1737–837; PRO: FO 371/125 138/ZP 23/2/G, bound volume with the British minutes of the bi- and trilateral meetings and conversations (Documents 1 to 13). (See particularly the reports of the first day of the conference, Dec. 4; see also Moran, *Churchill*, pp. 505–6, 508; diary entries, 5.12.1953 and 7.12.1953); Shuckburgh, *Descent to Suez*, pp. 112–17; diary entries, early Dec. 1953; Colville, *Fringes of Power*, pp. 681–90; diary entries, early Dec. 1953; J. W. Young, "Churchill, the Russians and the Western Alliance: the three-power conference at Bermuda, December 1953", *English Historical Review*, vol. 101 (1986), pp. 902–12.

99   On the Berlin Conference see PRO: FO 371/109 269–302; ibid., PREM 11/664, 665; FO 800/761; FRUS, 1952–54, Vol. 7, pp. 601ff., 871–7, 1177–80; A. Eden, *Full Circle: Memoirs*, London 1960, pp. 53–76; Adenauer, *Erinnerungen*, pp. 245–59; H.-J. Rupieper, "Die Berliner Außenministerkonferenzy von 1954. Ein Höhepunkt der Ost-West-Propaganda oder die letzte Möglichkeit zur Schaffung der deutschen Einheit?", in: *Vierteljahrshefte für Zeitgeschichte*, vol. 34 (1986), pp. 427–53; R. Steininger, "Deutsche Frage und Berliner Konferenz 1954", in: W. Venohr (ed.), *Ein Deutschland wird es sein*, Erlangen 1990, pp. 39–88; N. Katzer, "*Eine Übung im Kalten Krieg*". *Die Berliner Außenministerkonferenz von 1954*, Cologne 1995.

100   According to Eden this was now "the most urgent question". PRO: CAB 128/27, Part I, C.C.(54)10th conclusions, minute 1, 22 Feb. 1954. See in detail Dockrill, *Britain's Policy*, pp. 134–8; also K. Maier, "Die Auseinandersetzungen um die EVG als europäisches Unterbündnis der NATO 1950–54. Die EVG als supranationales Instrument für die kontrollierte Bewaffnung der Bundesrepublik", in: L. Herbst et al. (eds.), *Vom Marshall Plan zur EWG. Die Eingliederung der Bundesrepublik Deutschland in die westliche Welt*, Munich 1990, p. 455. See also B. R. Duchin, "The Agonizing Reappraisal – Eisenhower, Dulles, and the European Defence Community", in: *Diplomatic History*, vol. 16 (1992), pp. 201–21.

101   See for example PRO: PREM 11/667, Makins, Washington, to FO, No. 1258, 24 June 1954.

conference with Malenkov and Eisenhower.[102] In July 1954 Churchill and Eden travelled to Washington. Eisenhower had indicated his desire to talk to him and to his Foreign Minister in Washington to improve the increasingly tense Anglo-American relations at the Geneva conference on Indochina.[103] Churchill, however, primarily intended to use the opportunity to persuade Eisenhower of the benefits of a top-level meeting with Malenkov. Yet, he did not suggest German reunification as the main topic of conversation with the Soviet leaders anymore, but the much less contentious issues of the threat of the H-bomb and the Austrian question.[104] Since the Bermuda Conference, Churchill, whose health was rapidly deteriorating, had given up his plans for altering the entire western cold war concept. He had resigned himself to the fact that he was unable to change the status quo of a divided Europe.[105] Churchill was increasingly occupied with merely attempting to mellow down the international atmosphere, and to decrease the probability of the outbreak of war and the destruction of all civilization by such a conflict.[106] Above all, he was now much less concerned with the issues involved, than with establishing his reputation as a statesman who had not only succeeded in wartime, but also instigated a process of détente and disarmament by means of a summit conference. Moreover, he now clearly worked for a summit conference in order to postpone his impending retirement and to make a final dramatic impact on world affairs.[107]

102   See PRO: PREM 11/1074, 16.4.1954; Boyle (ed.), Correspondence, p. 139: Churchill to Eisenhower, 22.4.1954; Moran, Churcill, p. 559: diary entry, 24.6.1954; Colville, Fringes of Power, p. 691: diary entry, 24.6.1954. See for the events in 1954 G. V. Gersdorff, Adenauers Außenpolitik gegenüber den Siegermächten 1954, Munich 1994, pp. 187 ff.; Felken, Dulles, pp. 246 ff.

103   See for example Boyle (ed.), Correspondence, pp. 136–8, 139, 140: Eisenhower to Churchill, 4.4.1954, 23.4.1954, 26.4.1954.

104   See FRUS, 1952–54, Vol. 6, p. 1111: memorandum of a conversation between Dulles and Churchill, 27 June 1954. See also for example PRO: FO 371/109 292/C 1071/704, minute Roberts to Eden, 22 Feb. 1954; minute Roberts to Eden and Kirkpatrick, 23 Feb. 1954; also G. Bischof, "Eisenhower, the Summit and the Austrian Treaty, 1953–55", in G. Bischof and S. E. Ambrose (eds.), Eisenhower: A Centennary, Baton Rouge (La) 1995, pp. 136 ff.

105   PRO: FO 800/761, Con/54/6, Churchill to Eden in Geneva, 27 Jan. 1954.

106   See Boyle (ed.), Correspondence, pp. 122–4, 131–3: Churchill to Eisenhower, 9.3., 29.3., and 1.4.1954. See also H. Macmillan, Tides of Fortune, 1945–55, London 1969, p. 530; Shuckburgh, Descent to Suez, pp. 153–7: diary entries, 26.3.–31.3.1953; and the two parliamentary speeches in which Churchill elaborated on the issue, H.C. Deb., 5th series, Vol. 525, 30 March 1954, cols. 1840–9 and Vol. 526, 5 April 1954, cols. 45–7.

107   Already at the end of January 1954, J. K. Penfield, Counsellor at the US Embassy in London, told the State Department: "Churchill does, however, still apparently have a very strong feeling that when he steps down it must be after one last dramatic gesture on the world stage. (. . .) it may be assumed that Churchill will not remain as Prime Minister in another Government, but it is virtually impossible to predict when and how such an extraordinary individualist of such unique talents will retire". NA: 741.13/1-2854. No. 2589, 28 Jan. 1954.

Under the impression that Eisenhower had not been as hostile to his summit ideas as before,[108] Churchill, on his return journey to London from Washington, sent a telegram to Molotov inquiring whether Moscow would accept such an invitation and whether the British Prime Minister should first come to Moscow for an informal visit. Eden only agreed to the telegram because Churchill had promised to retire immediately after such a meeting had taken place.[109] However, the British Cabinet had not been consulted. Back in London, Churchill was confronted with a very serious cabinet crisis, as most members were opposed to his initiative and the possibility that the ailing Prime minister might conduct bilateral negotiations in Moscow without American participation. Lord Salisbury and two other members of the Cabinet threatened to resign. Churchill also considered that option.[110] In the end, the crisis was resolved by an entirely unforeseen (and, for the British cabinet, very fortunate) Soviet invitation to a thirty-two nation conference on European security. In the West this was not regarded as a genuine offer of negotiation by Moscow. It was, of course, impossible that the British Prime Minister would travel to Moscow while the West was contemplating how to react to this move, which seemed to open a new propaganda war between East and West.[111] Churchill wrote to Molotov that he was unable to visit Moscow at present.[112]

108   See Colville, *Fringes of Power*, p. 692: diary entry, 25.6.1954; Moran, *Churchill*, p. 561: diary entry, 25.6.1954; Seldon, *Indian Summer*, p. 405. Churchill's impression is, however, not confirmed by the minutes of his talks with Eisenhower. See for example FRUS, 1952–54, Vol. 6, p. 1098, 26 June 1954; and also pp. 1111–12: memorandum of a conversation with Dulles, 27.6.1954. Without doubt, Eisenhower was still strongly opposed to Churchill's summit diplomacy.

109   See Colville, ibid., pp. 697–8: diary entry, 2 July 1954; Moran, ibid., pp. 573–4: diary entries, 3 and 4 July 1954; Macmillan, *Tides of Fortune*, pp. 534–41; J. W. Young, "Churchill's bid for Peace with Moscow, 1954", History, vol. 73 (1988), pp. 434–44; Seldon, ibid., pp. 406–7; James, Eden, pp. 380–1; D. Carlton, *Anthony Eden: A Biography*, London 1986, pp. 351–5; Gilbert, *Never Despair*, pp. 996ff., 1018ff.

110   PRO: CAB 128/27, Part II, C.C.(54)47th conclusions, minute 4, 7.7.1954. See also Seldon, ibid.; Colville, ibid., p. 437: diary entry, 7 July 1954; Shuckburgh, *Descent from Suez*, p. 222: diary entry, 7 July 1954; PRO: CAB 128/27, Part II, C.C.(54)48th conclusions, minute 3, 8 July 1954, confidential annex; FO 371/125 139/ZP 24/11/G, FO to British delegation at the Geneva conference, No. 1486, Churchill to Eden; CAB 128/27, Part II, C.C.(54)50th conclusions, minute 2, confidential annex, 13 July 1954; CAB 127/28, Part II, C.C.(54)52nd conclusions, minute 3, confidential annex, 23 July 1954.

111   See PRO: FO 371/125 139/ZP 24/17/G, minute Churchill to Eden, M/138/54, 4 Aug. 1954; FO 371/111 706/NS 1073/13, minute Richardson, FO, 31 Aug. 1954; PREM 11/668. On the Soviet note dated 24 July see also: RIIA (ed.), *Survey of International Affairs, 1954*, London 1957, pp. 157–8; ibid., *Documents on International Affairs*, 1954, London 1957, pp. 46–51.

112   PRO: FO 800/762, FO to Embassy Moscow, No. 987, Churchill to Molotov, 26 July 1954. See also FO 371/125 139; CAB 128/27, Part II, C.C.(54)53rd conclusions, minute 2, confidential annex, 26 July 1954; Churchill, "Oral Answers. International Situation", H.C. Deb., 5th series, Vol. 531, 27 July 1954, cols. 232–3.

It is still unclear why the Kremlin did not accept Churchill's proposal. After all, the Soviet leaders must have known of the displeasure about Churchill's ideas in the western capitals. Perhaps Moscow simply did not trust Churchill and his "cold warrior" reputation. The Soviet leaders appear genuinely to have thought that the Prime Minister's summit diplomacy constituted a western trap. At least, a statement by the Soviet diplomat Rodionov supports this interpretation. In a conversation with British diplomat Frank Roberts in mid-August 1954 Rodionov admitted that Moscow had to bear some of the responsibility for the failure of Churchill's summitry. He indicated:

> that the Russian leaders were by no means sure what the Prime Minister really wanted to do at such a meeting and, with their naturally suspicious outlook, were reluctant to commit themselves to something the outcome of which they could not quite foresee.[113]

In the following months Churchill attempted several times to continue his work for a summit conference.[114] However, partly due to skillful manipulation by Foreign Office officials the opportunity did not arise.[115] Above all, the final refusal of the French Parliament to ratify the EDC treaty in August 1954 led to a crisis in the western capitals which made all summit diplomacy impossible. An alternative solution for West German rearmament and integration with the West had to be found. Eventually, at two conferences in London and Paris in September and October 1954, Eden succeeded in realizing the so-called NATO/WEU solution which Churchill supported as well. This was basically the solution both the Attlee and Churchill administrations as well as the Foreign Office had always hoped to achieve. In May 1955 the Federal Republic became a member of NATO and at the same time obtained its semi-sovereignty. Its integration with the West had been realized.[116] Churchill's constant advertisement of the NATO

---

113   PRO: FO 800/823, minute Kirkpatrick to Churchill with enclosed memorandum about the conversation between Roberts and Rodionov on 14 Aug. 1954, PM/IK/54/131, dated 16 Aug. 1954 (Churchill circulated the memorandum in the course of the cabinet meeting on 18 Aug. 1954: CAB 129/70, C.(54)271).

114   He still spoke of the necessity of a "parley at the summit". See Boyle (ed.), *Correspondence*, p. 167: Churchill to Eisenhower, 8 Aug. 1954.

115   In March–April 1955, for example, the officials prevented a visit by Eisenhower to London which would have given Churchill an opportunity to postpone his retirement once again. He would undoubtedly have attempted to persuade the President once again of the necessity to convene a summit conference. See *Bodleian Library, Oxford*: Woolton Papers, 3, diary 1942–60, p. 150, 15 March 1955; PRO: FO 800/763; PREM 11/893; CAB 128/28, C.C.(55)23rd conclusions, 14 March 1955: Gilbert, *Never Despair*, pp. 1102–11; Seldon, *Indian Summer*, pp. 52–3; Colville, *Fringes of Power*, pp. 705–6.

116   For the nine power London conference (28 Sep.–3 Oct. 1954), the most important meeting to work out an alternative solution to the EDC to realize the western integration of

solution between 1952 and 1954 may well have contributed to the fact that in the end such a solution was seen as the only reasonable alternative to the EDC. Eden's successful crisis diplomacy was above all the result of the careful search for alternatives by the British experts throughout 1953 and 1954. The simultaneous inclusion of West Germany into the reformed Western European Union (WEU) to control the amount of armaments and troops the Federal Republic possessed and Britain's agreement not to withdraw its two divisions stationed in Germany without the consent of the WEU members, for example, had been worked out a long time before the events of August 1954. Diplomat Frank Roberts wrote in his memoirs about the London Conference: "Although this has never yet been mentioned, it had always been a part of the British plan that we would commit ourselves to certain force levels on the Continent (. . .)".[117]

Conclusion

When West Germany became a member of NATO Churchill had already retired on 5 April, 1955, without having been able to convene a summit conference. After the downfall of Malenkov in February 1955 and because of his increasingly failing health, Churchill had given up. He was no longer able to confront the opposition to his plans from Eden and the Foreign Office, Eisenhower and Adenauer, which was still as strong as ever.[118]

Despite Churchill's vague plans for a united Europe during the war and his ambiguous calls for European unity as leader of the opposition, his last years as Prime Minister clearly demonstrate that at least in a narrow federalist sense he was not a committed pro-European. Churchill was never in favour of creating a supranational Europe – and certainly not one which involved British participation. When he referred

the Federal Republic, see PRO: FO 371/125 146 (Sep.–Oct. 1954); FO 371/109 773–76 (Oct. 1954). For secondary literature see notes 81 and 133 above; also H. Ehlert et al. (eds.), *Die NATO-Option*, Munich 1993; Gersdorff, *Adenauers Außenpolitik*, pp. 249 ff.
117   *Dealing with Dictators: The Destruction and Revival of Europe, 1930–70*, London 1991, p. 172. See also FRUS 1952–54, vol. 5, pp. 1723–5: Aldrich, London, to Dulles, 27 Nov. 1953; PRO: CAB 128/26, Part 2, C.C.(53)72nd conclusions, minute 4, 26 Nov. 1953; CAB 129/64, C.(53)332. During the Bermuda conference, early in Dec. 1953, Churchill had also already hinted at some elements of the 1954 NATO/WEU solution. See FRUS ibid., p. 1781, 5 Dec. 1953; *Birmingham University Archive*: Avon Papers, AP 20/1/29, diary Eden, 1953, 5 Dec. 1953.
118   See Shuckburgh, *Descent to Suez*, pp. 249–50: diary entries, 11 and 12 Dec. 1955; Moran, *Churchill*, pp. 631–2, 634: diary entries, 2 and 16 Feb., 1 March 1955; see also R. Cockett (ed.), *My Dear Max. The letters of Brendan Bracken to Lord Beaverbrook, 1925–58*, London 1990, p. 177: Bracken to Beaverbrook, 21 Feb. 1955.

to a united Europe it almost always excluded Britain. Moreover, his last years as Prime Minister clearly demonstrated that Churchill was more than ready to sacrifice any progress in European integration in order to obtain a Big Three summit conference. After all, it was his prime ambition to enable postwar Britain to remain one of the world's leading powers. As early as 1946 Churchill had come to the conclusion that this could best be achieved by working for a settlement with the Soviet Union to end the Cold War. In this way, Churchill was representative of the majority of the British population and the country's political elite in that he was utterly convinced that a speedy end to the Cold War would ensure a more peaceful and a more stable world which would allow Britain to catch up with the two superpowers in the economic sphere thereby enabling it to remain a great power itself.

This explains why Churchill believed that a neutral unified Germany was preferable to a divided Germany and the Federal Republic's western integration. He was convinced that the latter scenario would ensure the continuation of the Cold War. Particularly in the post-Stalin era the creation of an united and neutral Germany seemed to him the only possibility of obtaining Moscow's agreement to settle the Cold War amicably. The Prime Minister, together with most of his countrymen, did not believe that British participation in an ever stronger continental and integrated Europe would best serve Britain's interests. It was even believed that such involvement would be counter-productive and have a damaging effect on Britain's standing as a world power.

There is, of course, a good deal of truth in the often repeated statement that Britain missed the European bus between the late 1940s and the mid 1950s.[119] However, it had not occurred to Churchill that there was a bus which needed to be caught. On the whole, it is therefore difficult to disagree with Roy Jenkins's assessment that "it could hardly have been expected that a second Churchill government, inevitably existing in a glow of nostalgia for the first and greater one, would make the necessary break with the trappings of world power".[120] This would have to wait for another decade and longer.

119   Charlton, *Price of Victory*, pp. 124 ff.
120   Jenkins, "Churchill", p. 502.

5

Khrushchev and Kennedy: The Taming of the Cold War

Vladislav Zubok and Constantine Pleshakov

Originally appeared in *Inside the Kremlin's Cold War: From Stalin to Khrushchev*. Harvard University Press, © 1996 by the President and Fellows of Harvard College.

A perceptive Russian historian, witness to the rise and fall of Khrushchev, once observed that the leader's future biographer "would not escape a chapter featuring another prominent figure, John Kennedy."[1] Khrushchev's relationship with John Fitzgerald Kennedy evolved rapidly and was characterized by periods of friendliness and animosity.

During the US presidential elections of 1960, Khrushchev rooted for the young Democratic candidate and regarded him as a promising partner for future talks. Khrushchev appreciated Kennedy's saying that he would not have sent the U-2 on the eve of the summit and would have apologized to Khrushchev in Paris for the incident. In his memoirs Khrushchev wrote, "I was very glad Kennedy won the election."[2] After the Bay of Pigs Invasion in April 1961, in which a US-sponsored invasion of Cuba failed, Khrushchev began to perceive Kennedy as a "weak president," not entirely in control of the state machinery. He stopped underestimating the US president only after the Cuban missile crisis, in October 1962.[3]

This crisis marked the watershed between the first, virulent stage of the Cold War and the second, long period of truce, when the competition between the two superpowers was constrained by a mutual fear of

1 Mikhail Gefter, *Iz tekh i etikh let* [On the past and present years] (Moscow: Progress, 1991), p. 335.
2 Strobe Talbott, ed., *Khrushchev Remembers* (Boston: Little, Brown and Co., 1970), p. 458.
3 Interview with Oleg Troyanovsky, 30 March 1993, Washington, DC.

nuclear force. Just as the new global order had emerged from World War II, this Cold War truce arose out of the labors to avoid a nuclear war in October 1962. Its architects were Nikita Khrushchev and John F. Kennedy. The partnership of these two leaders during the crisis became one of the most remarkable developments in the history of the Cold War.

Despite the wealth of literature covering the crisis, its prelude and aftermath, there is still much uncertainty about Khrushchev's side of the story. How did he come to the conclusion that nothing short of Soviet missiles on Cuban soil would stop US aggression against the Castro regime? What other factors made him risk war for his country and the whole world? Why did he initially underestimate the dangers of the US response to the Soviet deployment, and then, even as the most perilous phase of the crisis passed, continue to make unilateral concessions, infuriating his Cuban friends?

In all the scenarios and analyses of Khrushchev's behavior and thinking one crucial factor has not yet been given the attention it deserves. This factor is Khrushchev himself and how he viewed his competition with Kennedy. This competition was not only about Cuba, although the island did possess tremendous symbolic and emotional significance for the Soviet Chairman; it was also about the status quo of the Cold War and what it implied for the future of the world.

Sizing Up a Partner

After the debacle of the Paris summit and his conflict with Eisenhower's Republican administration, Khrushchev began to root for the Democratic party and its presidential candidate. As the still unknown Kennedy emerged as the front-runner in the Democratic field, Khrushchev began to view him as a preferred alternative to Richard Nixon. In July 1959, during Nixon's presentation of an American exhibition in Moscow, the Soviet leader clashed with him in a debate on the comparative benefits of socialism and capitalism. Nixon offended Khrushchev by insisting on the superiority of American technology and consumer culture. Thereafter the Chairman branded the US vice president "a McCarthyite."[4] Any candidate would be better than Nixon.

Never before had Khrushchev followed a US presidential campaign so closely. Alexander Feklisov, then the KGB station chief in Washington under the alias "Fomin," recalls that "the *rezidentura* [station] had been instructed to inform the Center periodically about the development of

4   *Khrushchev Remembers*, p. 367.

the electoral campaign, and to propose measures, diplomatic, propagandist, or [any] other, to encourage Kennedy's victory." A KGB agent, according to Feklisov, even tried to contact Robert Kennedy, but met a polite rebuff.[5] In the end, Khrushchev did influence the US presidential elections by his belligerent rhetoric, as well as by demonstrating that a constructive US – Soviet dialogue would be impossible so long as Eisenhower or Nixon remained in the White House. Twenty years before the revolutionary leadership of the Islamic Republic of Iran used American hostages to influence a US presidential campaign, Khrushchev did the same by holding captive two pilots of the US reconnaissance plane RB-47, shot down in July 1960 over the Soviet North. Along with fears of the "missile gap," Kennedy successfully exploited the issue of the captive pilots in his barbs against the Eisenhower–Nixon administration.

When Kennedy won the presidential election on November 4, Khrushchev was delighted, and even joked that this was a present to him on the anniversary of the Great October Socialist Revolution. Later, when Khrushchev met Kennedy in Vienna, he did not hesitate to boast that he had helped the Democrat win an extremely narrow race with Nixon.[6]

Yet Khrushchev knew precious little about Kennedy as a man or a politician. Soon after Kennedy was nominated at the Democratic Convention in Los Angeles, the Soviet embassy in Washington sent Khrushchev a profile of the future president. According to the report, "Kennedy, in his general philosophical views, is a typical pragmatist . . . In his political activity he is governed not by any firm convictions but by purely pragmatic considerations, defining his positions in any given concrete circumstances and, most important, in his own interests." Kennedy, the report continued, does not like to go out on a limb politically (he avoided condemning McCarthyism), his liberalism "is rather relative," his position on the relations between the United States and the USSR, "like his position on domestic policy," "is quite contradictory," inconsistent.[7]

The report contained another important passage: "Considering that . . . there is a conflict of 'basic national interests' between the United States and the USSR and that because of this one cannot expect [any]

5   Alexander Feklisov, *Za okeanom i na ostrove: Zapiski razvedchika* [Overseas and on the island: the notes of an intelligence agent] (Moscow: DEM, 1994), pp. 199–200, 201.
6   Sergei N. Khrushchev, *Nikita Kruschev: Krizisi i raketi* [Nikita Khrushchev: crises and missiles] (Moscow: Novosti, 1994), pp. 88–9, 89–90.
7   The profile of Kennedy was sent by Chargé d'Affaire M. Smirnovsky to Gromyko on 26 July 1960. Gromyko sent it to Khrushchev on 3 August 1960 with a note: "This is of interest." TsKhSD, f. 5, op. 30, d. 335, pp. 92, 93, 96, 100. Translated passages are from the full text published in the *Bulletin* of CWIHP, no. 4 (1994), pp. 65–7.

fundamental change in their relations, Kennedy nevertheless grants the possibility of a mutually acceptable settlement . . . on the basis of a joint effort to avoid nuclear war." In the text, found in the Moscow archives, someone underlined the following key sentence: "Kennedy, in principle, is in favor of talks with the Soviet Union, rejecting as 'too fatalistic' the opinion that 'you can't trust' the Soviet Union, that it 'doesn't observe treaties,' and so on."

Khrushchev must have liked what he read. For the first time he was to deal with someone not anchored to a set of hostile, preconceived notions about the USSR and the Russian Revolution. From the report (and, no doubt, many others, sent along from intelligence and diplomatic channels) emerged the portrait of a flexible and prudent politician, attuned to changing circumstances and realities. The biggest question mark was Kennedy's ability to be a leader independent from the will and advice of others. The embassy's profile noted that "Kennedy himself and his supporters now are trying every way possible to create the impression that he is a strong personality of the caliber of Franklin D. Roosevelt," that the Democratic candidate is capable of making "the final decision on serious problems himself, not entrusting this function to his underlings." Yet it also claimed that he "is more of a good catalyst and consumer of others' ideas and thoughts than a creator of independent and original ideas" and "very attached to the institution of advisors."[8]

During his tumultuous stay in New York in the fall of 1960, Khrushchev called the Soviet ambassador Menshikov and his new deputy Georgi Kornienko and asked them if Kennedy would win, and, if so, could he become another Roosevelt? Menshikov answered that Kennedy was an "upstart," he would never make a great leader. Kornienko objected: Kennedy was a truly bright and outstanding politician. His presidency might be a very promising one, although no one knew if he would become another Roosevelt. Several months later Khrushchev met Kornienko in the lobby of the Central Committee in Moscow and said, "You were right about Kennedy, and others were wrong."[9]

Khrushchev was prone to optimistic (and often wishful) thinking, and in the early months after Kennedy's election he had an irresistible temptation to see "his" new president in the best light. He tried many

8 TsKhSD, f. 5, op. 30, d. 335, pp. 103–5, 106, 107; the *Bulletin* of CWIHP, no. 4 (1994), p. 67.
9 G. M. Kornienko, "Novoie o Karibskom krizise [New facts on the Cuban missile crisis]," *Novaya i noveishaya istoriya*, 3 (1991), p. 82. Kornienko had told Arthur M. Schlesinger, Jr., about this episode; see Schlesinger, *A Thousand Days: John F. Kennedy in the White House* (Boston: Houghton Mifflin, 1965), p. 378.

channels to convey to Kennedy that his presidency could open a new era in US–Soviet relations.[10]

On the eve of Kennedy's inauguration, Khrushchev shifted the gears of Soviet foreign policy abruptly toward détente. On January 26 he released the captive American pilots. Khrushchev approved a set of measures to improve Soviet–American public diplomacy that included the creation of an Institute of American Studies in Moscow, granting permission to five hundred elderly Soviet citizens to join their relatives in the United States, payment of honoraria to the American writers whose works were published in the Soviet Union (Moscow pirated books and movies, staying outside all international conventions on copyright), reopening the Jewish theater, reestablishing periodicals closed down by Stalin, and instituting student exchange programs.[11] (Incidentally, this was the second time the issue of Jewish immigration was raised. After the Camp David summit, the KGB had been instructed "to decide positively" on the applications for immigration, with the exception of security risks. The instruction was disregarded after the U-2 incident.)[12]

Communication between the Soviet and the US leader increased daily. The US ambassador in Moscow, Lewellyn (Tommy) Thompson, became a frequent guest of Khrushchev's in the Kremlin. In addition, the Chairman and the Kennedy brothers were able to maintain contact through the GRU colonel Georgi Bolshakov, working in Washington undercover as a press secretary of the Soviet embassy. Soon he, on one side, and Robert Kennedy, on the other, started passing personal messages from one leader to the other. On the Soviet side, the GRU reported to Minister of Defense Malinovsky, who briefed Khrushchev. Mikoyan and Adzhubei, Khrushchev's son-in-law, also knew about Bolshakov's channel. The Soviet ambassador Menshikov did not know about it, however. Foreign Minister Gromyko received only a brief oral summary from Malinovsky, or no information at all.[13]

10   One channel was, via Walt Rostow, Abrasimov to Gromyko (for Khrushchev), 8 February 1961, TsKhSD, f. 5, op. 30, d. 365, pp. 19, 26–7, 29. On a channel via Alexander Korneychuk, Khrushchev's friend, see "Zapiska Sovetskikh obshchestvennikh deiatelei ob itogakh poezdki v ShA [Report of Soviet public figures on the results of the trip to the United States]," sometime late November 1960, TsKhSD, f. 4, op. 16, d. 944, st. 172/15 (special dossier of the Secretariat of the Central Committee) for 24 January 1961, pp. 30, 36.

11   "Zapiska Sovetskikh obshchestvennikh deiatelei"; Boris Ponomarev to the Central Committee, 19 January 1961; the Secretariat's decision on the proposals, 27 January 1961, in TsKhSD, f. 4, op. 16, d. 944, pp. 27, 38–9, 40–53, st. 172/15 for 24 January 1961.

12   TsKhSD, f. 4, op. 16, d. 944, pp. 41–2.

13   Anatoly Dobrynin, *In Confidence: Moscow's Ambassador to America's Six Cold War Presidents (1962–1986)* (New York: Random House, 1995), pp. 52–4; V. Zubok's interview with Alexei Adzhubei, July 1990, Moscow.

Other developments put Khrushchev on alert. Kennedy interpreted the Soviet leader's "wars of national liberation" speech in January 1961 as a direct threat to the "free world," a gauntlet that Khrushchev had thrown down and Kennedy had to pick up. On February 6, Robert McNamara, Kennedy's secretary of defense, declared that there was no "missile gap" in favor of the Soviet Union. Yet on February 27, 1961, Kennedy sent a letter to Khrushchev, proposing an early summit meeting. Khrushchev agreed to meet in Vienna, Austria. Immediately thereafter, the usual presummit fever gripped Khrushchev and infected Soviet officials. In Washington, Feklisov told his contact from the *Washington Post* that some agreements might be possible at the upcoming meeting, among them a compromise on the stalled test-ban talks.[14]

Once again, however, an unpredictable event broke the presummit mood. On April 17, CIA-trained and financed counterrevolutionary volunteers ("contras") launched an operation to overthrow Castro's regime. The offensive ended in disaster; the result was a major loss of prestige for the United States, not only among the countries of Latin America, but also among its NATO allies.

There is some indication that Khrushchev had been forewarned about the Bay of Pigs Invasion. On February 14, 1961, the Soviet leader had perused an annual report of the KGB's chairman, Alexander Shelepin, marked "Top Secret – Highly Sensitive." Shelepin proudly enumerated, among the main achievements of Soviet intelligence, obtaining "evidence of preparations by the United States for an economic blockade of and military intervention against Cuba."[15]

One American historian suggests that Khrushchev knew about the invasion, but speculates that he miscalculated its timing.[16] But Castro's border troops were well prepared, tipped off by Moscow (and the *New York Times*, for that matter). The Chairman had clearly learned about "Operation ZAPATA." The real question is why he kept silent on this matter in his correspondence with Kennedy until the offensive was under way.

The incident took place at a time when Khrushchev – like Stalin at the end of World War II – was at the peak of his power and faced alone

14   Michael Beschloss, *Kennedy and Khrushchev: The Crisis Years* (New York: Harper-Collins, 1991), pp. 65–6, 78, 80–81, 83–4. Feklisov told Robert Estabrook, the editorial page editor of the *Washington Post*; Estabrook memo to the president, 20 March 1961, JFKL-NSF:CO:USSR, box 176.
15   "Otchet Komiteta Gosudarstvennoi Bezopasnosti pri Sovete Ministrov SSSR sa 1960 [The report of the Committee of State Security at the Council of Ministers of the USSR for the year 1960]," 14 February 1961, st. 179/42c (special dossier of the Secretariat), dated 21 March 1961, TsKhSD, f. 4, op. 12, d. 74, p. 147.
16   Beschloss, *The Crisis Years*, p. 88.

a pivotal moment in world history. It still did not appear that complications with the Chinese Communists would result in the "loss of China." At the same time, the Soviet sphere of influence included a growing number of Third World countries. Indicators of growth in the Soviet economy were still counted in the double-digits. On February 21, a much more advanced Soviet intercontinental ballistic missile, R-16 (SS-7), had been tested successfully, and Khrushchev ordered its mass production and the construction of underground silos.[17] On April 12, just days before the Bay of Pigs Invasion, the Soviet space program achieved its biggest triumph, sending the Soviet military pilot Yuri Gagarin around the Earth in a spaceship – making him the first human being to travel around the globe. As a shrewd politician, Khrushchev had to know that worse things might ensue in Cuba, but as a revolutionary romantic, mesmerized by the tide of events that seemed to flow in the Soviet Union's favor, he pushed this knowledge to the back of his mind.

Khrushchev learned of the contras' invasion on his sixty-seventh birthday. By noon of the next day the Chairman had sent a letter to Kennedy, after receiving the approval of the Party Presidium, warning that the Cuban events jeopardized "the peace of the whole world," and admonishing the US president "to avoid the irreparable." Khrushchev was blunt and direct about the Soviet position – the Cuban people and their government would get "all necessary assistance to repel the armed attack." To this Khrushchev added a veiled threat: if the flame of military conflict in the Caribbean continued to burn, then "a new conflagration may flare up in another area."[18] It required no special analysis to understand that by "another area" Khrushchev meant West Berlin.

When Kennedy refused to engage the US Air Force and Marines to save the Cuban contras, Khrushchev had reason to believe that his diplomacy of deterrence had worked again, as it had in the Suez crisis of 1956. This time, however, the victory was more significant, and the taste of triumph was unmitigated. Cuba's closeness to the United States could be compared to Hungary's geographical proximity to the USSR, yet in 1961 the United States failed to achieve what the Soviet Union had done in 1956 – prevent a breach in its sphere of influence.

Even more than in the U-2 affair, Khrushchev tended to attribute the responsibility for the Bay of Pigs not to Kennedy but to his underlings,

17   Vladimir Platonov, "Shchit i mech 'Satani': Strategicheskoye oruzhie Mikhaila Yangelia," *Sovershenno Sekretno*, no. 1 (1993), p. 12.
18   The letter was handed by Vladimir Semyonov to the American chargé d'affaires in Moscow, Edward Freers, at 12:15 p.m.; a collection of Khrushchev-Kennedy correspondence, declassified in 1993, is available on file at the National Security Archive, Washington, D.C.

"the dark forces" who had vested interests in the arms race and an ideological commitment to the Cold War. On April 10, 1961, in conversation with Walter Lippmann, Khrushchev personalized these forces, reducing them to one name: "Rockefeller."[19] He was referring to the governor of New York, Nelson Rockefeller, a scion of one of the wealthiest capitalist dynasties in the United States. On March 10 the KGB reported to Khrushchev and the Party Secretariat that a special slander campaign would be directed at "the reactionary militarist group in US ruling circles – [Nelson] Rockefeller, [Lauris] Norstad, A. Dulles, E. [J. Edgar] Hoover, as well as their allies in pushing an aggressive course in other countries."[20]

Khrushchev believed that the young and inexperienced president had been "taken in" by these circles. According to Troyanovsky, there was a sigh of relief in the Kremlin when the Bay of Pigs incident was over, but also almost a feeling of pity for Kennedy's discomfiture. Old Ike, at least, would have brought the Cuban affair to its successful completion.[21]

On the eve of the summit in Vienna, scheduled for June 3–4, Khrushchev convened a special session of the Politburo (Presidium) and told his colleagues that he intended to exert as much pressure as possible on Kennedy. He believed that after the Bay of Pigs incident he would be able to force the young and inexperienced American president to make concessions, in particular on Berlin. When Mikoyan tried to argue that a reasonable and constructive dialogue with Kennedy would be more likely to improve Soviet–American relations, Khrushchev exclaimed that the favorable situation must be exploited. The rest of the Kremlin leadership, who knew little about Kennedy and the course of secret diplomacy, supported Khrushchev.[22]

The Chairman's Miscalculation

Khrushchev met with Kennedy in Vienna as a prima donna meeting a first-time starlet. "I heard you were a young and promising man," Khrushchev greeted the forty-three-year-old president.[23] The difference in age was almost a quarter of a century. This generation gap grows into an abyss, if one thinks of all the milestones of Russian history as well

19   "Khrushchev to Lippmann – Face to Face," *New York Herald Tribune*, 17 April 1961.
20   KGB to CC CPSU, 10 March 1961, in st. 199/10c (special dossier of the Secretariat), dated 3 October 1961, TsKhSD, f. 4, op. 13, d. 74, p. 149.
21   Interview with Oleg Troyanovsky, then a foreign policy aide of Khrushchev's, 30 March 1993, Washington, D.C.
22   Dobrynin, *In Confidence*, pp. 43–4, 45.
23   Memorandum of a Conversation at the Vienna Meeting between the President and Chairman Khrushchev, 3 June 1961, 12:45 p.m., John F. Kennedy Library, POF:CO:USSR, box 126, folder 12, p. 1.

as the personal experience that had shaped Khrushchev, and of which Kennedy had only a limited understanding. The only two links between the leaders were World War II and the nuclear polarization of the Cold War.

Kennedy's main goal in his meeting with Khrushchev was to suggest a retreat from the Cold War, the broadening of the zone of neutrality between the two established blocs. Something along these lines had been proposed in the United States by Walter Lippmann and advocated by Maxim Litvinov in 1944.[24] Kennedy did not believe it would be feasible to change the status quo in divided Europe or in the Far East. Therefore he spoke in very general terms about the desirability of informal co-operation to prevent the spread of bipolar competition into the Third World. He told Khrushchev he would not object to having more Social-ist Yugoslavias, Indias, or Burmas – the nonaligned countries that would not affect the existing geostrategic balance between the two super-powers. Kennedy also targeted Laos, where a struggle was on among the Communist guerillas, the pro-American strongman, General Phoumi Nosavan, and a neutral group. In Kennedy's opinion, if both superpowers could convince their respective clients to move toward neutrality in Laos, the country might provide a model for settlement in future Third World conflicts.

Kennedy's attitude was in striking contrast to Eisenhower and Dulles's strategy of encirclement of the USSR and their antagonism to the idea of neutrality in the Cold War, in Europe and elsewhere. But to Khrushchev it seemed as if the US president were suggesting to the First Secretary of the Communist Party of the USSR that he renounce his beliefs in the revolutionary transformation of the world and the path to socialism and communism.

For two days the leaders were engaged in an academic and mis-guided dialogue on the history of the Cold War. They spoke about the issues of war, peace, and revolution, but the most important things at the summit were left unsaid.[25] The two men's encounter was similar to an immortal scene written by the great French satirist François Rabelais – "the debate" between the stiff British scholar and the jester Panurgue. In the end, Khrushchev (Panurgue) overwhelmed Kennedy (the scholar) – not by the force of argumentation, but by his formidable temperament and vigor. Some American observers, interestingly, attributed Kennedy's setback at the summit to his physical handicap, a bad back.[26]

24   See Chapter 1, and Walter Lippmann, *U.S. War Aims* (Boston, 1944).
25   Troyanovsky, interview with V. M. Zubok, 27 May 1993, Moscow.
26   Beschloss, *The Crisis Years*, pp. 206, 235.

Khrushchev, however, was not a mere jester or an idle talker. He was guided by the dictates of Communist ideology and his profound convictions. His passionate view of history and the world was very different from the detached and slightly fatalistic outlook of the US president. Khrushchev was ready to meet the level of historical discussion offered by the Harvard graduate. He even did his homework and mastered the art of historical parallels. A century and a half earlier in Vienna, he reminded Kennedy, Czar Alexander I had presided over the "Holy Alliance," a reactionary concert of rulers who wanted to put the genie of national revolutions back into the bottle.[27] In vain! The world order envisioned in 1815 eventually broke down as a result of revolutionary outbursts. The revolutionary situation in the world today, Khrushchev explained, had nothing to do with the Soviet Union. It was just a response to a Western "Holy Alliance" led by the United States and organized by John Foster Dulles to protect the status quo. But in fact America itself, continued Khrushchev, had been born in a war of national liberation. The Soviet Union should not reach agreement at the expense of other people; such an agreement could not bring peace.

While lecturing Kennedy, Khrushchev repeatedly pressed salt into his wounds by raising the Bay of Pigs fiasco. Although Castro is not a Communist, Khrushchev said, "you are well on the way to making him a good one." Indeed, having initially come to power with little sympathy toward the Communist sectarians in Cuba, Castro, under heavy American pressure, decided to lean toward the Socialist camp. Khrushchev saw the United States at this moment as a power historically on the wane. Washington could shore up its faltering global positions only through the use of military force, building "dams against the flow of ideas."[28]

Today it is hard to believe that the Secretary of the Communist party could launch these criticisms with the complete confidence of a man riding the crest of history. Yet Kennedy succumbed to this onslaught. He took a defensive line, arguing that when systems "are in transition," be it from feudalism to capitalism, or from capitalism to communism, "we should be careful, particularly today, when modern weapons are at hand." The president admitted that social transformation could not be stopped by force, and if the Shah of Iran resisted change he would perish like Fulgencio Batista, the last ruler of Cuba before Castro's revolution. It is dangerous when superpowers, capable of destroying each other, involve themselves in violent social change. Such involvement might

27   Memorandum of a Conversation at the Vienna Meeting, 3 June 1961, 12:45 p.m., box 126, folder 12, pp. 3–4.
28   Ibid., p. 4; Memorandum of a Conversation at the Vienna Meeting, 3 June 1961, 3:00 p.m., box 126, folder 12, p. 3; Beschloss, *The Crisis Years*, p. 196.

lead to "miscalculations" with catastrophic consequences. Our judgments of events may not always be correct, he said, and as an example,
he confessed that the Bay of Pigs affair was his "mistake."[29]

Kennedy's words had the opposite effect of what he had hoped to
achieve. In Khrushchev's opinion, the United States had an unchallenged capability of nuclear blackmail for a decade, and American politicians had been teaching the Soviet Union by example how to behave.
Secretary of State Dulles had not worried in those days about the danger
of "miscalculations." And now, just when the Soviet Union acquired
the means of retaliation, the Americans changed their approach: they
began to view the Soviet leader as a child playing with fire. "Miscalculation!" Khrushchev burst out in anger. "All I ever hear from your people
and your news correspondents and your friends in Europe and every
place else is that damned word." The United States, he continued, simply
wanted the USSR "to sit like a schoolboy with his hands on his desk."
"We don't make mistakes." (Stalin made them, but we will not.) "We will
not make war by mistake."[30]

After the first day of talks, Khrushchev's advisors, who waited for his
return in front of the Soviet embassy, asked him about his impressions
of Kennedy. Khrushchev waved his hand dismissively. Kennedy, he said,
was no match for Eisenhower; he lacked the broad horizons and the
statesmanship of the earlier president.[31]

Even on the second day of talks Kennedy hesitated to use his aces
against Khrushchev: he never mentioned that Soviet missile forces were
lagging disastrously behind those of the United States, and he hardly
played on the eruption of the Sino-Soviet conflict. Both developments
were corroborated to the American side by Oleg Penkovsky before the
Vienna summit.[32] In a familiar Cold War pattern, crucial intelligence did
not affect the important meeting. Instead, Kennedy said that "they" in
the US administration "regard the present [state] of power between
Sino-Soviet forces and the forces of the United States and Western
Europe as being more or less in balance."[33] Khrushchev found these
words both pleasing and mocking. The Chairman had long tried to con-

29   Memorandum of a Conversation at the Vienna Meeting, 3 June 1961, 3:00 p.m., box
126, folder 12, p. 2; ibid., 3 June 1961, 12:45 p.m., p. 6.
30   Ibid., 3 June 1961, 12:45 p.m., p. 6; Beschloss, *The Crisis Years*, pp. 196–7.
31   Interview with Oleg Troyanovsky, 30 March 1993, Washington, DC.
32   The first successful satellite reconnaissance of *Discoverer* was accomplished by the CIA in
August 1960, *Corona: America's First Satellite Program*, ed. Kevin C. Ruffner, History Staff
Center for the Study of Intelligence, Central Intelligence Agency, Washington, DC., 1995, pp.
22–4. The transcripts of the CIA debriefings of Penkovsky, July 1961, are on file at the National
Security Archive, Washington, DC.
33   Memorandum of a Conversation at the Vienna Meeting, 3 June 1961, 12:45 p.m., box
126, folder 12, p. 6.

vince everyone that the balance of power between the two superpowers could not be measured on scales, that the exact number of missiles "did not matter anyway."[34] But he also knew that by the Vienna summit there could be nothing resembling joint "Sino-Soviet forces."

Again, both leaders operated on a completely different plane. Kennedy viewed the nuclear deadlock through the prism of geopolitics, as an invitation to a more cautious and prudent policy for both superpowers, perhaps even a kind of partnership between them. He felt he was offering a fair deal from a position of substantial strategic superiority (in terms of deliverable nuclear warheads). But Khrushchev saw this as a recognition by the leader of the most powerful imperialist country that the forces of socialism had now caught up with the forces of the old world. As a true believer, he took it as another sign that the imperialist camp was doomed and in retreat. For the rest of the meeting the Soviet leader was on the offensive, acting increasingly arrogant.

At last Khrushchev turned to the question of Germany. One of his main expectations was that Kennedy and his advisors would divorce their position on the German question from the "policy of Adenauer," would look at it from what Khrushchev knew was a common ground between the superpowers – mistrust of German militarism.[35] The Chairman received confusing signals: at one point US Ambassador Thompson told him that the Americans "would rather deal with the Russians" in Central Europe than "leave it to the Germans," and added, "I refuse to believe that your Germans are any better than ours." Khrushchev laughed and, reaching over the table, said impulsively, "Let's shake on that."[36]

In Vienna, however, Kennedy did not show any signs of flexibility. He explained to Khrushchev America's vital interest in maintaining the present status of West Berlin. The Soviet leader insisted that he had come to Vienna to reach some agreement with Kennedy similar to "the interim agreement" that he had discussed with Eisenhower. The USSR, he said, was prepared to accept such an arrangement even now. "Now" was the key word. Khrushchev would accept no delay. The alternative would be a separate peace treaty with the GDR.[37]

34   Ibid., 3 June 1961, 3:00 p.m., p. 9.
35   In the documents of the CC CPSU Secretariat, we found some of these signals on the new flexibility of the Kennedy circle (Arthur M. Schlesinger, Jr., Walt W. Rostow). See Vladislav M. Zubok, "Khrushchev and the Berlin Crisis," CWIHP Working paper no. 6, p. 17.
36   This portion was excised from the published version; see Thompson to State Department, Telegram from the Embassy in Moscow, 24 May 1961, FRUS: Berlin Crisis, pp. 66–9. We thank William Burr from the National Security Archive for bringing this to our attention.
37   Memorandum of a Conversation at the Vienna Meeting, 4 June 1961, 10:15 a.m., box 126, folder 12, pp. 17, 18.

Kennedy ignored the message and the hint about an interim agreement. The president acted on advice received from de Gaulle: it should be left to the Soviet leader to press for change in Central Europe. But unlike de Gaulle, who always believed Khrushchev was merely bluffing in Berlin, Kennedy was not so sure.[38] The Soviet Chairman grew impatient. He told Kennedy how many lives the USSR had lost in the war with Germany and reminded him that his own son had been one of those killed. Finally he snapped. "Perhaps the USSR should sign a peace treaty [with the GDR] right away and get it over with," he said. The Soviet Union would "never, under any conditions, accept US rights in West Berlin after a peace treaty had been signed." In the frenzy of brinkmanship Khrushchev said that the USSR would not start a war, but if the United States was going to unleash war, then let it be now, before the development of even more destructive weapons. This passage was so reckless that it was not included in either Soviet or American records of the conversation.[39]

Khrushchev, of course, was bluffing. But again Kennedy did not call the Chairman's bluff. Khrushchev left the meeting saying that "if the United States [refused] an interim agreement," Moscow would sign the peace treaty in December. "it will be a cold winter," said Kennedy.[40] These were the last words Khrushchev heard from the president. They never met again.

Some in the Kennedy administration were convinced that the president had reinforced the impression of his weakness that had arisen from the Bay of Pigs fiasco.[41] They were correct. The outcome of the Vienna summit encouraged Khrushchev to launch the most serious campaign of brinkmanship around Berlin. Years later he said he "could tell" that Kennedy was a reasonable man, interested "in avoiding conflict with the Soviet Union." He was sure that Kennedy would not start "a war over Berlin."[42] Upon returning from Vienna he ordered the publication of a

38   Cyril Buffet at the conference on the Berlin crisis, Woodrow Wilson International Center for Scholars and the Nuclear History Project, Washington, 21 May 1993.
39   *FRUS: Berlin Crisis, 1961–3*, XIV, pp. 87–94. G. M. Kornyenko, "Upushchennaia vozmoshnost: Vstrecha N. S. Khrushcheva i J. Kennedi v Vene v 1961 g. [The missed opportunity: the meeting of N. S. Khrushchev and J. Kennedy in Vienna in 1961]," *Novaiia i noveishaia istoriia*, no. 2 (1992), p. 101.
40   Memorandum of a Conversation at the Vienna Meeting, 4 June 1961, 3:15 p.m., box 126, folder 12, p. 3.
41   Dean Rusk, *As I Saw It*, ed. Daniel L. Papp (New York: Norton, 1990), pp. 220–1; Theodore C. Sorensen, *Kennedy* (New York: Harper & Row, 1965), p. 549; Arthur M. Schlesinger, Jr., *A Thousand Days: John F. Kennedy in the White House* (Boston, 1965), p. 361, and *Robert Kennedy and His Times* (Boston: Houghton Mifflin, 1978), p. 427. On other sources and the essence of the debate, see Richard Ned Lebow and Janice Gross Stein, *We All Lost the Cold War* (Princeton: Princeton University Press, 1994), pp. 23, 71, 408–10.
42   *Khrushchev Remembers*, p. 458; *Khrushchev Remembers: The Last Testament* (Boston: Little, Brown and Co., 1974), trans. and ed. Strobe Talbott, pp. 562–72.

confidential Soviet memorandum to the US administration restating the ultimatum of 1958 on West Berlin. This time Khrushchev threatened to sign a separate treaty with the GDR by the end of 1961, and he pulled all stops to prove that he meant it.

The Chairman miscalculated: the pressure he put on Kennedy pushed him to the limits of bluff and nuclear rhetoric, but failed to change the position of the United States on the German question. Khrushchev's words and actions did, however, result in the most heated summer and fall since the beginning of the Cold War in Europe.

Brinkmanship and the Wall

Confident as he was that the revolutionary-imperial paradigm would lead the USSR from one historic victory to another, Khrushchev soon discovered that in Berlin and Germany as a whole, social forces that elsewhere seemed to justify Soviet optimism threatened to undo Soviet geopolitical positions. In the spring of 1961 the flight of people from the GDR to West Germany via Berlin and the resulting economic disruption created a situation in which the East German Communist regime might collapse without a single shot fired from the Western side. Ironically, it was the very same crisis, unleashed by Khrushchev, that destroyed the status quo in East Germany and sent a wave of panic through the population of the GDR: many fled, fearing that the gate to the West would eventually close. The Soviet embassy in Berlin informed Moscow on a weekly basis about this human exodus, and in April 1961 calculated that during the 1950s the population of the GDR was reduced by 1.2 million.[43]

The seriousness of the situation was not lost on Khrushchev's entourage. One of his speechwriters, however, an expert on Germany, showed his black humor, saying that soon there would be no one left in the GDR, except Ulbricht himself.[44] Experts observed that the USSR's "friends" in the GDR received more Soviet assistance per capita than West Germany received from the Americans.[45] The embassy reported that West Berliners and Western tourists were buying a huge number of goods in East Berlin, profiting from subsidized prices and the favor-

43   From the diary of V. Suldin, the first secretary of the Soviet embassy in the GDR, TsKhSD, op. 49, d. 380, pp. 13–14, 47, 70–72, 92–3; "On the Issue of the Exodus of the GDR Population to West Germany" (embassy's materials), 7 April 1961, TsKhSD, op. 49, d. 380, p. 60.
44   Interview with Oleg Troyanovsky, 30 March 1993, Washington, DC.
45   By 1962 Soviet loans to the GDR amounted to 6.8 billion deutschemarks; Yuri Andropov to the Presidium of the Central Committee, Report of the International Department, 16 March 1962, TsKhSD, f. 4, op. 18, d. 103, p. 129.

able ratio between the DM and the mark of the GDR. The longer the GDR suffered, the higher the bill for the Soviet economy and morale.

Ulbricht himself brought this naked truth to Khrushchev's attention. Since October 1960 he had been asking for "emergency aid," claiming that the Bonn government was about to sever a trade agreement with the GDR. He requested 50 million dollars in cash and compensation for the consumer goods that the GDR refused to buy in West Germany. Later the Soviets learned that total losses of hard currency for 1961 amounted to 540 million DM.[46] In November, when Ulbricht attended the world Communist forum in Moscow, Khrushchev invited him to the Council of Ministers. Alexei Kosygin, a leader of Gosplan (the State Planning Committee at the Council of Ministers), complained that the requests of the GDR created difficulties for the Soviet economy. The hundreds of tons of butter and meat that the GDR asked for, he said, were in extremely short supply in the Soviet Union itself.[47]

Khrushchev was uneasy about Ulbricht's growing appetite. When the East German leader asked him to send Soviet *Gastarbeiter*, or seasonal labor, to the GDR, Khrushchev snapped: "We won the war," he reminded the East German Communist. "Our workers will not clean your toilets."[48] He refused to touch the Soviet gold reserve to get the GDR out of trouble. "Don't encroach on our gold, don't thrust your hands into our pockets," he said.[49] But, his temper notwithstanding, Khrushchev remained generous toward his East German "friends," since their collapse would mean a Soviet defeat in the Cold War.

Ulbricht knew this as well. Like the Chinese Communists, he did not conceal his critical attitude toward Khrushchev's foreign policy, and he put increasing pressure on the leader to change his priorities. He called the plan to disarm within three years "demoralizing palaver" and was shocked by drastic reductions of Soviet troops in the GDR. The U-2 affair and the debacle of the Paris summit allowed him to argue for tougher, decisive actions in West Berlin. East German activists, according to a Soviet diplomat, were ready to storm West Berlin "tomorrow" – naturally in the rear guard of Soviet tanks.[50] At the meeting in November, Ulbricht made it clear to Khrushchev that another détente with the United States, at the expense of the interests of the GDR, would be a dis-

46   Pervukhin to Gromyko, 6 December 1961, AVP RF, f. 082, op. 57, por. 388, papka 119, p. 32.
47   Memorandum of a Conversation of Comrade N. S. Khrushchev and Comrade W. Ulbricht, 30 November 1960, AVP RF, f. 0742, op. 6, por. 4, papka 43, pp. 18, 19, 20, 21.
48   MNSK (1993), no. 10, p. 68.
49   AVP RF, f. 0742, op. 6, por. 4, papka 43, p. 13.
50   First secretary of the embassy in the GDR (A. Avalduev) on his conversation with O. Neumann, member of the SED Central Commitee, 9 June 1960, TsKhSD, f. 5, op. 50, d. 226, p. 122.

aster. "What will happen in 1961?" he asked Khrushchev after Kennedy was elected to the White House. "We cannot repeat our campaign in favor of a peace treaty as we did before the Paris summit . . . We can only do this in the event that we actually achieve something." When Gromyko accused him of provocative conduct toward West Germany, Ulbricht pretended not to hear.[51] The GDR government prepared detailed plans for a "purge" from West Berlin of "a number of persons and organizations hostile to the GDR."[52] At a minimum, Ulbricht wanted to control all intersectoral traffic in the city and to discourage his people from looking for jobs in capitalist sectors of the city.

Khrushchev initially used the threat of a separate peace treaty with the GDR to jolt Western powers out of complacency on the German question. He was an angler, holding Adenauer and the Western powers on his hook. But suddenly Ulbricht directly involved himself in the affair, and the Chairman had to face the truth: if he signed a separate peace treaty with the GDR, the situation in Berlin could become explosive. Ulbricht's "impatience" with the status quo in the city would lead to Western economic sanctions against the whole Soviet bloc, as well as retaliation from both sides.

The only way out of this impasse would be to protect the Soviet sphere of influence by forcefully closing the loophole through which people and resources escaped to West Berlin. The German experts at the ministry of foreign affairs, and Mikhail Pervukhin, the Soviet ambassador in the GDR, wrote that the closing of the border would be difficult technically and damaging politically, but "with the exacerbation of the political situation," dividing Berlin "could be necessary."[53] Until after the Vienna summit Khrushchev still hesitated to take this route to stabilizing the GDR. For him it meant an effective renunciation of his grand diplomacy. The border closing would render absurd his idea of Berlin as a free city. It would be a colossal propaganda defeat for the Communist system in its competition with capitalism. In other words, the political damage appeared forbiddingly high.[54]

It took another ultimatum – this time Ulbricht's – to make Khrushchev reassess his priorities. After the meeting in Vienna Ulbricht

51   AVP RF, f. 0742, op. 6, por. 4, papka 43; ibid., p. 12.
52   Yu. Kvitsinsky, conversation with P. Papist, 21 October 1960, TsKhSD, op. 49, d. 288, p. 278.
53   Yuli Kvitsinsky's recollections, in Hope M. Harrison, "Ulbricht and the Concrete 'Rose'": New Archival Evidence on the Dynamics of Soviet-East German Relations and the Berlin Crisis, 1958–1961," Working paper no. 5, CWIHP, Washington, D.C. (May 1993), p. 39; letter from Ambassador Pervukhin to the minister of foreign affairs of the USSR, Comrade A. A. Gromyko, 4 July 1961, AVP RF, referentura po GDR, op. 6, por. 34, papka 46.
54   Harrison, "Ulbricht and the Concrete 'Rose'"; Zubok, "Khrushchev and the Berlin Crisis," p. 20.

urged Khrushchev to convene a summit of the leaders of the Warsaw Treaty Organization to discuss the situation in the GDR. The previous such meeting, in March, had been inconclusive. Khrushchev deferred unpleasant decisions in expectation of the coming meeting with Kennedy. This time, however, Ulbricht was determined not to let Khrushchev's preoccupation with Soviet–US relations get in the way of a favorable settlement for the GDR. In early July he asked the Soviet ambassador to report to the Kremlin that "if the present situation of open borders remains, collapse is inevitable"; Ulbricht made it clear that he "refuses all responsibility for what would then happen."[55]

The decision to build the Wall to separate the GDR from West Berlin was the benchmark of Khrushchev's statesmanship; although something like it was expected, the decision was made spontaneously, coming as a surprise to friends and foes alike. In his memoirs Khrushchev described how the plan unfolded. "I spoke to Pervukhin, our ambassador in Germany, about the establishment of border control." The Soviet ambassador was ill prepared for the operation. "He gave me a map of West Berlin. The map was very poor." Khrushchev then asked Pervukhin to share the idea with Ulbricht, "and also to ask Marshal Ivan I. Yakubovsky [the commander of the Soviet troops in Germany] to send me a new map." When Pervukhin disclosed the strategy to Ulbricht, he "beamed with delight." To the surprise of the Soviet ambassador, the GDR chief immediately laid out a detailed plan of action: barbed wire and fencing must be set along the entire border, the U-Bahn and S-Bahn to West Berlin must be stopped, and the main Friedrichstrasse train station should be divided by a glass wall. Ulbricht even had a code name for the operation: "Rose."[56]

At about the same time, on July 25, the day President Kennedy publicly announced military mobilization to meet a Soviet challenge in Berlin, Khrushchev invited the president's disarmament advisor, John J. McCloy, on a diplomatic mission to Moscow, to fly to his spacious resort at Pitsunda, on the Black Sea. The next morning the Soviet leader staged a spectacle for his visitor, one minute playing the "man of peace," and the next the tough leader. He wanted to send McCloy back to Washington scared and pleading for a compromise. The following day Kennedy's envoy cabled from the US embassy in Moscow that, although "the situation is probably not yet ripe for any negotiation," it is "too dangerous to permit it to drift into a condition where lack of time for balanced

55   A younger Soviet diplomat, Yuli Kvitsinsky, was present at this meeting and described it in Julij A. Kwitzinskij, *Vor dem Sturm: Erinnerungen eines Diplomaten* (Berlin: Siedler Verlag, 1993), p. 179; quoted in Harrison, "Ulbricht and the Concrete 'Rose,'" p. 47.
56   Harrison, "Ulbricht and the Concrete 'Rose,'" pp. 47, 51; MNSK (1993), no. 10, p. 69; Kwitzinskij, *Vor dem Sturm*, pp. 179–80.

decision-making could well lead to unfortunate action."[57] "I know he [McCloy] reported accurately," Khrushchev smugly commented to the Communist leaders.[58]

The Warsaw Treaty allies gathered in secrecy in Moscow on August 3. A transcript of Khrushchev's speeches from the meeting was found in the party archives in Moscow in the summer of 1993. Khrushchev's message was rambling and incoherent. The situation was slippery, he told the group, but as long as he, Khrushchev, was in control, it could be managed. True to his nature, Khrushchev waved the bloody shirt of revolutionary rhetoric. "I wish we could give imperialism a bloody nose!" he said to the Communist leaders. He even compared the risk of signing a separate peace treaty with the GDR to the risk that the Bolsheviks had taken in 1917 when they seized power in Russia.[59]

In his speech of July 25, Kennedy "declared war on us and set down his conditions," said Khrushchev. He told the audience how McCloy (who of course had known about the speech, being a messenger from the White House) first pretended he had not heard about it, but then tried to convince the Soviet leader that "Kennedy did not mean it, he meant to negotiate."[60] Khrushchev shared with the Communist leaders his confusion about the seemingly odd nature of US politics. The American state, he said, is "barely governed." Kennedy himself "hardly influences the direction and development of policies."[61] Power relations in the United States were characterized by chaotic infighting among factions, where the "faction of war" was still greater than the "faction of peace." "Therefore anything is possible in the United States," Khrushchev admitted. "War is . . . possible. They can unleash it. The situation in England, France, Italy, and Germany is more stable." Khrushchev even had to admit, contrary to much of his previous rhetoric, that German militarism was much more under check than US militarism![62]

The new US president was no match for the huge military-industrial complex that his predecessors had nourished. Khrushchev expressed

57 Beschloss, *The Crisis Years*, p. 263.
58 The conference of the first secretaries of the Central Committee of Communist and workers parties of Socialist countries for the exchange of views on questions related to the preparation and conclusion of a German peace treaty, 3–5 August 1961 (transcripts of the meeting were found in the miscellaneous documents of the International Department of the Central Committee), TsKhSD (hereafter, Transcripts), p. 144. Khrushchev hinted more than once that the KGB services intercepted cables sent by foreign embassies in Moscow. Excerpts of the document were translated by V. Zubok and published in *Bulletin* of CWIHP, no. 3 (Fall 1993), pp. 59–61.
59 Ibid., p. 178.
60 Ibid., pp. 142, 143.
61 Ibid., p. 157.
62 Ibid., pp. 157, 158.

sympathy for the young, inexperienced Kennedy, who, for all his best intentions, was "too much of a lightweight." The US state (*gosudarstvo*) "is too big, powerful, and it poses certain dangers."[63] At this moment Khrushchev seriously questioned whether Kennedy would be able to keep "the dark forces" of his country at bay while he negotiated for a long truce.

Khrushchev's uncertainty about Kennedy's power and character did not stop him from employing his two favorite political tools – nuclear brinkmanship and strategic deception. On July 10 Khrushchev hosted a meeting for the leaders and scientists of the Soviet nuclear complex to announce an end to the nuclear moratorium. To those who listened to the First Secretary, the decision was unmistakably linked to the Berlin crisis. The best scientists from Arzamas-16, Yakov Zeldovich and Andrei Sakharov, informed Khrushchev that they were eager to test a "new idea," a 100-megaton thermonuclear bomb. Khrushchev jumped at the suggestion. "Let this terrible weapon become the Sword of Damocles hanging over the imperialists' necks," he said to the assembly.[64]

The image of a superbomb and nuclear missiles as the ultimate expression of Soviet power had always remained of paramount importance to the Kremlin ruler, along with the arguments borrowed from the arsenal of Marxist–Leninist "teaching" on revolutionary change. He once told the US ambassador that if he got down on his knees and prayed in a "Holy Orthodox Church" for peace, the West would not believe him. But if he walked toward the West with "two missiles under my arms, maybe I'd be believed."[65] After Vienna the Chairman made the nuclear threat his ultimate argument. From July on he methodically shocked NATO diplomats in Moscow by briefing them in a casual manner on how many hydrogen bombs he thought would be assigned to the task of burning their home countries to the ground. Khrushchev relied on the West Europeans' outrage at the idea that they might be forced to die for the sake of two and a half million Germans in Berlin. . . .

On August 13, two and a half million West Berliners and a quarter of a million East Berliners who crossed the internal border every day

63 Ibid., p. 159.
64 An account by Sakharov and Zeldovich to Yuri Smirnov, who then worked on Sakharov's research team in Arzamas-16. Interview of V. M. Zubok with Smirnov, Antibes, France, 26 June 1993. This story contradicts the version of Andrei Sakharov, *Vospominaniia* [Memoirs] (New York: Chekhov, 1990), pp. 285–90. According to Smirnov, Sakharov at that time was still an enthusiast of nuclear testing. The opposition and the clash with Khrushchev happened later.
65 27 January 1959, "Memorandum of Henry C. Ramsay on Ambassador Thompson's Remarks at the Planning Board, 13 January 1959." Declassified by the U.S. Department of State on 24 February 1995, on file at the National Security Archive, Washington, DC. We would like to thank William Burr of the National Security Archive, who brought this document to our attention.

were separated by barbed wire from East Berlin. A month later workers began to build a cement wall. For a while Khrushchev based in the seeming success of the operation. The US administration resisted the public uproar over the Wall, especially in West Germany, and did nothing. The disintegration of the GDR, economically and politically, was stopped and reversed. There was no longer the possibility of a quiet *Anschluss* of the GDR to West Germany. Adenauer's foreign policy, based on this tacit expectation, lost credibility among the Social-Democratic opposition leaders, including the mayor of West Berlin, Willy Brandt. They were angry at the United States, which seemed to pay only lip service to the idea of German reunification, and in reality was relieved when the Wall was built. Soon the opposition leaders began to contact Soviet representatives and search for new ways of dealing with the problems of the dismembered nation.[66]

Kennedy did, indeed, feel that the Wall was preferable to a war over Berlin.[67] He authorized his Secretary of State, Dean Rusk, to begin secret communications with Gromyko on the Berlin situation. Khrushchev noticed and appreciated this move. During his vacation in September he summoned Bolshakov, his GRU messenger, to his Black Sea resort in Pitsunda and handed him a long letter addressed to Kennedy, with a modified proposal for the "free city" of West Berlin. Khrushchev suggested that secret correspondence could be a means for ending the stalemate on the German question. He invited Kennedy to Moscow. Kennedy's reply came on October 16, shortly before the Party Congress. He declined Khrushchev's proposal, but agreed to continue a personal exchange of views through a confidential channel.[68]

The construction of the Wall, for all the vitality it gave to the Soviet sphere of influence in Central Europe, remained an ideological and propaganda defeat for Khrushchev in the struggle "between the two systems." The Soviet leader could not admit this, however, particularly not on the eve of the Twenty-second Party Congress, where he wanted to renounce Stalin's cult, bury the ghosts of the "antiparty group," and respond in kind to the challenge from Beijing. For this reason, Khrushchev still pretended that the Wall was not an alternative to, but just a preparation for, the inevitable signing of a separate peace treaty with the GDR.[69]

66   Timothy Garton Ash, *In Europe's Name: Germany and the Divided Continent* (New York: Random House, 1993), pp. 51, 59–62.
67   See Beschloss, *The Crisis Years*, pp. 310–12.
68   Khrushchev to Kennedy, 29 September 1961; Kennedy to Khrushchev, 16 October 1961, *FRUS: Berlin Crisis*. Declassified copies of the letters are available at the National Security Archive, Washington, DC.
69   Khrushchev's opening speech, 3 August, Moscow, Transcripts, p. 3.

Late in October, when the Party Congress approved Khrushchev's leadership and the Chinese delegation left Moscow in anger and dismay, Khrushchev delayed the deadline indefinitely. But not before he dramatically confronted American hard-liners. On October 21, when the Party Congress was still in full swing, Deputy Secretary of Defense Roswell Gilpatric announced to the public that the "missile gap" was a myth, and, in fact, the United States had vast strategic superiority over the Soviet Union. Simultaneously, Khrushchev learned from intelligence sources that Lucius Clay, a veteran of the Berlin blockade, whom Kennedy appointed as a commander of the Western garrison in Berlin, was making preparations to tear down the barbed wire between the Western and Eastern parts of the city.

In Khrushchev's eyes, this was a game between him and "the dark forces" to see who would call the other's bluff first. He informed his diplomatic advisors that he was sending Marshal Ivan Konev, a fierce and trigger-happy war veteran, to Berlin with "full authority" to fight back, if the Americans dared to storm the border.[70] In reality his instructions to the military were much less belligerent. American military jeeps should be let through the border, he said, as they had been before the Wall. And if the Americans moved in tanks, Soviet tanks should block their advance right across the border. Khrushchev seemed to be sure that the Americans would not risk a military clash over Berlin, and he was right. The famous tank stand-off lasted at Checkpoint Charlie on Friedrichstrasse for two days, where the Wall still had not been erected. Finally Kennedy "blinked": there was some kind of exchange (which is still classified) between him and Khrushchev, probably through Robert Kennedy and Bolshakov. The president was looking for a way out of the dangerous impasse. Khrushchev ordered Konev to pull the Soviet tanks back. The American tanks followed their example within twenty minutes.[71]

Khrushchev also sent a powerful nuclear signal to Washington at 11:32 a.m. on October 30, when a 50-megaton nuclear bomb was dropped from a Soviet plane at an altitude of 7.5 miles over the testing site in Novaya Zemlya. The flash of light from the monstrous explosion was visible at a distance of 700 miles, and a gigantic, swirling mushroom cloud rose as high as 50 miles. The bomb had been designed to yield only half of its potential. Had its maximum yield been tested, it would have generated a firestorm engulfing an area larger than the

70   MNSK (1993), no. 10, p. 69; Valentin Falin, *Politische Erinnerungen* (Munich: Droemer-Knaur, 1993), pp. 345–6.
71   MNSK (1993), no. 10, pp. 69–70. For traces of the secret exchange during the confrontation, see Beschloss, *The Crisis Years*, p. 335, and Khrushchev's letter to Kennedy, 9 November 1961, p. 9, National Security Archive, Washington, DC.

state of Maryland. When the telegram proclaiming the success of the test arrived at the Kremlin, Khrushchev and Minister of Defense Malinovsky presented this news to the delegates of the Party Congress as the Soviets' "crushing" response to the imperialists' talk of strategic superiority.[72]

The Berlin crisis of 1961 did not convert Khrushchev to the idea of a permanent truce. While Kennedy's ministers and advisors rehashed the prospect of a nuclear response to the Soviet blockade of West Berlin, no one in the Kremlin was thinking about the possibility of nuclear war.[73] This certitude was not undermined by Khrushchev's episodic uneasiness about the confusion of American politics. The events of the crisis did not shake his belief in his ability to use deliberate pressure and even brinkmanship in his diplomacy. With his approval, the KGB and the Ministry of Defense continued their operations directed at the "strategic deception" of the West.[74] He still regarded himself as capable, as John Foster Dulles had been, of reaching the brink without falling over it. Equally important, Khrushchev had still not made up his mind about Kennedy. Was he an educated wimp or a challenger capable of being Khrushchev's partner? In August Khrushchev told his Communist allies that, frightened by the possible consequences of the crisis, "people close to Kennedy are beginning to pour cold water [on the engine of military escalation] like a fire brigade."[75]

But the signs of American belligerence in October made Khrushchev think that perhaps the military, which was very influential in Washington, was putting some pressure on Kennedy. In a second personal letter to Kennedy, the First Secretary expressed the hope that the two would "plant a new orchard" on the ashes of the Cold War.[76] But what if "the dark forces" in the Pentagon, the CIA, and the State Department drew Kennedy into another Cold War adventure? The more Khrushchev thought about it, the more he worried that the hard-liners in America would take revenge by invading Cuba. And so he fixed his eyes on the

72   Viktor Adamsky and Yuri Smirnov, "Moscow's Biggest Bomb: The 50-Megaton Test of October 1961," the *Bulletin* of CWIHP, no. 4 (1994), pp. 3, 19; *XXII s'ezd kommunisticheskoi partii sovetskogo soiuza: Stenograficheskii otchet* [Twenty-second Congress of the CPSU, stenographic report] (Moscow: Gospolitizdat, 1962), vol. 1, p. 50; vol. 2, pp. 571–3.
73   Interview with Oleg Troyanovsky, 28 May 1993, Moscow; Dobrynin, *In Confidence*, p. 45.
74   Ivashutin and Malinovsky to CC CPSU (Khrushchev), 10 November 1961, in st (special dossier of the Secretariat), 2/35c, 14 November 1961, TsKhSd, f. 4, op. 14, d. 1, pp. 10–14; Zubok, "Spy vs. Spy," pp. 29–30.
75   Transcripts, p. 144; Honore M. Catudal, *Kennedy and the Berlin Wall Crisis: A Case Study in U.S. Decision Making* (Berlin: Berlin Verlag, 1980), p. 201.
76   Interview with Oleg Troyanovsky, 28 May 1993, Moscow; Khrushchev to Kennedy, 9 November 1961, *FRUS: Berlin Crisis*, p. 9.

island in the Caribbean Sea that could drastically change the geopolitics of the Cold War.

The Missiles in Cuba, the Riots in Russia

Operation "Anadyr," the code name for deployment of the Soviet missiles in Cuba that led to the showdown with the United States in October 1962, proved to be the most dangerous moment of the Cold War. Most details about the Soviet side of the crisis became known only recently, when ex-Soviet generals declassified the operation, which promised to deliver troops and missiles to the "Island of Liberty." They described in great detail how the ships deluded their American escorts, what the soldiers on those ships and in Cuba wore, ate, spoke, and wrote in their letters.[77] The cost of the operation, according to CIA estimates, amounted to one billion 1962 US dollars.[78]

Many still cannot grasp the fact that the lives of millions of Americans, Soviets, and indeed all people hung on one single thread, controlled by two mortal men, John F. Kennedy and Nikita Khrushchev.[79] Had either one of them pulled too hard, the crisis could have escalated into war. It is no surprise that the reasonable Harvardian felt he was on the brink of an abyss. What is remarkable, however, is that Khrushchev, the gambler of the decade, panicked and capitulated.

Why did Khrushchev send missiles across the ocean to America's backyard and put his purported "partner," Kennedy, in such a terrible bind? Recently, an American scholar has suggested that "his motivations for this initiative, like the motivations for his threats against Berlin, should not be attributed to any single policy aim; more likely, he

---

77   In the sea of publications it is important to emphasize the recent revelations: James G. Blight and David A. Welch, *On the Brink: Americans and Soviets Reexamine the Cuban Missile Crisis*, 2nd edition (New York: Noonday, 1990); Bruce J. Allyn, James G. Blight, and David A. Welch, eds., *Back to the Brink: Proceedings of the Moscow Conference on the Cuban Missile Crisis, January 27–28, 1989*, CSIA Occasional paper no. 9 (Latham, Md.: University Press of America, 1992); Arthur M. Schlesinger, Jr., "Four Days with Fidel: A Havana Diary," *New York Review of Books*, vol. 39, no. 6, 26 March 1992; Anatoly Dokuchaev, "100-dnevnyi yadernyi kruiz [One hundred days of nuclear travel]," *Krasnaya zvezda* (Moscow), 6 November 1992; also see Dokuchaev's "Operatsia 'Anadyr' [Operation 'Anadyr']," *Krasnaya zvezda*; 21 October 1992; Gribkov, "Karibskii krizis (Caribbean Crisis)," *Voenno-Istoricheskii Zhurnal* (Moscow), no. 10–12 (1992), no. 4 (1993); Gen. Anatoly I. Gribkov and Gen. William Y. Smith, *Operation Anadyr: U.S. and Soviet Generals Recount the Cuban Missile Crisis*, ed. Alfred Friendly, Jr. (Chicago: Edition Q, Inc., 1994).
78   Beschloss, *The Crisis Years*, p. 388.
79   Mark Kramer, "Tactical Nuclear Weapons, Soviet Command Authority, and the Cuban Missile Crisis"; James G. Blight, Bruce J. Allyn, and David A. Welch, "Kramer vs. Kramer," in the *Bulletin* of CWIHP, no. 3 (Fall 1993), pp. 40–41.

intended the move as a bold stroke that would alleviate pressures from several directions."[80] At the time of the crisis there were two interconnected problems being considered by the American government and experts: strategic balance and Berlin. Many in the Kennedy administration, especially the Pentagon's civilian officials, were obsessed with numbers of missiles, comparison of strategic arsenals, and war scenarios, a consequence of the major shift from Eisenhower-Dulles's "massive retaliation" to the new doctrine of "flexible response." They believed the Soviet leader had decided to rectify in one move the "missile gap" in favor of the Soviet Union and, once in a position of strength, to push the Western powers out of West Berlin. There could be only one response to this challenge: to liquidate the Soviet missiles in Cuba or force the Soviets to remove them under the threat of global war.[81]

This analysis underestimates two aspects of Khrushchev's beliefs. First, he was convinced that there was no third alternative between "peaceful coexistence" and all-out war between the Soviet Union and "the imperialists." Therefore, he saw the size of both sides' nuclear arsenals as important, but not crucial, to tipping the scale in international relations, not to mention the historic competition of the two systems. Second, he was fervently dedicated to preserving revolutionary Cuba against a possible US invasion for the sake of the victorious march of communism around the globe and Soviet hegemony in the Communist camp. It was not the temptation to use the Cuban Revolution as a chance to improve the Soviet position in the strategic balance of the superpowers that brought the Soviet missiles to San Cristobal, Cuba; rather, it was a new strategic capability that emboldened Khrushchev to launch an overseas operation to save the Cuban Revolution.[82]

The reverse would have been true of Stalin and Molotov: they would not have cared about the revolutionary process in the Caribbean unless it were directly linked to an increase in Soviet might. It is very hard to imagine that, from the "realist" and cynical platform, either Stalin or Molotov would have risked confrontation thousands of miles away from the fortress of the USSR. But Khrushchev was doing exactly that and even relished in advance how the United States would have to swallow "the same medicine" it had for a decade administered to the Soviets – enemy missiles in its backyard. Khrushchev believed that because the

---

80 James Richter, *Khrushchev's Double-Bind: International Pressures and Domestic Coalition Politics* (Baltimore: The Johns Hopkins University Press, 1994), p. 194; the discussion of the "reinforcing objective" is in Lebow and Stein, *We All Lost the Cold War*, pp. 60–62.
81 Among the strong believers in this hypothesis are Walt W. Rostow and Adam Ulam; V. Zubok's interview with John Auslund, Oslo, Norway, November 1993.
82 Interview with Oleg Troyanovsky, 28 May 1993, Moscow.

Americans had extended their influence into Europe, the Soviets had the right to extend theirs into the zone of the Monroe Doctrine.[83]

Despite the firm belief of an entire generation of American policy-makers and some prominent historians that Khrushchev's gamble in Cuba was actually aimed at West Berlin, there is little evidence of that on the Soviet side. True, many facts seem to indicate that Khrushchev and those around him used the Soviet leverage over West Berlin to deter the Kennedy administration from a Cuban invasion. During the crisis, there was pressure on Khrushchev to use this leverage. The new Soviet ambassador, Anatoly Dobrynin, recommended from Washington that the leader "hint unequivocally to Kennedy" about "our possible repression of Western powers in West Berlin (as a first step – the organization of a blockade of ground access routes, with aerial communication left intact, in order not to create a pretext for an immediate clash)." The KGB chief in Washington, Feklisov (Fomin), actually used this leverage when he talked with John Scali, his channel to the White House.[84] But we also know that when Vassily Kuznetsov, the first deputy of Gromyko, a cautious and pragmatic diplomat, reminded Khrushchev of this possibility at the height of the crisis, the Chairman barked at him: "We are here trying to get ourselves out of this *avantyura* [reckless gamble] and now your are pulling us into another one!"[85]

What pushed Khrushchev into his worst *avantyura* was not the pragmatic search for the well-being of the Soviet empire. On the contrary, it was his revolutionary commitment and his sense of rivalry with the United States. From this perspective, the Cuban adventure was linked to the Berlin crisis. Khrushchev's fear of losing Cuba was similar to his concern about the survival of the GDR. The geopolitical stake of the Soviets in East Germany was incomparably higher than that in Cuba, but what mattered for Khrushchev was to preserve the impression of communism on the march, which, in his opinion, was critical to dismantling the Cold War on Soviet terms. The loss of Cuba would have irreparably damaged this image. It would also have meant the triumph of those in Washington who insisted on the roll-back of communism and denied any legitimacy to the USSR. Khrushchev decided to leap ahead, despite the terrible risk, as he had done at the Twentieth Party Congress, revealing Stalin's crimes against the Party and communism.

83   *Khrushchev Remembers*, p. 494; interview with Oleg Troyanovsky, 28 May 1993, Moscow.
84   Dobrynin to Gromyko, 23 October 1962. From the collection of AVP RF, pp. 7–8. A. Feklisov's recollections of his meetings with Scalia, in "Neizvestnoie o razviazke Karbiskogo krizisa [Reminiscences of Alexander Feklisov, the chief of the KGB station in Washington in 1962]," *Voienno-Istoricheskii Zhurnal*, no. 10 (1989); also his presentation at the Conference on the Cuban Missile Crisis: New Evidence from the Archives, September 1994, Moscow.
85   Interview with Oleg Troyanovsky, 28 May 1993, Moscow.

In September, when Troyanovsky was alone with Khrushchev in his study, he told the Chairman that the Cuban enterprise was far too risky. "It is too late to change anything," said the leader of the USSR. Troyanovsky felt that his boss was a man driving out of control, gathering speed, and rushing God knows where.[86]

Khrushchev's daredevil attitude was not completely shared by many other Soviet elites. Even earlier, in July 1961, Oleg Penkovsky had reported to his Western handlers that higher Soviet officials grumbled: "If Stalin were alive, he would do everything quietly, but this fool is blurting out his threats and intentions and is forcing our possible enemies to increase their military strength."[87] The new gamble was "quiet," but the risk was enormous. Mikoyan and Gromyko were aware of it and initially voiced their concern that the reaction of the United States to the introduction of Soviet troops and missiles in Cuba would be fierce. The question of nuclear war was even raised at the Council of Defense, the special standing body consisting of key Politburo members and government officials. Khrushchev knew that he was taking a huge responsibility and wanted to share some of it with his subordinates. All members of the Politburo and the Secretariat took part in the final meeting of the Defense Council on May 24, 1962, when the minister of defense, Malinovsky, laid out the details of "Anadyr." On the list of speakers were Kozlov, Brezhnev, Mikoyan, Georgi Voronov, Dmitry Polyansky, Otto Kuusinen. The Chairman made everyone sign the directive to start the operation. When some members of the Secretariat of the Central Committee argued that they just did not know enough about the problem, Khrushchev dismissed their objections. They had to sign off, too.[88]

The blueprints for Operation "Anadyr" were still on the table of the Presidium-Politburo when Khrushchev's prestige, which had already fallen among the military and other elite cadres of the Party and the state, faltered among the Soviet general public, including workers and peasants. On May 31 the Soviet Chairman spoke on the radio announcing that the state-controlled prices on meat, sausages, and butter would be doubled. At the same time the minimal individual plan for workers was increased, in effect reducing the guaranteed disposable income of millions. After three years of rhetoric about "overtaking the United

86 Troyanovsky, "Nikita Khrushchev and Soviet Foreign Policy," p. 101.
87 Penkovsky's debriefings, second phase: July–August in London. July 18–19, p. 14, the collection of the National Security Archive, Washington, DC; see also Jerrold L. Schecter and Peter S. Deriabin, *The Spy Who Saved the World: How a Soviet Colonel Changed the Course of the Cold War* (New York: Scribner's, 1992), pp. 209, 241.
88 *Operation Anadyr*, p. 14.

States" and the soon-to-be abundance of goods, the economic (one is tempted to say imperial) overstretch was catching up with Khrushchev. Earlier he had saved the Ulbricht regime by sending carloads of Soviet food to the GDR. Now he had to ask his subjects to diminish their food rations.

A close aide tried to persuade Khrushchev not to stick out his neck, to order someone else to make the announcement. Khrushchev answered: If not me, who else will take the heat? This was the same Khrushchev who had risked denouncing Stalin before the Communist universe and its enemies, and sending missiles across the Atlantic Ocean. An inveterate fighter for the future of utopia, he dismissed the pragmatic advice, at great cost to his political future.[89]

The announcement produced widespread discontent. Leaflets and graffiti protesting the cutbacks appeared in and around Moscow, Leningrad, and many industrial centers of Ukraine, Georgia, Latvia, Southern Russia, the Urals, and Siberia. The KGB reported to the Politburo numerous calls to strike. In many instances protesters were outraged over economic aid to Soviet satellites and "progressive regimes." In their reports the KGB informers preserved some voices of that moment:

> *Azovsky, worker from Moscow*: Our government sends out gifts, feeds others, and now we have nothing to eat, so they are trying to solve their problems at our expense.

> *Zaslavsky, actor*: We will not die, but we should be ashamed to look abroad. If they could only stop boasting that we are overtaking America.

> *Kolesnik, driver from Archangel*: Life goes from bad to worse. Kennedy will be doing the right thing if he drops an atom bomb on the Soviet Union.[90]

The accountants of the KGB computed that "in the first half of 1962, 7,705 anti-Soviet leaflets and anonymous letters were distributed . . . twice as many as in the analogous period of 1961." Most of them were aimed at Khrushchev. "After a long period," the impassive KGB record read, "anonymous documents again are distributed praising the participants of the antiparty group. There is a dramatic increase in the number of letters containing terrorist intentions regarding the leadership of the Party and the government."[91]

89   Interview with Oleg Troyanovsky, 28 May 1993, Moscow.
90   "Information of V. E. Semichastny, the Chairman of the KGB, to the Central Committee on the Reaction of the Population," 2 June 1962, in "Novocherkasskaia tragediia, 1962 [The Novocherkassk tragedy, 1962]," *Istoricheskii arkhiv*, no. 1 (1993), pp. 114, 116.
91   Information from the KGB to the Central Committee, special dossier, top secret, 25 July 1962, in "Novocherkasskaia tragediia, 1962," *Istoricheskii arkhiv*, no. 4 (1993), pp. 170–71.

On June 1–3 in Novocherkassk, the former capital of the Don Cossacks that was now occupied by machine-building plants, the Soviet Communist regime was overthrown by thousands of workers, women, and children. The crisis of the Kremlin's legitimacy was so acute that Khrushchev sent his most able troubleshooter, Anastas Mikoyan, and the second-ranking man in the Party, Frol Kozlov, to Novocherkassk. Soon half of the Politburo gathered there hastily, along with senior KGB officials. Early on the morning of June 2, Kozlov called Khrushchev, who had stayed in Moscow, and received his permission to fire on the rebellious crowd.[92]

That same day Khrushchev was on the radio again, addressing a meeting of Cuban and Soviet youths. He wandered back and forth, from the imperialists threatening the Castro regime to the Novocherkassk rioters, whom he denounced (without mentioning the place of the riot) as "antisocial elements who spoil our lives," as "grabbers, loafers, and criminals." He called for the employment of Civil War methods to deal with dissenters. By then Mikoyan and Kozlov had failed to talk the people of Novocherkassk into submission. Khrushchev must have learned that the workers of the Novocherkassk locomotive plant had painted a chilling slogan on one of their engines: "Khrushchev's flesh for goulash." That day the Red Army moved its tanks into Novocherkassk and restored order. Twenty-three protesters, most of them aged eighteen to twenty-five, were shot dead, and eighty-seven were seriously wounded. Hundreds were arrested; a dozen "instigators" were court-martialed and shot.[93]

The man in charge of the Novocherkassk massacre was the commander of the North Caucasian military district, Army General Issa A. Pliyev. Born on the Caucasian borderland and resembling a character from Leo Tolstoy's *Cossacks*, this brave cavalryman had led many fierce charges against the Germans and the Japanese. Despite being a trained cavalryman, Pliyev was a man of great reserve. He waited for Khrushchev's personal authorization to move tanks and armored personnel carriers into Novocherkassk, and then he held back fire, waiting for another order from Khrushchev to shoot. When the order was issued, his troops dispersed the crowd with machine guns.[94]

92 A. V. Tretetskii, "Novocherkassk: Iyun 1962 goda [Novocherkassk: June 1962]," *Voenno-Istoricheskii Zhurnal*, no. 1 (1991), p. 70. The group of top officials included Alexandre Shelepin, Andrei Kirilenko, Kozlov, Mikoyan, Ilyichev, Dmitry Polyansky, and Piotr Ivashutin.
93 *Pravda*, 3 June 1962; *Istoricheskii arkhiv*, no. 1 (1993).
94 Pliyev received authorization to use arms from Kirilenko and Shelepin on 1 June, after Kirilenko's telephone conversation with Khrushchev. The decision was approved by Mikoyan and Kozlov the next day, and also, by phone, by the minister of defense, Malinovsky. A. V. Tretetskii, "Novocherkassk," pp. 69, 72.

When the czarist officers would put down peasant revolts, the czars would promote them to higher ranks or called them to the Court. A grateful Khrushchev had a better idea for Pliyev. He appointed him head of the provisional contingent of Soviet troops in Cuba, seven thousand miles from Moscow. The Soviet leader personally instructed Pliyev, who knew more about horses than missiles, what to do with the latter once they were deployed on the island. The rocket division of medium-range R-12s and R-14s (some of which Khrushchev had once compared to "sausages") could be used only on the personal order of Nikita Sergeevich. Khrushchev told Pliyev he could use the tactical missiles, called *Luna* (Moon), exclusively in the event of a US sea landing, to prevent the larger missiles from falling into the enemy's hands.[95] When the crisis erupted and the US joint chiefs of staff proposed a preventive strike on the Soviet installations in Cuba, Pliyev had a nuclear option at his discretion.[96]

The guns of Novocherkassk and the missiles of San Cristobal entrusted to the general by Khrushchev were the means of deterrence and retaliation. Did the Chairman realize that the latter could trigger nuclear war? If he did, then the chances of failure in Novocherkassk and Cuba must have seemed infinitesimal to him. He did not believe that Novocherkassk could be a harbinger of the fall of the Soviet order. Nor did he imagine that six *Luna* missiles in Pliyev's hands could bring about a nuclear holocaust. The whole experience of the Berlin crisis assured him he could stay in control. But this time he pushed his luck too far.

Again, as after the revolutions of 1956 in Poland and Hungary, Khrushchev had to build back the muscles of the Stalinist state he sought to dismantle. On July 19 he ordered the KGB to mobilize its reserves for possible future riots on a large scale. Special rapid deployment forces were to be created for "guarding official buildings, communications, banks, and prisons." The situation was so serious that the KGB leadership solemnly "warned" all its officials that the "stepping up of the struggle" against anti-Soviet elements did not mean the reversal of de-Stalinization.[97]

---

95   Gribkov, "Karibskii krizis," p. 31; Mark Kramer, "The 'Lessons' of the Cuban Missile Crisis for Warsaw Pact Nuclear Operations," the *Bulletin* of CWIHP, no. 5 (1995), pp. 110, 112.
96   For a discussion of whether this threat was real or exaggerated, see Kramer, "Tactical Nuclear Weapons"; Blight, Allyn, and Welch, "Kramer vs. Kramer."
97   "Predlozheniia Khrushcheva i drugikh ob usilenii borbi s vrazhdebnimi proiavleniiami antisovetskikh elementov: Vypiska iz protokola N. 42 zasedaniia Prezidiuma TsK ot 19 iulia 1962 g. [Khrushchev's proposal of July 19]," the Central Committee of the CPSU, top secret, special dossier, TsKhSD, f. 89, op. 6, doc. 22, pp. 1–2. Also cited from this file are the draft order of the KGB chief and the collective proposals of the leadership of the state police – surveillance, prosecution, and the penitentiary system (Shelepin, Semichastny, Ivashutin, Zakharov, Tikhunov, Rudenko, Mironov), ibid., pp. 10, 11, 15.

Khrushchev's attention was also riveted on several Soviet ships in the open sea. Those ships were transporting 42 missiles to Cuba and 42,000 Soviet officers and soldiers to protect them. In a separate operation, 3 ships, *Indigirka*, *Alexandrovsk*, and *Archangel*, set out from the Kola Peninsula in the North with a cargo of 164 nuclear charges on board. They passed the British Isles and the Bahamas, and on October 4 the first of the ships, *Indigirka*, arrived at Port Mariel in Cuba.[98]

In September, just as one year before, the Chairman was vacationing at his Black Sea resort and fetched the GRU colonel Bolshakov, his messenger to the Kennedy brothers. This time the Chairman wanted to know if the Americans would go to war with Cuba in the near future. Bolshakov said it was a possibility. "We in Moscow want to know everything," urged Khrushchev. But he did not tell Bolshakov (or Ambassador Dobrynin in Washington) anything about the missiles on their way to Cuba. Perhaps he even used Bolshakov's channel to mislead Kennedy.[99] Some later thought that Khrushchev's belief in secrecy was misplaced. But it is unimaginable that the Soviet leader, given his view of Kennedy and his political surroundings, could even contemplate a public announcement that he was sending missiles and thousands of Soviet troops over an ocean dominated by the US Navy.[100] His plan was to announce his "deterrent" to Kennedy only after the November mid-term elections in the United States. Even if there were tremendous pressure on Kennedy to do something, Khrushchev reasoned, the president had enough common sense to be daunted by the threat of nuclear war over Cuba.[101] According to the schedule, the missiles were to be operational on October 25–27. Just two weeks before that, a tropical storm in the Caribbean subsided, clouds melted over San Cristobal, and a U-2 flew over unfinished Soviet missile installations. Khrushchev was not alarmed. He was so sure of his success that he did not even bother to tell Gromyko, who flew to New York to attend the UN General Assembly, to prepare convenient explanations in case the whole plot became public.

Gromyko met with Kennedy and repeated the official lie: there were not and would not be any "offensive weapons" in Cuba. Kennedy already knew about the missiles but gave no sign of it. Gromyko and Khrushchev felt encouraged: the US president, whatever he knew about

98   Based on the account of Col. Nikolai Beloborodov, at the Conference on the Cuban Missile Crisis of 1962, New Evidence from the Archives, Moscow, 27–29 September 1994; see also *Operation Anadyr*, pp. 62–3. Beloborodov was responsible for the transportation and storage of all nuclear munitions on Cuba.
99   Col. V. T. Roshchupkin, "Moskva hotela znat' vse [Moscow wanted to know everything]," *Voenno-Istoricheskii Zhurnal*, no. 9 (1992), pp. 59–60; Dobrynin, *In Confidence*, p. 54.
100   For a discussion of this issue, see Lebow and Stein, *We All Lost the Cold War*, p. 80; Kornienko at the Conference on the Cuban Missile Crisis of 1962, Moscow, September 1994.
101   Dobrynin, *In Confidence*, p. 72.

the Soviet operation, seemed to prefer keeping silent about the build-up in Cuba until the mid-term elections were over. The Soviet foreign minister reported to Khrushchev that "the situation was satisfactory in general." "The government, as well as the ruling American circles as a whole, are astonished at the boldness of the action of the Soviet Union in rendering assistance to Cuba." And in these new circumstances, he concluded, "a military *avantyura* of the United States against Cuba is next to impossible."[102] The minister reported what Khrushchev wanted to hear.

While Soviet soldiers in Cuban T-shirts worked around the clock to finish the rocket positions, and some higher officers in charge of "Anadyr" played tennis or hid from the scorching sun, the crisis exploded.

The Moment of Truth

The "black week" of October 1962 forced Khrushchev to make a fateful choice: between hegemony in the Communist world and peaceful accommodation with the United States. Before the crisis the Soviet Chairman believed the two goals were compatible, provided that the United States respected Soviet nuclear power. But during the crisis Khrushchev lost his faith in the nuclear deterrent: chaos and uncertainty overpowered the audacious ruler. Vassily Kuznetsov, the same diplomat who had proposed a counterattack in Berlin, later remarked that "Khrushchev shit his pants."[103] In his first letters to Kennedy (October 23 and 24), Khrushchev tried to cover his dismay with unabashed bravado, although he was gripped with fear as he read KGB reports from Washington informing him that the US military was pushing Kennedy toward a military showdown in the Caribbean.[104] He believed that Kennedy was too weak to stem the onslaught of the hardliners. Some Soviets, including Ambassador Dobrynin (who replaced Bolshakov as chief messenger), attempted to get a "fair deal" from Kennedy by trading the Soviet missiles for the US missiles in Turkey. But as soon as the brink seemed too close, Khrushchev was prepared to accept any terms of settlement.[105]

102   Gromyko to the CC CPSU, 19 October 1962, from the declassified collection of the AVP RF, on file at the National Security Archive, Washington, DC.
103   Georgi Kornienko, "Novoie o Karibskom krizise," *Novaiia i noveishaia istoriia*, no. 3 (May–June 1991), p. 85; Kornienko, interview with Zubok, April 1990, Moscow.
104   Kornienko, "Novoie o Karibskom"; Feklisov, "Neizvestnoie o razriadke Karibzkogo krizisa."
105   Dobrynin, *In Confidence*, pp. 86–91.

This happened for the first time on the night of October 25–6, when Khrushchev received erroneous intelligence reports that the US invasion of Cuba was imminent. The next morning Khrushchev dictated a conciliatory letter to Kennedy that did not mention the missiles in Turkey. We must prevent the invasion, and later return to the missiles in Turkey, he explained to Kuznetsov and the other assistants who stayed with him on the night watch in the Kremlin. This "later" came in a few hours. As soon as Khrushchev realized that the reports were false and must have been planted deliberately by the Americans, he sent another letter to Washington in which he insisted on inclusion of the Turkish missiles in any deal over Cuba. For a moment, pride and arrogance again took the upper hand over prudence: he could not look weak in the eyes of his subordinates.

But on October 27 another war scare gripped Khrushchev. Through a failure in the chain of command, Soviet air defense shot down a U-2 over Cuba. Major Rudolf Anderson, Jr., the pilot, was killed. Cries of revenge reverberated all over the United States. Castro shouldered responsibility for the shooting. But at that moment Khrushchev understood that nuclear war could result from a simple accident. He told Malinovsky to send a ciphered message to Pliyev categorically forbidding any use of nuclear weapons. At the same time, at his request twenty-three key Kremlin officials, including the Presidium and Secretariat members, gathered in his dacha at Novo Ogarevo and stayed there all day and night discussing what to do if an American attack were imminent.

The final wave of panic shook the Kremlin on Sunday, October 28, when Khrushchev feared that Kennedy would make another speech on national television at noon, announcing the US invasion of Cuba. As it turned out, this was just a replay of his quarantine speech. Khrushchev immediately accepted Kennedy's terms – a unilateral withdrawal of "all Soviet offensive arms" from Cuba. A courier was sent from Novo Ogarevo at breakneck speed, beating the Moscow traffic, to the State Broadcasting Committee to announce the concessions on the radio. At 6:00 p.m. Moscow time, only two hours before the rebroadcasting of Kennedy's address, the whole world was listening to Khrushchev's submission. The Soviet military immediately began to dismantle missile sites and prepare them for the long trip back to the Soviet Union (nuclear warheads for missiles were evacuated later, by December 1). In his haste Khrushchev even forgot to consult with Castro.[106]

106   Oleg Troyanovsky, "Karibskii krizis: Vzgliad iz Kremlia [The Caribbean crisis: a view from the Kremlin]," *Mezhdunarodnaiia zhizn*, no. 3–4 (1992), p. 174. On the Soviet nuclear charges stored in Cuba, see the account of Beloborodov, the Conference on the Cuban Missile Crisis of 1962, Moscow, 27–29 September 1994.

In an instant the Soviet leader seemed to have forgotten how fiercely he had just recently reacted to minor slights to Soviet honor. He also forgot about the pride and prestige of Castro and his revolutionary friends. He acted in the chillingly "realist" manner of Stalin: walking over the egos and bodies of those who had helped in the implementation of his grandiose designs, but then just happened to be in the way of retreat. Khrushchev further infuriated Castro when he single-handedly made two more concessions to Kennedy: he withdrew from Cuba Soviet IL-28 tactical bombers, his "comradely aid" to the Cuban army, and finally all Soviet troops with the exception of one training brigade. Only on November 20, after the Soviet withdrawal was complete, did Kennedy order the lifting of the US blockade around Cuba. He reneged on his promise, made through confidential channels, to make a public pledge of nonaggression against Cuba. The Irishman from Boston left the boastful Russian from Kalinovka hanging on the ropes.

The making and handling of the Cuban missile crisis tarnished Khrushchev's reputation among well-informed members of the Soviet elite, and certainly among his allies. The rift between the Soviet military corps and Khrushchev, produced by his drastic cuts in early 1960, had grown deeper during the hasty withdrawal of Soviet troops from Cuba. Khrushchev ordered his military to put all missiles on the decks of Soviet ships so that US pilots could count them. For the Soviet generals and admirals this was a humiliation they could not forgive Khrushchev even many years later.[107]

Humiliated, Castro refused to cooperate with the UN inspectors who had to supervise the dismantlement of Soviet installations in Cuba. A new fissure appeared in the Soviet alliance system: relations with Cuba deteriorated to such an extent that Castro was thinking about taking the side of Beijing in the great opposition within the Socialist camp. Khrushchev sent Mikoyan to Havana just as Mikoyan's wife, Ashkhen, was dying in a hospital in Moscow. Khrushchev wanted Mikoyan to show Castro his secret correspondence with Kennedy during the crisis and tell him that, in his view, the crisis ended in a "victory of socialism" – Cuba was saved, and the crisis did not end in a nuclear war that might have led to the destruction of not only capitalist but Communist countries.[108]

---

107   Beloborodov and Gribkov at the Conference on the Cuban Missile Crisis, September 1994, Moscow.
108   Memorandum of a conversation between A. I. Mikoyan and Fidel Castro, Oswaldo Dorticos Torrado, Raul Castro, Ernesto Guevara, Emilio Aragones, and Carlos Rafael Rodriguez, 4 November 1962. From the collection of AVP RF, pp. 1–17; published in *Bulletin* of CWIHP, no. 5 (Spring 1995), pp. 94–101.

But the flowery rhetoric about "proletarian solidarity" rang hollow in the ears of the Cubans, who were disgusted at finding themselves impotent onlookers in the superpowers' deadly waltz. The fiery Ernesto (Che) Guevara felt betrayed. He told Mikoyan that the outcome of the crisis "baffled" the revolutionaries of Latin America, and had already led to their split into pro-Moscow and pro-Beijing factions. In his opinion, "two serious mistakes" – bargaining with the United States and retreating openly – undercut good chances of "seizing power in a number of Latin American countries."[109] Fidel Castro also barely concealed his rage at being treated like a puppet in the grand game. He wondered wryly why Moscow swapped the Soviet missiles for the US missiles in Turkey, not for an American base in Guantanamo. Ten days later, when Mikoyan came to tell him about Khrushchev's decision to take IL-28 bombers back, Castro interrupted his long-winded explanation: "Why explain the rationale? Just say bluntly what the Soviet government wants."[110]

Another fissure appeared in the Warsaw Treaty, as a result of Khrushchev's failure to inform East European leaders about "Anadyr." A Rumanian ambassador secretly told Washington officials that his government dissociated itself from Khrushchev's actions that had just led to the confrontation and similar steps that might produce another such crisis in the future.[111]

In light of these developments, the Soviet leader chose what seemed to be the only strategy: he posed as a great "peacemaker" and tried to utilize the new chemistry between Kennedy and himself for the benefit of "peaceful coexistence." If you cannot defeat the enemy, try to win him over. Khrushchev quickly forgot his ambivalence about Kennedy. He convinced himself that Kennedy was a leader of world stature, wise and magnanimous, in a word, "another Roosevelt." In Vienna he had shrugged off Kennedy's lecture on "miscalculations," believing that it would force him to swallow Soviet missiles in his backyard. Now he praised Kennedy's reserve. "My role was simpler than yours," he wrote in a letter to the US president, "because there were no people around me who wanted to unleash war."[112]

109   Memorandum of a conversation between A. I. Mikoyan and Oswaldo Dorticos, Ernesto Guevara, and Carlos Rafael Rodriguez, 5 November 1962, evening, from the collection of AVP RF, pp. 20–21.
110   Memorandum of a conversation between A. I. Mikoyan and F. Castro, 12 November 1962, from the collection of AVP RF, p. 5.
111   Raymond Garthoff, "When and Why Romania Distanced Itself from the Warsaw Pact," *Bulletin* of CWIHP, no. 5 (1995), p. 111.
112   Khrushchev's letter to Kennedy of 30 October 1962, from the collection of Khrushchev-Kennedy correspondence, declassified by AVP RF in 1991, published in *Problems of Communism* (Spring 1992), Special Edition, p. 65. Copies of the originals are on file at the National Security Archive, Washington, DC.

In the aftermath of the crisis, Khrushchev felt an irresistible temptation, in a sort of catharsis, to offer Kennedy a grand deal. He commented with satisfaction that Nixon, Kennedy's strongest Republican rival, was "pinned down to the mat" in California's elections, and predicted that Kennedy would be reelected to a second term. "Six years in world politics is a long period of time," he wrote, "and during that period we could create good conditions for peaceful coexistence."[113] The Soviet Chairman consistently referred to three issues that were high on his postcrisis agenda: a nonaggression pact between NATO and the Warsaw Treaty Organization, disarmament, and a German peace treaty. This was his "orchard" to replace the "poisonous plants" of the Cold War.

Quietly, Khrushchev abandoned his grandiose plan for general and complete disarmament, which had been designed to win propaganda contests, and returned, instead, to the old Soviet proposals that Moscow had put forward on May 10, 1955 – the first serious production of the emerging Soviet arms control bureaucracy. The Soviet leader also suggested reaching a quick agreement on the banning of all nuclear tests, although he still resisted the idea of on-sight inspections as a channel for Western espionage.[114]

As Khrushchev was retreating in the fields of the Cold War, he tried to save face. In his inimitable style – naiveté blended with arrogance – he proposed that the superpowers jointly pressure Chancellor Adenauer. "Should you and we – two great states," Khrushchev wrote only twenty days after the US-Soviet clash, "submit, willingly or unwillingly, our policy, the interests of our states, to an old man who both morally and physically has one foot in the grave?"[115]

The Soviet leader continued to believe that cooperation with the United States and the support of revolutionary regimes were not mutually exclusive goals. Khrushchev, in correspondence with Kennedy, called the Cuban revolutionary leaders "young, expansive people; in a word, Spaniards," but he took very seriously their questioning his credentials as the world Communist leader.[116] The prospect of Cuba's defection to the side of Beijing could strengthen China's claim to hegemony in the Communist world and was simply intolerable to the Chairman. During the next several months the Soviet leader made it one of his priorities to mend fences with Castro, and convince him of his sincere friendship – with vodka, bear hugs, a visit to the super-secret silo

113   Letter to Kennedy to 11 November 1962; letter to Kennedy of 10 December 1962; *Problems of Communism*, pp. 84, 114.
114   Letter to Kennedy to 11 November 1962; letter to Kennedy of 30 October 1962; *Problems of Communism*, pp. 65, 83, 84.
115   Letter to Kennedy of 10 December 1962; *Problems of Communism*, p. 116.
116   Letter to Kennedy of 22 November 1962; *Problems of Communism*, p. 108.

of intercontinental ballistic missiles, and more billions of rubles from the Soviet state coffer.[117] The comparative reading of Khrushchev's letters to Kennedy and Castro provides a fascinating insight into the widening gap between the revolutionary legacy and pragmatic considerations in the mind of the Kremlin leader. He tried with obvious sincerity to convince the Cuban leader that Soviet economic and military assistance to Cuba was dictated by "internationalist duty," not by "mercantile goals." He mentioned more than once that Soviet leaders understood the Cuban Revolution as a validation of Russia's revolutionary experience – it was part of the same struggle against the West; it reflected the same difficulties in creating a "new society." In a spirit of Communist camaraderie, Khrushchev wrote to Castro: "What could be more sublime, from the point of view of fulfilling proletarian internationalist duties, than the actions undertaken by our country on behalf of another Socialist country, on behalf of the common Marxist–Leninist cause?"[118]

This battle cry was more faint than those Khrushchev had uttered before he built the Wall in Berlin. In his unique way, he believed he could make the objectives meet under a happy banner of "peaceful coexistence." To Kennedy he proposed cooperation to defuse the potential sources of the Cold War crises. At the same time he believed this cooperation could be beneficial to the Communist cause. In the short term, it would safeguard revolutionary Cuba and, possibly, would lead to US recognition of the People's Republic of China. In the long term, it would promote stability for economic competition between the two systems – a competition in which (as Khrushchev never doubted) socialism would prevail. In his correspondence with Castro the Soviet leader explained that peaceful coexistence with the United States allowed them to gain time. "And gaining time is a very important factor," he explained, "because the correlation of forces is everyday more favorable to socialism."[119] Before his own colleagues, hastily convened to approve the deal with Kennedy, Khrushchev again used the term "peace of Brest–Litovsk," a notorious treaty that Lenin had signed with the German militarists in 1918 to win time for world revolution.[120]

By the end of the crisis, Khrushchev began to lean on the idea of joint management of the world with the United States much more than his Communist creed and his – albeit very crude – sense of social justice per-

117   Khrushchev's letter to Castro of 31 January 1963, esp. pp. 3–4, 7, 11.
118   Letter to Castro of 31 January 1963, p. 10.
119   Letter to Castro of 31 January 1963.
120   Personal interview with Boris Ponomarev, a long-term chief of the International Department of the Central Committee, Moscow, 5 June 1990. The meeting took place in Novo-Ogarevo, the Party retreat near Moscow.

mitted. The Cuban missile crisis did not convert him from the Communist Saul into the peace-building Paul. Still, Khrushchev's truce with Kennedy after the crisis was not a marriage of convenience, as had been the agreement between Stalin and Hitler in 1939. It was not another "Yalta," like Roosevelt's concessions to Stalin in 1945. It was a step toward peace, not war. The taming of the Cold War, fifteen years after its inception, and almost a decade after Stalin's death, finally happened.

Part III

War and Détente

Introduction to Part III

Speaking before the US Senate Committee on Foreign Relations in 1974, Henry Kissinger, observed that "the challenge of our time is to reconcile the reality of competition with the imperative of co-existence".[1] Détente was, in Kissinger's eyes, not a process with a definite end point but a strategy for constructive management of Soviet–American relations within the parameters of irreconcilable ideological conflict. The Cuban Missile Crisis of 1962 had provided a sharp reminder that in the thermonuclear age the overarching objective of foreign policy was to avoid war at all cost. By the end of the decade a complex web of political, economic and social factors, both domestic and external, inclined the American and Soviet leaderships to seek in détente a less antagonistic strategy for managing East–West tensions.

Détente was viable at this stage of the Cold War precisely because there had been a substantial shift in the balance of power between the major players. The United States in this period was in relative economic decline, a process not helped by its heavy overseas burdens and especially its costly and seemingly limitless commitment to the war in Vietnam. Moreover, the conservative outlook which had sustained the growth of the national security state during the 1950s and early 1960s was under increasing intellectual challenge from the New Left which questioned the United States' hegemonic tendencies and sought to heighten public consciousness of America's competitiveness in the Cold War conflict. This debate resonated strongly in Europe. France overtly rejected American

1 US Congress, Senate, *Détente, Hearings before the Committee of Foreign Relations*, 93rd Congress, 2nd Session, 1974, pp. 247–60.

hegemony in 1966 by declaring its independence of NATO; the West German government, more discreetly, began to cultivate closer relations with its east European neighbours through cultural and economic exchanges. The Soviet Union, meanwhile, was battling with reformers within its own camp. Having achieved almost military parity with the United States by the end of the 1960s, the Prague Spring and the subsequent Soviet invasion of Czechoslovakia which prevented the country from leaving the Warsaw Pact sent a chill through the communist leaderships in eastern Europe. It also encouraged Moscow to seek to barter its leverage with the North Vietnamese for recognition of the post-war division of Europe and the European borders as determined at Yalta and Potsdam.

Perhaps the most significant change of all, however, was the emergence of China as a potential third superpower. Estranged from the Soviet Union since 1958, it was only at the end of the 1960s that the United States realised the potential of the Sino-Soviet dispute for achievement of its own foreign policy objectives, including Nixon's and Kissinger's search for a negotiated exit from Vietnam. By exploring Washington's pursuit of a triangular relationship Richard Crockatt demonstrates how the emergence of détente in its widest sense was dependent primarily upon the altered perceptions of the respective leaderships in Washington and Moscow of their own interests and the changing balance of power between the two superpowers.

Several views of the explanation for the collapse of détente emerge from the current literature. Many scholars make domestic developments in the United States, e.g. the rise of the Neo-Conservatives with their strong anti-Communism in the mid 1970s, responsible for undermining the American public's support of détente. However, much of the blame for the collapse of détente at the end of the 1970s has also been heaped on the Carter administration. In particular the emphasis placed by Carter's National Security Adviser, Zbigniew Brzezinski, on the Soviet "threat" has been much criticized. Indeed, the notion that the United States should deal equally with China and the Soviet Union without getting too close to either can be regarded as the key to the Nixon–Kissinger strategy which was subsequently undermined by the firm anti-Soviet line taken by Brzezinski. He encouraged Carter to enter into formal diplomatic relations with the post-Mao regime in China in 1979, thus reinforcing the Soviet Union's apparent isolation. Kissinger, himself, however, points to the Soviet–Cuban intervention of Angola in 1975, and its resistance to the Human Rights basket of the Helsinki Final Act as determining factors for the collapse of détente.

Raymond Garthoff, himself a practitioner actively engaged in the Strategic Arms Limitations Talks, explains that the balance in the argument lies somewhere between these interpretations. Détente, he argues, began to unravel from the mid 1970s as a consequence of a series of failures, perhaps the most fundamental of which was the differing conceptions of détente held in Washington and Moscow. Furthermore, Garthoff compares the cynicism and naïveté of American public opinion in assessing their country's foreign policy with the more subtle and sophisticated outlook of European public opinion which recognised Washington's active role in Cold War competition. Thus, while Soviet–American détente collapsed in 1979/80 after the Soviet invasion of Afghanistan, détente in Europe managed to survive.

6

The Vietnam War and the Superpower Triangle

Richard Crockatt

Originally appeared in Richard Crockatt, *The Fifty Years War: the United States and the Soviet Union in World Politics 1941–1991*. Routledge, 1995.

Viewed from the West, and more especially from the United States, the Vietnam War has been regarded as a peculiarly American problem. The popular view of the war, as represented in films, documentaries, novels, and first-hand accounts, has issued from questions and anxieties about the war's effect on American society. Historians, with some notable exceptions, have tended to reinforce this perspective, addressing such questions as: How did the United States become involved in Vietnam? Why did America fail? What are the lessons of Vietnam?

It is easy to understand this emphasis. Taken as a whole, the American experience in Vietnam was a decisive event in its post-war history in both domestic and foreign affairs. The year 1968 marked not only a crisis in the conduct of the war itself – witness the North Vietnamese "Tet" offensive which penetrated the US Embassy compound in Saigon – but also within American society, as race riots and student protests reached a peak, and in the eyes of many American leaders threatened the foundations of American society. Symbolizing the government's crisis of confidence at home and abroad was Lyndon Johnson's withdrawal of his candidacy from the presidential election of 1968.

When Americans uttered the word "Vietnam" (and the same holds true today) they generally meant, not a country several thousand miles from their shores but a whole complex of social conflicts associated with a great divide in the American experience. The fact that with hindsight we can see that the lines of division were actually more complex than these perceptions suggest – public opinion polls show that the fissures were less clear-cut than portrayed by the media images – did not erase the dominant impression of crisis and division (Erikson et al. 1980: 70–1, 94, 162, 172).

Talk of the "Vietnam syndrome" in the years following the war reinforced the sense that in foreign relations, as in domestic affairs, the war provoked a serious rupture. Initial involvement in Vietnam and the subsequent escalation of the war had rested on a measure of consensus on the need to counter the global threat of communism. The costs of implementing that policy in Vietnam ultimately eroded the consensus, producing a retreat from the assumptions which had underpinned it and ushering in a period of indecision about the means and ends of American power. Once again, there is room for doubt about how deep the divide between Vietnam and post-Vietnam policies actually went. There are good grounds for arguing that the basic pattern of US policy was sustained through the aftermath of the war, despite the shock of defeat. Nevertheless, the dominant perception was of discontinuity and this – above all the fact that it was a defeat – has tended to reinforce the emphasis on the war as an episode in the American experience.

For the historian of international relations the specifically American experience is only one among a range of issues to be addressed. In order fully to understand the war, Gabriel Kolko has written, "we need constantly to examine and recall the larger trends and interrelations, treating them all as integral dimensions of a vast but unified panorama" (Kolko 1986: 6). The most obvious feature of the panorama relevant to American involvement in Vietnam by the late 1960s was the growing conflict between the Soviet Union and the People's Republic of China (PRC). Its roots lay in the 1950s, but reached a climax as Richard Nixon entered the White House in 1969. Over the next four years, as the United States sought to achieve "peace with honour" in Vietnam, it also pursued *détente* with the Soviet Union and the PRC, aiming to exploit the Sino–Soviet split without alienating either. Triangular diplomacy and Vietnamization were linked policies. With this in mind, an understanding of the Vietnam War rests on answers to two questions: (1) how did the United States come to believe that vital American interests were at stake in Vietnam? and (2) what were the connections between those interests and the changing pattern of relations between the United States, the Soviet Union, and the PRC? Underlying both questions is the brute fact of North Vietnamese persistence in pursuing the goal of reunifying Vietnam under communist rule.

Vietnam and the American National Interest

Conceptions of the American national interest in Vietnam did not remain static. Indeed the shifts in the American definition of its objectives tell much about the course of the war. Furthermore, examination of stated policy objectives alongside the policies actually pursued exposes difficulties faced by policy-makers in matching means to ends. Rather than give a chronological account of the war, we shall examine American policy in terms of the goals which were most frequently cited by policy-makers.

The first of these, which goes at least as far back as 1952, was "to prevent the countries of Southeast Asia from passing into the Communist orbit" (*Pentagon Papers* 1971: 27). Here, in line with the domino theory, the emphasis is regional rather than national and, in line with the main thrust of American cold war foreign policy, targets communism as the generalized enemy. Also important is the ambiguity of the goal itself – between containment of communism within its existing boundaries and neutralizing its effectiveness as an expansive force, which might imply a more positive or aggressive attack at its roots.

Containing communism, of course, was not of itself a policy, far less a strategy, only a broad goal. A strategy, as John Gaddis has put it, is "the process by which ends are related to means, intentions to capabilities, objectives to resources" (Gaddis 1982: viii). By this standard the escalation of the war by Lyndon Johnson, which saw an increase from 16,000 US advisers in 1963 to over 500,000 ground troops in 1968, represented a vast expansion of means which were poorly designed to achieve the desired objective. Henry Kissinger put his finger on the problem in an influential essay published in the month Nixon was inaugurated. American military strategy, he noted, "followed the classic doctrine that victory depended upon a combination of control of territory and attrition of the opponent". US forces were deployed along the frontiers of South Vietnam to prevent North Vietnamese infiltration and in those areas where the bulk of traditionally organized North Vietnamese forces were located. Destroy the enemy's forces and the guerrillas would "wither on the vine". Unfortunately, he continued, the policy failed to recognize the difference between guerrilla war, which depended upon control of populations, and conventional war, which depended upon control of territory. The bulk of the South Vietnamese people lived in the Mekong Delta (in the far south) and the coastal plain, while most US troops were deployed in the frontier regions and the Central Highlands which were virtually unpopulated. Kissinger concludes:

As North Vietnamese theoretical writings were never tired of pointing out, the United States could not hold territory and protect the population simultaneously. By opting for military victory through attrition, the United States strategy produced what came to be the characteristic feature of the Vietnamese war: military successes that could not be translated into permanent political advantage . . . As a result, the American conception of security came to have little in common with the experience of Vietnamese villagers. (Kissinger 1969: 102–3)

Furthermore, the pacification programme, designed to promote the South Vietnamese government's control of the countryside, failed in its objectives. The Rural Development Programme, follow-up to the Strategic Hamlet scheme developed under Kennedy, had the effect of destroying the local community structures (and creating millions of refugees who poured into the cities) without achieving the military/political goal of winning the stable allegiance of the local populations (Kolko 1986: 236–51).

What in fact might "defeating communism" mean if not destroying its roots – that is to say, defeating the North Vietnamese? The problem was that communism had roots in the South too in the form of the "Vietcong" (or Vietnamese communists) and its political organization the National Liberation Front (NLF). Frustration at slow progress in defeating the Vietcong in the South, and the continued supply of Vietcong forces from the North via Laos and Cambodia, inevitably led to consideration of stepping up pressure directly on the North. From 1965 bombing of the North became an integral part of American military strategy, though initially care was taken to avoid attacks on Hanoi and its port Haiphong. Under Nixon's presidency bombing of the North, including Hanoi and Haiphong, assumed a more central role both because it was seen as necessary compensation for the phased withdrawal of US troops under the Vietnamization policy and because it was regarded as a means of leverage to bring the North Vietnamese to the negotiating table.

The common thread running through American strategy, despite the enormous commitment of troops and the intensive air war on the North, was the concept of limited war inherited from Korea. Johnson's escalation of the war, gradual and partially disguised from American public opinion as it was, was carried out with one eye on the Chinese and the other on domestic opinion. Defeating communism was never a live option if that meant risking all-out war with China and full American mobilization on to a war footing. But the other option of containment of communism in Vietnam was hamstrung by two fundamental difficulties, neither of which had operated in Korea: (1) the

North Vietnamese held a strong footing in the South in the form of North Vietnamese cadres who had been infiltrated since the late 1950s and among South Vietnamese peasants who were either apathetic to American efforts to win their allegiance or were alienated by those efforts; (2) the geography of Indo-China which made it virtually impossible to insulate South Vietnam from its neighbouring states, Cambodia and Laos. Richard Nixon was surely right about at least one feature of the war: namely, that it was an Indo-Chinese and not simply a Vietnamese war, and to that extent his decision to invade Cambodia in 1970 and to insert troops into Laos had a logic behind it, damaging and ineffective as these tactics proved to be. As an extension of the existing policy of limited war, however, Nixon's policies could not surmount the familiar constraints of growing dissent at home and the capacity of the North Vietnamese to absorb punishment and continue fighting.

A second American objective commonly cited by policy-makers was "an independent non-Communist Vietnam" or, in another formulation, "to permit the people of SVN (South Vietnam) to enjoy a better, freer way of life" (*Pentagon Papers* 1971: 278, 432). This goal might seem synonymous with the one already discussed, but there are important distinctions to be made between them. For one thing, the second objective was the positive one of nation-building rather than the negative one of keeping communism out. For another, it focused on the task of political consolidation of the South Vietnamese government rather than on the military task of clearing communists from South Vietnam. True, there was an important military dimension to this goal, as we shall see, but the ultimate test of success would be the creation of self-sustaining, stable self-government in South Vietnam. Crucial to this aspect of American policy were its relations with the South Vietnamese government and that government's relations with its own people.

In three respects the American presence in Vietnam worked to undermine these objectives. In the first place, the American stake in successive South Vietnamese governments, particularly since the overthrow of Diem in 1963, was such as to render questionable the idea of an independent self-governing Vietnam. Of course, the United States could not always call the tune. Continual pressure on Diem's successors to institute reforms, to eradicate corruption and nepotism, and to broaden the base of the administration's support among the South Vietnamese people came to very little. The United States was caught in the bind of, on the one hand, seeking effective control over the South Vietnamese government in order to achieve its own ends and, on the other hand, recognizing that if South Vietnam was to survive once the United States withdrew it must be capable of standing on its own. The result was a half-way house in which American influence over the South Vietnamese government was substantial enough to undermine its autonomy but insufficient to act as a substitute for a genuinely independent and stable regime. In this, as in the economic and military aspects of US–South Vietnamese relations (the other two limiting factors on the creation of an independent and stable South Vietnam), the "Vietnam" war became in large part an American war.

Economically South Vietnam became largely a creature of the United States, dependent on it not merely for direct aid but for the infrastructure necessary to support the war effort. That the war destroyed much of the agricultural production in South Vietnam only served to increase its dependency on American imports. Corruption was rife among the officials responsible for administering American aid. The likelihood of a self-supporting South Vietnam emerging from these conditions receded as the war progressed (Kolko 1986: 223–30).

Similar problems plagued the South Vietnamese military effort. From the early stages of the war when American servicemen were present only (at least in the technical sense) as advisers, relations between the South Vietnamese generals and their American advisers had been difficult. Low morale among the South Vietnamese troops and the generals' premium on keeping casualties down meant engaging in low-risk ventures which frequently left their American advisers deeply frustrated (Sheehan 1989: Book III). The Americanization of the war under Johnson "solved" the problem by transferring effective military command to the United States but created another one by depriving the Vietnamese army of all but the fiction of autonomy. When the South Vietnamese army was called upon to undertake an offensive in Laos in 1971 without American ground support – a Congressional amendment having been passed the previous year forbidding the use of American troops in Cambodia and Laos – the operation failed miserably. Vietnamization was hardly likely to succeed so long as, in Stanley Karnow's words, the South Vietnamese general officers "represented a regime that rewarded fidelity rather than competence" (Karnow 1984: 630).

The combined effect of these political, economic, and military confusions in the relations between the United States and South Vietnam was progressively to undermine the goal of creating a self-sustaining South Vietnam. One indication of the difficulty of achieving this aim was a remarkable re-ordering of American priorities in the mid-1960s. In March 1964 Defense Secretary McNamara wrote to President Johnson that the chief US objective was "an independent non-Communist Vietnam" (*Pentagon Papers* 1971: 278). Only a year later, McNamara's Assistant Secretary for International Security Affairs, John McNaughton, listed American priorities as follows:

70% – To avoid a humiliating US defeat (to our reputation as a guarantor).
20% – To keep SVN (and the adjacent) territory from Chinese hands.
10% – To permit the people of SVN to enjoy a better, freer way of life.

(Pentagon Papers 1971: 432)

Even if one accepts that this represents the opinion of only one official within the administration and that others might have assigned the percentages differently, it offers striking evidence of the degree to which reputation and prestige had become a factor in American decision-making. It operated as a powerful negative, inclining policy-makers effectively to rule out the option of unilateral withdrawal which was the rallying cry of the anti-war movement. But jut as significant is the extent to which the means of achieving the goal of an independent South Vietnam had become an end in itself, producing a circular justification for American involvement. America was there because she was there. Vietnam itself became incidental to the larger priority of reinforcing American power and prestige in the eyes of friend and foe alike.

Such a stance, adopted on the threshold of Johnson's escalation of the war, could only widen the gap between means and ends and render any realistic assessment of the chances of achieving American goals less and less likely. It locked the administration into a strategy in which the only conceivable alternative to pulling out was to increase the commit-ment of troops. Lyndon Johnson's final realization that the strategy was not working came only at the moment when, in the aftermath of the Tet offensive in February 1968, the American Commander in Vietnam, General Westmorland, requested a further 206,000 troops to the 543,000 already committed to South Vietnam. That the Tet offensive was a costly military defeat for the North Vietnamese was less signifi-cant, as far as American credibility was concerned, than the fact that they had been able to mount it at all and that they had managed to penetrate deep into South Vietnam, indeed into the American Embassy compound. As Richard Nixon put it in a retrospective account of the war, "the debate over whether we should expand our intervention in the Vietnam war ended with the Tet offensive and the November 1 bombing halt. These foreclosed the option of committing ourselves even deeper. Whatever the merits of our cause and whatever our chances of winning the war, it was no longer a question of whether the next President would withdraw our troops but of how they would leave and what they would leave behind" (Nixon 1986: 96).

At the point, then, when Richard Nixon entered the presidency in January 1969 each of the American aims – containing communism in

Southeast Asia, creating a stable, self-sustaining South Vietnam, and maintaining American credibility in the eyes of alliés and enemies – had run into the ground. Vietnamization was designed to deal with all three. As a maximal strategy it was intended to achieve these aims in conjunction with an American withdrawal and peace negotiations with the North Vietnamese, with the goal, as Nixon put it, of achieving "peace with honour". Minimally, however, it would provide the United States with a way out of Vietnam which, it was hoped, would safeguard at least some vital interests.

Not least of the pressures on the Nixon administration was domestic public opinion. Demonstrations against the war reached new heights in the spring of 1970 in the wake of the incursion into Cambodia. In May four students were killed by National Guardsmen at Kent State University, provoking widespread public outrage. The timing of these events was significant. In February of the same year Kissinger had opened secret talks in Paris with Le Doc Tho, a senior North Vietnamese official, in an effort to reach a negotiated settlement. For the next three years Kissinger would shuttle to and from Paris, keeping the details of his conversations with Le Doc Tho largely secret from his colleagues in the administration, reporting only to Nixon himself.

His efforts, however, were seriously weakened by a number of factors. In the first place, time was on the side of the North Vietnamese. They had been fighting the French and then the Americans for over twenty-five years, and could afford to spin out negotiations and wait for the Americans to tire. By contrast, Nixon's time was strictly limited – by what Congress and the American public was prepared to stand and by the demands of electoral politics. As the Presidential election of 1972 drew closer, American urgency increased, a fact which was not lost on the North Vietnamese who in the Spring of 1972 launched a massive offensive which lasted until June, exerting further pressure on Kissinger to reach a solution. Only American bombing and helicopter support prevented military disaster for the hard-pressed South Vietnamese army. By this stage only a few thousand American combat troops remained in South Vietnam (Karnow 1984: 640–3).

The time factor reinforced the short-term and long-term military problems which had bedevilled the American effort from the beginning. In the long term, one military expert has written, American containment had always taken the form of strategic defence, punctuated by tactical offensives. The North Vietnamese, on the other hand, had pursued strategic offence while on occasion adopting tactical defence in order to consolidate their positions (Summers 1982: ch. 10). The North Vietnamese willingness to accept huge casualties in pursuit of their goal of victory, an option not open to the Americans, further strengthened the

North's long-term advantage. In the short term, in line with the phased withdrawal of American ground troops, the United States was forced to rely on bombing both as a lever in the negotiations and in support of South Vietnamese ground operations.

Bombing, however, had not in the past yielded clear positive results, because of the capacity of the North Vietnamese to shift their command centres and the lack of substantial economic targets in the North. Furthermore, during Johnson's administration the North Vietnamese had been able to rely on American public opinion's distaste for the bombing policy to limit both the geographical limits and the scale of the air war. Johnson resisted the pleas of military advisers to allow them to pound Hanoi and its port Haiphong. Nixon was less inclined to resist such pleas and at two critical points in negotiations with the North Vietnamese during 1972 he ordered B-52s to attack the Hanoi area. The first, which took place in May, helped to produce a breakthrough in the negotiations and the second, during December, triggered the final agreement which had been stalled in the latter months of 1972. Significant, however, as the bombing may have been, it was not the only factor in producing a conclusion to the negotiations. Chinese and Soviet pressure on North Vietnam was equally important, as will become clear in the next section. Moreover, not only was the bombing policy highly controversial in the United States then and since, but it undercut the fiction of Vietnamization.

The terms of the final agreement reached by the United States and North Vietnam in January 1973 revealed the fragile political and military foundations on which the American war effort had been based. From the American point of view, the measure of a successful agreement would be the extent to which the United States managed to extricate itself from Vietnam "with honour", leaving behind a militarily and politically secure regime in the South. In the event, while the formalities of agreement ensued, peace did not.

On the face of it the agreement was made possible by a major North Vietnamese concession – the abandonment of their earlier insistence that political and military issues be resolved together and more specifically the demand that President Thieu be removed from the leadership of the South as the price of a cease-fire. So long as the North Vietnamese set these conditions for a settlement, the Americans would not agree to a cease-fire, since it would leave the political future of South Vietnam in the balance. Nor would Thieu be likely to accept such a proposal, and for all the American doubts about Thieu's leadership, an agreement made at Thieu's expense would put in question the whole rationale of the war effort. As Nixon wrote to Kissinger, "Thieu's acceptance must be wholehearted so that the charge cannot be made that we forced him into a settlement" (Isaacson 1992: 454). In actuality Thieu's acceptance was less than wholehearted, and in the months leading up to the January 1973 agreement Kissinger and Nixon were forced to expend almost as much effort in persuading Thieu to accede to the proposals as in bargaining with the North Vietnamese. In the face of the American determination to reach agreement Thieu simply had no choice. In line with American wishes the agreement separated military and political issues. The first provided for a cease-fire, American troop withdrawal, and an exchange of prisoners; the second for bilateral negotiations between North and South Vietnam leading to the establishment of a "council of national reconciliation" and subsequently elections to reunify the country (Karnow 1984: 648). This optimistic scenario, however, could not hide the substantial concession made by the United States which permitted North Vietnamese troops to remain in the South following the cease-fire. It left South Vietnam with few defences against a resumption of the war by the North, particularly in the light of a Congressional resolution, passed in March 1973, cutting off funds for any further intervention by the United States in the event of North Vietnamese violations of the cease-fire or non-compliance with other parts of the agreement. Thieu and South Vietnam were in effect left to their own devices – the last and most decisive test of Vietnamization. The denouement came two years later when North Vietnamese troops took Saigon and achieved their aim of reunifying Vietnam by force of arms.

Kissinger wrote in his memoirs that "I believed then, and I believe now, that the agreement could have worked." He shared Nixon's conviction that "in the end, Vietnam was lost on the political front in the United States, not on the battlefront in Southeast Asia". Kissinger put it down to the collapse of executive authority which resulted from Watergate; Nixon was more inclined to blame "a spasm of Congressional irresponsibility" (Kissinger 1979: 1470; Nixon 1986; 15, 165). In truth, however, a "credibility gap" had long existed between publically stated policy, which was relentlessly optimistic about the chances of achieving American goals, and the military and political realities on the ground in Vietnam. The *Pentagon Papers*, a lengthy in-house study of the war commissioned by 1968 by Defense Secretary McNamara and leaked to the *New York Times* in 1971, reveal a consistent pattern of self-deception as much as public deception among American officials from the Kennedy administration onwards. In an analysis of the Papers Hannah Arendt remarked on the policy-makers' imperviousness to facts. Time and again intelligence reports and advice which ran counter to government plans for the war would be ignored or suppressed. Policy-makers, she suggested, lived in a defactualized world in which the politics of image took over from the politics of reality. She ascribed this to "two new genres in the art of lying" – "the apparently innocuous one of the public relations managers in government who learned their trade from the inventiveness of Madison Avenue", and that of the "professional problem-solvers" who were drawn into government from the universities and think-tanks. Both groups had a hatred of "contingency", an unshakeable commitment to an order which could only be brought about by ignoring the facts or manipulating them. The gap between the facts and the desired order was filled by public relations (Arendt 1971: 30–1, 34).

Another perhaps less contentious way of making the same point is to say that the United States had difficulty in conceiving of limits to its own power. Nothing is more striking than the contrast between this posture and that of the North Vietnamese, whose history, it has been observed, had long been characterized by "subjugation and tributary status", pre-eminently to the Chinese (McGregor 1988: 12). North Vietnam's limited material resources, consciousness of the enormous gap in power and resources between itself and the United States, and consequent dependence on Chinese and Soviet aid enforced a certain realism in North Vietnamese political and military strategy. Above all, while these constraints served to concentrate the North Vietnamese mind on the overriding goal of ridding Indo-China of Western imperialism, they also encouraged tactical flexibility and a good deal of political ingenuity.

North Vietnam and Sino–Soviet Conflict

In the hands of a less skilful leader North Vietnam might well have been crushed between the USSR and the PRC. As it was, Ho Chi Minh pursued policies and military strategies which were designed to promote North Vietnamese interests without alienating either of the communist superpowers. As far as possible Ho Chi Minh maintained neutrality in the Sino–Soviet split and exploited the desire of both powers to be seen to be active sponsors of North Vietnamese interests (Zagoria 1967: 102–4). Among other reasons, geography dictated the maintenance of good relations with both powers: while North Vietnam was dependent primarily upon the Soviet Union for heavy military equipment, the main supply route for these deliveries lay through China. Frequent clashes between the Soviet Union and China over the arrangements for delivery during the Cultural Revolution and the deepening Sino–Soviet split (1965–9) put deliveries seriously at risk without, however, wholly disrupting them. Neither the PRC nor the Soviet Union could afford to let this happen (Funnell 1978: 147–50).

Similar disputes between 1965 and 1968 over military strategy and peace initiatives found North Vietnam in the unenviable position of having to tread a narrow path while, as it were, looking over both shoulders simultaneously. Militarily, Beijing favoured the Maoist strategy of protracted guerrilla war, while the Soviet Union counselled the employment of conventional force strategy, a reflection of the ideological biases as well as material resources of both powers. Worse still, this divide reinforced a rift between the Hanoi leadership and the NLF in the South over military strategy. On the question of peace talks too Soviet and Chinese pressures were opposed: the Soviets pressing for an end to the war and a political settlement and the Chinese urging North Vietnam to "persevere in a protracted war and oppose capitulation and compromise" (Funnell 1978: 156–60, 161). Coming in the wake of the Soviet invasion of Czechoslovakia, which the Chinese stridently condemned, this statement showed the strain exerted on North Vietnam by the Sino–Soviet split at its most extreme point to date. Hanoi's support for the Soviet invasion of Czechoslovakia worsened relations between Hanoi and Beijing, though not to the point of an open breach. While there were thus clear signs by 1969 of a tilt in North Vietnamese policy towards the Soviet Union – Hanoi's largest benefactor by a considerable margin (Pike 1987: 106 and ch. 6) – it was not yet such as to sever the connection with China.

It would be misleading to regard the complex Soviet and Chinese machinations with respect to Hanoi as arising only from the war in Vietnam. Each power had larger fish to fry. Vietnam was never more than one factor in their calculations, which centred rather on perceptions of global advantage in their relations with each other and with the West (Zagoria 1967: 27–30). North Vietnam was the gainer from these conditions to the extent that, while they inclined both powers to continue aiding North Vietnam, they also acted as a limitation on Soviet and Chinese desire to dictate a solution. North Vietnam could continue to extract maximum advantage from its measure of independence from both powers, knowing that neither would risk all its foreign policy resources in the Vietnam conflict. On the other hand, North Vietnam's scope for manoeuvre was limited by these same conditions, and one important limiting condition was the relations of the communist superpowers with the United States.

The American Opening to China

The vector of forces shifted substantially with Nixon's assumption of the presidency in 1969. We have already seen that *détente* with the Soviet

Union was begun in part with a view to enlisting Soviet pressure on North Vietnam to negotiate an end to the war. The opening to China had similar aims, though as with Soviet *détente* it also looked a good deal further than Vietnam. Indeed, well before Nixon came to power the United States and the PRC had signalled their desire to prevent the Vietnam War escalating into a Sino–American war in the form of an understanding, the so-called "stand-off" agreement, reached in 1966. Reportedly the PRC set three conditions, to which the United States agreed: "(1) that the United States not attack China; (2) that it not invade North Vietnam; and (3) that it not bomb the Red River dike system" (Litwak 1984: 40). It was the first indication of the United States' reconsideration of its policy of non-recognition of Communist China, and during the following three years further tentative moves were made towards an opening of negotiating channels.

That these saw fruition under Richard Nixon's presidency has always provoked surprise and even astonishment. No one had been louder in condemnation of the Chinese communists following the Revolution of 1949, no one more publicly opposed to recognition of the PRC nor stronger in support of Chiang Kai-shek's Nationalist government on Taiwan than Congressman, Senator and later Vice-President Nixon. Perhaps, as Seymour Hersh suggests, "as with other major foreign policy issues, Nixon's views on China had always been more pragmatic than ideological" (Hersh 1983: 350). As early as 1954 we find Nixon taking a middle position between those who believed that the United States had no alternative but to launch a war against the Communist Chinese and those who advocated recognizing Mao's China and opening up trading links in order to woo China away from the Soviet Union (Chang 1990: 111–12). Furthermore, if one judges by Nixon's own record of his thinking during his long period as a private citizen from 1961 to 1968, he had come to believe that the reality of Communist China could no longer be ignored. It was the PRC's growing strength as a nuclear power, as a political force in Asia and above all in independence from the Soviet Union, which inclined him to realism (Nixon 1978: 272–3, 282–3, 371–4). In a 1967 article entitled "Asia after Vietnam" he had observed that in the light of the growing strength of China "for the short run ... this means a policy of firm restraint, of no reward, of a creative counterpressure designed to persuade Peking that its interests can be served only by accepting the basic rules of international civility. For the long run, it means pulling China back into the world community – but as a great and progressing nation, not as the epicenter of world revolution" (Nixon 1978: 285).

Nixon's timetable was brought forward by three things: (1) evidence that China itself was interested in talking to the United States; (2) a preoccupation with finding a way out of the Vietnam War (coupled with a revision of the earlier conventional wisdom that Chinese aggression lay behind the actions of North Vietnam); and (3) his sense, once he had achieved election to the presidency, that he was in a position to make a personal diplomatic coup.

China's motives

Despite the intense preoccupation with internal affairs during the Cultural Revolution, elements within the Chinese leadership continued to seek ways out of China's diplomatic isolation. Their motives were not entirely due to worsening relations with the Soviet Union. In line with China's growing sense of itself as a major power, it lobbied intensively in the late 1960s for admission to the United Nations, recognizing that there was growing support in the General Assembly for a rectification of the anomaly of Taiwan's position as representative of all China. (The PRC was finally admitted in 1971 after the United States abandoned its fruitless efforts to resist.) China's need for technological aid to develop oil resources also counted for a good deal, and that ultimately meant an opening to the United States as the leader in oil technology. In 1966, just prior to the Cultural Revolution, there had even been an American proposal, prompted by American academic specialists on China but taken up by the Secretary of State, that Chinese scholars and scientists be permitted to visit the United States. This was shelved with the opening of the Cultural Revolution (Spence 1990: 628–9). Mention has already been made of the stand-off agreement between the United States and China in 1966 regarding Vietnam. Finally, within a few days of Nixon's election to the presidency in November 1968 China requested a reconvening of talks between the US Ambassador to Poland and Chinese diplomats which had taken place intermittently since the mid-1950s. Tentative and still-born as some of these moves were, they display a consistent shift in Chinese policy towards the West. The Sino–Soviet border crisis of 1969 and the declining intensity of the Cultural Revolution quickened its momentum.

The larger pattern behind these individual moves, however, rested on Mao's perception of the changing balance of power among the three superpowers. The combination of relative American decline, increasing Soviet strength, and China's own growing power had produced a fundamental shift in the international correlation of forces. The chief threat to China by the late 1960s was the Soviet Union, not the United States. As John Gittings has suggested, Mao applied the same argument

in the late 1960s as he had done in the 1930s in the face of Japan's bid
for hegemony in Asia: "one had to identify the 'principal contradiction'
or major enemy (Japan then and the Soviet Union now) and make
common cause against it with those who posed the lesser threat
(American imperialism in both cases)" (Gittings 1982: 74). In effect,
Mao's vision was a realization of the hope which some American policy-
makers had harboured in the 1950s – that Mao might become an Asian
Tito. That it had taken so long to materialize was in part due to Mao's
own difficulty in establishing Chinese independence from the Soviet
Union and in part because the Americans had taken so long to perceive
the implications of the Sino–Soviet split.

Finding a way out of Vietnam

The Nixon administration's determination to conclude the war in
Vietnam was one important factor in the opening to China. In abandoning the view of previous administrations that North Vietnam was a
stalking horse for Chinese expansionism, Nixon was in a position to
exploit China's own desire to improve relations with the United States
by seeking Chinese help in reaching a Vietnam settlement. While rhetor-
ically the Chinese leadership continued to berate the United States, particularly during the expansion of the war into Cambodia and Laos in
1970 and 1971, behind the scenes the Beijing leadership maintained
channels of communication which had been opened soon after Nixon
came into office, convinced as they were by Nixon's troop withdrawals
that "the United States was serious about withdrawing from Vietnam".
Furthermore, the Chinese evidently did, as Garthoff records, "make a
concentrated effort to persuade the Vietnamese to compromise"
(Garthoff 1985: 255). That the Chinese were willing to run the risk
of alienating the North Vietnamese demonstrated where their chief
priority now lay.

Nixon: the personal factor

Nixon's personal stake in the opening to China was immense. It was his
own rather than Kissinger's initiative, though he employed Kissinger as
his emissary in the latter's secret visit to Beijing in July 1971 which laid
the groundwork for Nixon's own visit six months later. "Kissinger",
notes his most recent biographer, "was at first sceptical about any quick
opening to China and it was Nixon's dogged vision that propelled the

initiative" (Isaacson 1992: 336). Before these path-breaking moves, however, careful preparation had been necessary. Via renewed ambassadorial talks in Warsaw in early 1970 and further contacts with China through intermediaries (Presidents Ceaușescu of Romania and Yaya Khan of Pakistan) Nixon conveyed the message that he was prepared to talk about the status of Taiwan, the main sticking point in China's relations with the United States. In April 1970 came a surprise invitation to the American table tennis team to visit Beijing – the advent of so-called "ping-pong diplomacy" – to which Nixon responded by easing restrictions on Sino–American trade.

Nixon set off for China with a heady sense that he was making history. A few days before he left, he had received the French writer André Malraux at the White House. Malraux had known Mao Zedong and Zhou Enlai during the 1930s and had maintained intermittent contact with them. The writer's final words to Nixon, faithfully recorded in the President's memoirs, doubtless fed his sense of destiny. " 'I am not De Gaulle,' " declared Malraux, " 'but I know what De Gaulle would say if he were here. He would say: All men who understand what you are embarking upon salute you.' " Later, during the flight to China, Nixon noted in his diary that "there was almost a religious feeling to the messages we received from all over the country" (Nixon 1978: 559). Despite notes of caution and realism in his account of his China trip, these hardly hide his pride of accomplishment. *Détente* with the Soviet Union was business; important business but business nevertheless. The opening to China was pleasure, born of satisfaction with a bold personal achievement which promised much and yielded much, at least symbolically. He warmed to Prime Minister Zhou Enlai in a way he did not to Brezhnev. Brezhnev, he noted had "a great deal of political ability and a great deal of toughness". Zhou Enlai, though, "had the combination of elegance and toughness, a very unusual one in the world today" (Nixon 1978: 619).

Doubtless some of Nixon's satisfaction arose from the pressure his China visit put on the Soviets who, in the wake of Nixon's trip, moved quickly to fix a date for the US–Soviet summit later in the year. Equally important was the achievement of a form of words on the Taiwan issue which allowed each side to edge towards the other without sacrificing basic principles. Of course, the outline of the American position had been prepared well before Nixon's visit, indeed by Kissinger, drawing, as he admitted, on an unused State Department memorandum dating from the 1950s (Kissinger 1979: 783). The result on the face of it was stalemate. In the Shanghai Communiqué which concluded the talks, the American and Chinese positions on Taiwan were simply stated alongside each other, their differences plain to see. The Chinese asserted that "Taiwan is a province of China", that "the liberation of Taiwan is China's internal affair in which no other country has the right to interfere", and that "all US forces must be withdrawn from Taiwan". For its part, the United States declared that:

> the United States acknowledges that all Chinese on either side of the Taiwan Strait maintain there is but one China and that Taiwan is a part of China. The United States Government does not challenge that position. It reaffirms its interest in a peaceful settlement of the Taiwan question by the Chinese themselves. With this prospect in mind, it affirms the ultimate objective of the withdrawal of all US forces and military installations from Taiwan. In the meantime, it will progressively reduce its forces and military installations on Taiwan as the tension in the area diminishes. (Grenville and Wasserstein 1987: 305)

The largest concession lay on the American side – its commitment, though at an unspecified date, to withdraw troops from Taiwan – but the US–Taiwan security treaty dating from 1955 remained in force as a reminder of America's continuing role as guarantor of Taiwan's independent status. Furthermore, the final words of the communiqué ("as tension in the area diminishes") reflected the American expectation that the Chinese now had a stake in ending the chief source of tension – the Vietnam War (Garthoff 1985: 238).

Clearly the agreement on Taiwan and on other issues fell far short of full normalization of Sino–American relations. Diplomatic recognition would only come in 1978 under Carter's administration. The resumption of contact, however, after two decades of icy coexistence, was a measure of the enormous external and internal changes which both powers had experienced. Kissinger concluded his account of these events with the remark that "the bipolarity of the postwar period was over" (Kissinger 1979: 1096).

The impact on Nixon's political fortunes was less clear-cut. While he was able to ride out the storm of protest from the Right over his "abandonment" of Taiwan, his triumph in China did not over the next two years immunize him against the erosion of his domestic credibility as the Watergate story broke and finally engulfed him. The Chinese, like the Soviets, were mystified that a statesman with such achievements to his credit should be sacrificed on the altar of domestic politics. Mao had made much in his talks with Nixon of his preference for dealing with "Rightists" among capitalist leaders. "I voted for you during your last election", Mao told him (Nixon 1978: 562). Mao's "vote" may have counted in the international arena, but at home what counted was a solid base of support, and the very means which Nixon used to promote his foreign policy initiatives – back-channel diplomacy, secrecy, and surprise – contributed to the fragility of that base even as it smoothed the path to diplomatic solutions.

Vietnam: The Costs of Victory

Accounts of the Vietnam War commonly end with discussion of America's defeat and its implications for policy-making in the 1970s. We shall have much to say about that in the following chapter. For the moment, however, we must consider the implications of the communist victory not only in Vietnam itself but in Indo-China as a whole, since in 1975 Ho Chi Minh's dream of Indo-Chinese liberation was finally achieved with communist victories in Cambodia and Laos following swiftly on the fall of Saigon. Rather than producing unity among the communist regimes in Southeast Asia and between the PRC and the Soviet Union it exposed all the more clearly the differences between them. So long as the American presence in Southeast Asia had lasted, it had served to paper over the many conflicts of purpose among the interested powers in the region.

China had always had ambiguous feelings about Vietnamese nationalism. Aid to North Vietnam in the war against the United States, John Gittings points out, had been offered "with the purpose of maintaining the north as an effective buffer zone rather than to bring liberation to the South" (Gittings 1982: 85). A strong and united Vietnam, particularly one backed heavily by the Soviet Union, posed a threat to China's desire for pre-eminence in Southeast Asia. Vietnam's military and political influence in Laos throughout the period of the war further limited Chinese power, and inclined Beijing to seek influence in Cambodia as a counter-weight. Ideological affinity between Chinese communism and the Cambodian Khmer Rouge, who had led the insurgency against the American-backed Lon Nol since 1970 and finally came to power in 1975, created a deep fissure within Southeast Asia. As the Khmer Rouge leader, Pol Pot, embarked in 1977 upon a murderous campaign to "democratize" Cambodia and mounted raids and massacres in disputed territories on the Cambodian–Vietnamese border, Vietnam responded in December 1978 by invading Cambodia (or Kampuchea, as it was now called). When the Vietnamese took Phnom Penh, the Kampuchean capital, and ousted the Khmer Rouge, for all their misgivings about Pol Pot, China continued to recognize the Khmer Rouge as the legitimate government (as did the United States) and mounted a brief counter-invasion of Vietnam. With Vietnam receiving strong backing from the Soviet Union – a Soviet – Vietnamese Treaty was signed in 1978 – the Sino–Soviet split thus achieved its final destructive denouement in Southeast Asia (McGregor 1988: 35–41).

Vietnam's harvest of victory was thus another war at a time when it was attempting to rebuild the nation after thirty years of conflict. The refusal of the United States to accede to Vietnam's demand for $3 billion dollars in war reparations as a precondition for talks on reconciliation cut Vietnam off from a much-needed source of aid for reconstruction (Karnow 1984: 28). As the Vietnamese economy floundered and political repression deepened, thousands of Vietnamese fled the country in boats, many of them falling prey to piracy and starvation, further increasing Vietnam's isolation and economic disarray. The outcome could hardly have been further from Ho Chi Minh's vision of liberation and peace. Nor, it must be said, did the actuality correspond to the long-held American fears of the consequences of a communist victory in Southeast Asia. If ever there were proof that the chief force at play in Southeast Asia was nationalism rather than communism, then the aftermath of the war provided it.

That in the critical year of 1978 the United States played its "China card" by opening formal diplomatic relations with the PRC illustrated the global ramifications of this regional conflict. Soviet anger at the American move worsened US–Soviet relations at a moment when progress on SALT II was already stalled. Was it a paradox that *détente* should have flourished at a time when the United States was heavily embroiled in Vietnam and that it should have begun to unravel once the war was over? Or was it rather logical that *détente* was most likely to succeed when the parties were conscious of limits to their bargaining power? Clearly there was more involved in the rise and decline of *détente* than Vietnam. But there was surely more than a coincidental connection between the two. Arguably the Vietnam War was an enabling condition for *détente*. It sustained a measure of common purpose between the PRC and the Soviet Union, if only to the extent that it inclined both to compete for influence in Hanoi and in Washington. The outer limits of competition were set by the need to be seen to be supporting a critical liberation struggle. The United States for its part needed Chinese and Soviet help in extricating itself from Vietnam, and American negotiators were careful to assure the Soviets that the opening to China was not to be regarded as an anti-Soviet move. Once the Vietnam issue was resolved, at least to the extent of removing the United States from the equation, lines of conflict which had always been present were free to flourish. If only for a brief period in the late 1960s and early 1970s, the Vietnam War was the pivot of the triangular superpower balance. With the pivot removed the balance collapsed.

References

Arendt, H. (1971) "The Art of Lying: The Pentagon Papers", *New York Review of Books*, 18 November, 30–9.

Chang, G. (1990) *Friends and Enemies: The United States, China, and the Soviet Union, 1948–1972*, Stanford: Stanford University Press.

Erikson, S., Luttberg, R. and Redin, K. (1980) *American Public Opinion: Its Origins, Content, and Impact*, 2nd edition, New York: Wiley.

Funnell, V. (1978) "Vietnam and the Sino–Soviet Conflict, 1965–1976", *Studies in Comparative Communism* XI, Nos. 1 and 2, Spring/Summer: 142–69.

Gaddis, J. (1982) *Strategies of Containment: A Critical Appraisal of Postwar American Security Policy*, New York: Oxford University Press.

Garthoff, R. (1985) *Détente and Confrontation: American–Soviet Relations Nixon to Reagan*, Washington, DC: Brookings Institution.

Gittings, J. (1982) "China: Half a Superpower", in N. Chomsky et al., *Superpowers in Collision: The New Cold War*, Harmondsworth: Penguin.

Grenville, J. and Wasserstein, B. (eds) (1987) *The Major International Treaties Since 1945: A History and Guide With Texts*, London: Methuen.

Hersh, S. (1983) *The Price of Power: Kissinger in the Nixon White House*, New York: Simon and Schuster.

Isaacson, W. (1992) *Kissinger: A Biography*, New York: Simon and Schuster.

Karnow, S. (1984) *Vietnam: A History*, Harmondsworth: Penguin.

Kissinger, H. (1969) *American Foreign Policy: Three Essays*, London: Weidenfeld and Nicolson.

Kissinger, H. (1979) *The White House Years*, London: Weidenfeld and Nicolson.

Kolko, G. (1986) *Vietnam: Anatomy of a War*, London: Allen and Unwin.

Litwak, R. (1984) *Détente and the Nixon Doctrine: American Foreign Policy and the Pursuit of Stability, 1969–1976*, Cambridge: Cambridge University Press.

McGregor, C. (1988) *The Sino–Vietnamese Relationship and the Soviet Union*, London: International Institute for Strategic Studies, Adelphi Paper 232.

Nixon, R. (1978) *The Memoirs of Richard Nixon*, London: Sidgwick and Jackson.

Nixon, R. (1986) *No More Vietnams*, London: W. H. Allen.

Pentagon Papers (1971), New York Times Edition, New York: Bantam Books.

Pike, D. (1987) *Vietnam and the Soviet Union: Anatomy of an Alliance*, Boulder: Westview Press.

Sheehan, N. (1989) *A Bright Shining Lie: John Paul Vann and America in Vietnam*, London: Jonathan Cape.

Spence, J. (1990) *The Search for Modern China*, London: Hutchinson.

Summers, H. (1982) *On Strategy: A Critical Analysis of the Vietnam War*, Novato, Calif.: Presidio Press.

Zagoria, D. (1967) *Vietnam Triangle: Moscow, Peking, Hanoi*, New York: Pegasus.

7

The Failure of
the Détente of the 1970s

Raymond L. Garthoff

Originally appeared in *Détente and Confrontation: American–Soviet Relations from Nixon to Reagan*, revised edition. The Brookings Institution, Washington, D.C., 1999.

Differences in Basic Conceptions

Foremost among the causes of the ultimate failure of détente in the 1970s was a fatal difference in the conception of its basic role by the two sides. The American leaders saw it, in Kissinger's words, as a way of "managing the emergence of Soviet power" into world politics in an age of nuclear parity. The Soviet leaders envisaged it as a way of managing the transition of the United States from its former superiority to a more modest role in world politics in an age of nuclear parity. Thus each saw itself as the manager of a transition by the other. Moreover, while the advent of parity ineluctably meant some decrease in the ability of the United States to manage world affairs, this fact was not sufficiently appreciated in Washington. And while it meant a relatively more important role for the Soviet Union, it did not mean acquisition of the kind of power the United States wielded. Finally, both had diverging images of the world order, and although that fact was well enough understood, its implications were not. Thus, underlying the attempts by each of the two powers to manage the adjustment of the other to a changing correlation of forces in the world there were even more basic parallel attempts by both to modify the fundamental world order – in different directions.

The Soviet leaders, conditioned by their Marxist–Leninist ideology, believed that a certain historical movement would ultimately lead to the replacement of capitalism (imperialism) in the world by socialism (communism). But they realized this transition would have to occur in a world made incalculably more dangerous by massive arsenals of nuclear weapons. Peaceful coexistence and détente were seen as offering a path to neutralize this danger by ruling out war between states, permitting historical change to occur, as the Soviets believed it must, through fundamental indigenous social-economic-political processes within states. While Marxist–Leninists did not shun the use of any instrument of power if it was expedient, they did not see military power as the fundamental moving force of history. On the contrary, they saw it as a possible ultimate recourse of the doomed capitalist class ruling the imperialist citadels of the West. There was, therefore, no ideological barrier or reservation in pursuing a policy of détente aimed at preventing nuclear war. Quite the contrary – détente represented a policy aimed at providing stability to a world order that allowed progressive historical change.

The American leadership and the American people, not holding a deterministic ideology, while self confident, were much less sure of the trend of history. Insofar as they held an ideology for a global order, it was one of pluralism. That ideology did not assume the whole world would choose an American-style democratic and free enterprise system. The world order has been seen as one that should provide stability and at least protect the democratic option for peoples. Occasionally during the Cold War there were crusades to extirpate communism in the world; a fringe represented, for example, by Norman Podhoretz in the 1980s when he criticized even the Reagan administration for failing wholeheartedly to rally a new assault on communism and against the Soviet Union. But the dominant American aim was to contain and deter Soviet or Soviet-controlled communist expansion at the expense of a pluralistic and, in that sense, "free" world order. What varied and periodically was at issue was the relative weight to be placed, on the one hand, on containment achieved by building positions of counterposing power, and on the other, on cooperation, pursued by seeking common ground for mutual efforts to reduce tension and accommodate the differing interests of the two sides. There were varied judgments in both countries about whether objective circumstances permitted the latter approach or required the former, and therefore about whether détente was feasible or confrontation was necessary.

When Nixon and Kissinger developed a strategy of détente to replace a strategy of confrontation, the underlying expectation was that as the Soviet Union became more and more extensively engaged in an organic network of relations with the existing world order, it would gradually become reconciled to that order. Ideological expectations of global revolutionary change would become attenuated and merely philosophical rather than actively political. Avoidance of the risks of nuclear war was essential; hence there was acceptance of peaceful coexistence and of efforts at strategic arms limitations and other negotiations to reduce the risks.

The common American and Soviet recognition of the need to avert war was of fundamental significance. But there remained radically different visions of the course world history would follow and, therefore, of the pattern of world politics. This divergence in their worldviews naturally affected the policies of the two powers. The difference was well-known in a general way; its implications for the two superpowers' respective actions, and therefore for their mutual relations and for détente, were not, however, sufficiently understood. And this gap led to unrealistic expectations that were not met and that undermined confidence in détente.

The pursuit of absolute security by any state is not only unattainable but is based (whether recognized or not) on an unacceptable premise: absolute security for one state can only mean absolute insecurity for others. Absolute security is not attainable in today's world, but during the Cold War the nuclear threat was not sufficiently reassuring to those who feared that their adversaries sought it. While no doubt sincerely denying such an absolute aim, both the United States and the Soviet Union pursued their own military security in ways that gave rise to real concern on the part of the other. Whether in pursuit of military superiority or not, the natural dynamic of military planning in a bipolar world was to resolve conservatively the unavoidable uncertainties in measuring the military balance and the outcomes of hypothetical military conflicts. Each side always presumed the advantage in such cases to rest with the other side – a situation that then required unilateral efforts by each to overcome that advantage. Equally important, each was led to see the other side as seeking superiority, domination, and absolute security.

American perceptions of a Soviet drive for world domination were rooted in the US image of the ideological expectations of the Soviets for the future. The United States saw a relentless, inexorable Soviet drive for world communism under the leadership and control of Moscow, and military means as the most – some said the only – successful Soviet instrumentality and therefore the key. The Soviet leaders in turn, after the late 1970s, saw a reborn American pursuit of military superiority as the basis for a policy of intimidation (in US deterrence terms, an aggressive use of "escalation dominance"). The ultimate aim was seen as world domination in a Pax Americana. Rather than attributing to Americans an underlying ideological expectation for the future, they saw a nostalgia for the past, an atavistic reaching back for a time when imperialism ruled the world and, more proximately, for a time when the United States had nuclear superiority and, in the Soviet view, *did* carry out a policy of intimidation (for example, compelling the withdrawal of Soviet missiles from the territory of an ally, Cuba, in 1962).

The United States did not analyze critically the underlying postulates of either American or Soviet conceptions – nor, indeed, could that be done before they were more clearly articulated. For example, consider the proposition held by the Soviet leaders until 1986 that "the class struggle" and "national liberation struggle" were not and could not be affected by détente. With the exception of a minuscule minority that accepted the Soviet line uncritically, almost all Americans saw that proposition as communist mumbo jumbo being used as a transparently self-serving argument to excuse pursuit of Soviet interests. In fact, Soviet leaders considered that proposition to be a self-evident truth: détente was a policy, while the class struggle was an objective phenom- enon in the historical process that could not be abolished by policy deci- sion, even if the Soviet leaders wanted to do so. While there was a self-serving dimension to the Soviet proposition, it was not cynical artifice. To the contrary, it was sincerely believed. On a logical plane, to whatever extent the Soviet premise was true, it was crystal clear that any inevitable historical process could not be stopped by any state's policy or even agreement between states.

It was not necessary to assume a prior meeting of the minds of the leaders of the two powers on ideological conceptions as a prere- quisite to agreements based on calculated mutual advantage. While ideological conditioning and belief did influence policy, they did not determine it. Questions about the historical process can and should be left to history. The critical question was not whether there was a global class struggle or national liberation struggle, as defined by Marxism–Leninism, but what the Soviet leadership was going to do about it. While the Soviet leadership accepted a moral commitment to aid the world revolutionary process, it was also ideologically obliged to do so only in ways that did not weaken or risk the attainments of socialism in the USSR. Moreover, the ideology also held that world revolutionary processes were indigenous. Revolution could not be exported. Neither could counterrevolution. But both could be aided by external forces. Here the Soviet prescription naturally stressed the ultimate failure but present danger of an imperialist export of counter- revolution (for example, American support to the authorities in El Salvador, its destabilizing covert action against Nicaragua, and the invasion of Grenada). And while the Soviet Union expressed support for genuine revolutions and national liberation movements, it was careful and selective in what support it provided, as ideologically sanctioned prudence required.

In approaching the question of what was a proper and consistent code of conduct with respect to Soviet – and American – behavior in the Third World, each side needed to understand the perspective of the other. Each, naturally, retained its own view of the historical process, as well as its own national interests. Differences of concrete interests remained to be reconciled, but failure to understand each other's viewpoint seriously compounded the problem.

Failure to Use Collaborative Measures

A second cause of the collapse of détente was the failure to turn to greater use of collaborative measures to meet the requirements of security. National military power was bound to remain a foundation of national security in the foreseeable future. But it did not need to be the first, or usual, or sole, recourse. The American–Soviet détente involved efforts to prevent and to manage crises, and to regulate the military balance through arms control and arms limitation. In the final analysis, however, those efforts – while useful and potentially significant – were almost entirely dependent on the political relationship, and in large measure withered with it.

The effort to achieve strategic arms limitations marked the first, and the most daring, attempt to follow a collaborative approach in meeting military security requirements. It involved an unprecedented joint consideration of ways to control the most vital (or fatal) element of national power – the arsenals of strategic nuclear weaponry. Early successes held great promise – but also showed the limits of readiness of both superpowers to take this path. SALT generated problems of its own and provided a focal point for objection by those who did not wish to see either regulated military parity or political détente. The final lesson of the failure to ratify SALT II was that arms control could not stand alone nor sustain a political détente that did not support itself. Indeed, even the early successes of SALT I, which contributed to an upsurge of détente and were worthwhile on their own merits, became a bone of contention as détente came under fire.

The widely held American view that SALT tried to do too much was a misjudgment: the *real* flaw was the failure of SALT to do enough. There were remarkable initial successes in the agreement on parity as an objective and on stability of the strategic arms relationship as a necessary condition, and the control imposed on strategic defensive competition in ABM systems. But there was insufficient political will (and perhaps political authority) to bite the bullet and ban or sharply limit MIRVs – the key to controlling the strategic offensive arms race. Both sides share the blame for this failure, but especially the United States because it led a new round of the arms competition when it could safely have held back (in view of the ABM Treaty) long enough to make a real effort to ban MIRVS. The failure to control MIRVs was ultimately the key to the essential failure in the 1970s to stabilize military parity, and it contributed indirectly to the overall fall of détente.

Too little attention has been paid to the efforts in the 1970s to devise a regime of crisis management and crisis avoidance. Paradoxically, the relatively more successful steps in this direction are rarely remembered because they do not seize attention as do political frictions. The agreements of 1971 on averting war by accident or miscalculation and on upgrading the hot line, the agreement of 1972 on avoiding incidents at sea between the US and Soviet navies, and the agreement of 1973 on prevention of nuclear war played a positive role. (In addition, so did multilateral confidence-building measures in the European security framework.) The one instance sometimes charged to have been a failure of collaboration was in fact, if anything, a success: the defusing of the pseudocrisis between the two superpowers in October 1973 at the climax of the fourth Arab–Israeli war.

Failure to Define a Code of Conduct

A third cause of the failure of American–Soviet détente in the 1970s was the inability of the superpowers to transform the recognition of strategic parity into a common political standard to govern their competitive actions in the world. The divergent conceptions of détente and of the world order underlay this failure, but these were compounded by other factors. One was the unreadiness of the United States, in conceding nominal strategic parity, also to concede political parity. Another was a reciprocated hubris in which each superpower applied a one-sided double standard in perceiving, and judging, the behavior of the other. The basic principles of mutual relations and a code of conduct were never thrashed out with the necessary frank discussion of differing views, a failure that gave rise to a facade of agreement that affected not only public expectations, but to some extent even expectations of the leaderships. Expectations based on wishful thinking about the effects of the historical process, or based on overconfidence about a country's managerial abilities to discipline the behavior of the other side, were doomed to failure. Paradoxically, these inflated expectations coexisted – on both sides – with underlying excessive and projected fears and imputations to the other of aggressive hostility, which resurfaced when the expectations were not met. That this process influenced wider political constituencies (a much wider body politic in the United States) only compounded a situation that affected the leadership as well.

The United States applied a double standard to Soviet behavior in occupying Afghanistan (and earlier to a series of Soviet moves in the Third World). President Carter's pained confession of having learned more about Soviet intentions from that action than from anything else only illustrated the fact. The Soviet intervention in Afghanistan was *not* justified by the standards of a world order endorsed by the community of nations and in principle by the Soviet Union as well as by the United States. But this fact did not alter (although it effectively obscured) that in practice the United States and Soviet Union each applied fundamentally different standards to their behavior than they did to that of the rival superpower (and others). There also was also an important failure in the case of Afghanistan (as well as in many other cases) by both the United States and the Soviet Union to recognize the perceptions, motivations, and the security interests, of the other side, whether accepting them or not.

The dominant American perception of the motive behind the Soviet intervention in Afghanistan was that it was an egregious example of aggressive expansionism, unprovoked unless perhaps by a temptation that arose from declining American military power. The Soviets were seen as unaffected by détente unless they were using that policy to cover expansionist moves. The occupation of Afghanistan was seen as dangerous to American interests because it represented a stepping-stone for Soviet advancement toward a vital Western interest – assured access to oil from the Persian Gulf.

The official public Soviet justification for its move involved several elements: to assist the Afghan people and government in resisting indirect armed interference by external powers via Pakistan; to respond to the invitation of the Afghan government, with which the Soviet Union had a treaty of friendship and assistance; and counter the machinations of the traitorous President Amin, who, they claimed, was a CIA agent. This justification was hardly credible or even consistent.

The actual Soviet perception of the situation was as follows. First, Amin was personally ambitious and not reliable or responsive (from the Soviet standpoint). He was a potential Sadat who was already actively seeking contact with other powers. He had even lived for some time in the United States and had American contacts. Moreover, Amin was known to be highly suspicious of Moscow since the failure of an attempt to remove him from power in September 1979. Second, Amin was pursuing too radical a course of reforms and was antagonizing and alienating the people of Afghanistan. He had disregarded Soviet advice against this course and was objectively weakening and discrediting communist authority. Third, there was external encouragement and support for the growing tribal resistance, which operated from a sanctuary in Pakistan. Even more important, the United States and China, increasingly operating in anti-Soviet collusion, could be expected to seek to fill any political vacuum that developed. Afghanistan threatened to become another link in a grand US–NATO–Japan–China encirclement of the Soviet Union. Fourth, a fragmented nationalistic, religious regime in Afghanistan (as well as in Iran) would constitute a hostile and chaotic belt along the border adjoining the Muslim south of the Soviet Union. Fifth, decades of Soviet economic and political investment, and since the April 1978 Marxist coup and the December 1978 Treaty of Friendship with the Soviet Union, an ideological-political stake as well, would be lost unless the Soviets acceded to the repeated appeals of the Afghan leaders for Soviet military forces to bolster their position. Sixth, with Soviet military support and a change in command as Amin was eased out, a more reliable socialist regime could restore order. Seventh, *without* Soviet intervention, there would be no escape from a humiliating Soviet withdrawal and defeat. Finally, Soviet vital interests were at stake in this adjoining communist state, while the vital interests of the United States were not. The West had, moreover, accepted the accession of communist rule in Afghanistan in 1978, and the subsequent incorporation of Afghanistan into the Soviet security system, with scarcely a murmur. Soviet military forces were already present in the country; criticism in the West and the Third World of a larger Soviet military presence would be ephemeral. Nonetheless, the Soviet decision to escalate to direct intervention was most reluctant – the Soviet leaders did not see themselves as seizing an opportunity, but as reluctantly turning to a last resort in order to prevent a serious loss and potential threat.

The Soviet leaders, given their perception of events, saw the attribution to them of offensive purposes and threats to the Persian Gulf region, stressed in the prevailing American perception, not merely as incorrect, but as not representing a real assessment by the American leadership, and indeed as a hostile act. That view seemed to be borne out by the official American response, which included not only a new containment strategy (the Carter Doctrine) and a quasi alliance with China, but also the dismantling of virtually the entire set of American–Soviet relations developed over a decade of détente. The Soviet leaders concluded that this reaction represented the *preferred* American policy. The American administration used Afghanistan as a pretext for doing what it desired: to mobilize American (and to some extent world) opinion in support of

an intensified arms race and an anti-Soviet political line of confronta-
tion. This interpretation fitted the Soviet evaluation of the trend in
American policy. It also conveniently removed the Soviet action in
Afghanistan as a cause of the collapse of détente.

In the Soviet perception, it was the United States that was acting in a
manner inconsistent with the implicit code of conduct of détente. The
United States was not respecting vital Soviet interests in its security
sphere, as the Soviets had done with respect to Chile and Portugal,
where their criticism of American action had not been permitted
to interfere with state relations. On the contrary, the United States
was directly challenging them and unnecessarily converting the
Afghanistan affair into a broad global political challenge, while dis-
carding the achievements of détente.

In the Soviet perception, moreover, the United States was ignoring
Soviet parity as a superpower and applying a double standard. The
United States had, for example, introduced its own military forces, and
changed the leadership, in the Dominican Republic – a country on the
American periphery and in the American political, economic, and
security sphere. (How, the Soviet leaders might have asked, was the
Monroe Doctrine essentially different from the Brezhnev Doctrine?)
While voicing criticism, the Soviet Union had not made that or other
comparable American actions, including intervention in Vietnam, a
touchstone of Soviet–American relations. Indeed, it had not done so
even on the occasion of the American escalation in bombing Hanoi and
mining Haiphong in May 1972, which had not been permitted to derail
the first Brezhnev–Nixon summit meeting and the signing of SALT I.
Now the United States was putting the signed SALT II Treaty on the shelf
and cutting economic, consular, and even cultural and sports relations,
and in addition was mounting a strident propaganda campaign and
pressing its allies and others to join in a wide range of anti-Soviet
actions.

Indeed, the United States was applying a double standard to Soviet
actions not only as compared with US actions, but as compared with
those of China as well. After all, only months earlier the United States
had, while nominally expressing disapproval, done nothing when China
invaded a neighboring smaller communist country. The United States
even proceeded with a planned visit to China by its secretary of the
treasury, who while there signed an agreement for broadened bilateral
economic relations that provided most-favored-nation status – while
Chinese troops remained engaged in Vietnam.

The Soviet perception in this case was certainly not understood in the
United States. For their part, the Soviets failed to recognize American
perceptions in this whole episode.

The example of Afghanistan also illustrates Soviet difficulty in recognizing that Western actions were often reactions to things the Soviets had done, rather than part of a hostile design that would have led to those same actions under any circumstances. The reverse was also true – the West had great difficulty recognizing Soviet perceptions of a threat (one that it did not see itself) as the cause of some Soviet actions. Further, the West did not recognize that the Soviets often did not perceive sufficiently the reactive motive for Western countermeasures.

The consistent failure of each side to sense and recognize the different perspectives and perceptions of the other was strongly detrimental to the development of their relations, compounding their real differences. The dangers of the failure of each side to recognize the effects of its own misperceptions were also too little appreciated, as were the dangers of its failure to perceive the implications of differing perceptions and misperceptions. Frequently during the 1970s (as earlier, and during the 1980s) it was unconsciously assumed that the other side was bound to see something in a certain way. That belief led to serious errors and distortions in assessing the intentions and motivations of the other side. Rather than recognize a differing perception, judging it to be a valid alternative perception, or misperception, both sides typically ascribed a different and usually malevolent purpose to each other. This tendency, for example, characterized the assessments each made of the military programs of the other, as well as of many of its political moves. Even when attempts were made to take account of different ways of thinking, on each side the usual approach was to apply respective stereotypes of "communist" or "imperialist" modes of calculation to the other side, but in a superficial way that stressed the expansionist or aggressive image of the adversary. The result was usually no more than to provide a self-satisfying illusion that the perceptual factor had been taken into account.

In the United States, many in the 1970s saw a cumulative series of Soviet interventions, involving military means, often with proxies – Angola, Ethiopia, Kampuchea, Afghanistan – that they believed formed a pattern of Soviet expansion and aggrandizement inconsistent with the Basic Principles and détente. Moreover, many believed that these expansionist moves were encouraged by détente, or were at least induced by a weakness of US will and military power. Hence the need to rebuild that power and reassert that will; hence too the heightened suspicion of détente.

In fact, the history of diplomatic, political, and interventionist activity during the decade of the 1970s is much more extensive and complex – and much less one-sided. Certainly from the Soviet perspective, not only was the Soviet role more limited and more justified than the United States would concede, but the American role was more active and less benign. . . .

Americans need to recognize that not only the Soviet Union but also the United States was "waging détente" in the 1970s – and that it was not justified in concluding that the Soviet Union was violating some agreed, clear, and impartial standard to which the United States in practice adhered. This same point about the application of a double standard equally needed to be recognized in the Soviet Union, and equally was not.

Both sides in fact sought advantages. Surely Nixon and Kissinger, and Brezhnev and Gromyko, never believed that the other side, or that *either* side, would fail to seek advantages at the expense of the other just because they had agreed, in a document on Basic Principles on Mutual Relations, that "efforts to obtain unilateral advantage at the expense of the other, directly or indirectly, are inconsistent with these objectives" (those objectives being "reciprocity, mutual accommodation and mutual benefit").

Moreover, on the whole, after 1972 the leaders of the United States were probably at least as inclined as those of the Soviet Union to ignore the further elaboration of that same basic principle – "the recognition of the security interests of the Parties based on the principle of equality." Some Americans, including leaders, spoke and acted as though the Soviet Union had *no* legitimate security interests. Under the confrontational approach of the Reagan administration in its first term the very legitimacy of the Soviet system was repeatedly challenged by the president himself.

The United States and the Soviet Union failed to recognize the need for each to take into account the other's interests, not from altruism but in its own self-interest. Restraint and reciprocity can be useful guidelines only if they are applied by both sides, and by each to its *own* actions as well as to its expectations of the other. The United States, under all administrations in the 1970s (as earlier, and later) sought to encourage or to impose greater restraint on Soviet behavior in the Third World. Yet the United States failed to recognize that the Soviet Union also sought greater *American* restraint and reciprocity – and that it had grounds for seeing a lack of American restraint.

While both sides throughout the decade recognized their continuing competitive and even adversarial relationship (although the image of that relationship was distorted), they publicly muted this fact – until serious differences emerged. Then each sanctimoniously accused the other of violating an agreed code of conduct. Especially in the United States, this disjunction between private appreciation by its leadership of the political competition, and failure to acknowledge it publicly, contributed to later disillusionment with the détente process itself. In the Soviet Union it was easier to advocate détente while blaming the other side for renewing tensions.

Both the United States and the Soviet Union acted in ways contrary to the spirit and letter of a code of conduct for détente as set forth in the Basic Principles to which both had committed themselves in 1972. Each saw its own actions as compatible with pursuit of a *realistic* policy of détente. Each, however, sought to hold the other side to its own *idealized* view of détente. As a result, each was disappointed in and critical of the actions of the other. The Soviet leaders, however, adjusted their expectations more realistically, seeing no better alternative than to continue an imperfect détente. This was the Soviet judgment even though the United States was seen as taking advantage of détente in the continuing competition, and even though détente proved less of a restraint on the United States than the Soviets had hoped and expected. Hence Soviet advocacy of détente even after the US repudiation of détente in January 1980 and the subsequent election of Reagan. In the United States, on the other hand, dissatisfaction with the failure of détente to restrain Soviet behavior as expected, and to provide as much leverage on Soviet internal affairs as some had hoped it would, eroded public support for détente. Moreover, it was believed that some other course, containment (under Carter from 1978 on, above all in 1980) or even confrontation (under the Reagan administration in its first term), was a possible and preferable alternative. In practice, containment alone, or laced with confrontation, proved – as had an idealized détente – not to be "the answer," or even a viable policy, but that was not appreciated when détente was abandoned.

The essence of détente, as a practical proposition, was an agreement on mutual accommodation to a political competition in which each side would limit its actions in important (but unfortunately not well-defined) ways in recognition of the common shared interest in avoiding the risks of uncontrolled confrontation. Détente called for political adjustments, both negotiated and unilateral. It did not involve a classical division of the world into spheres of hegemonic geopolitical interests. Rather, it was a compact calling for self-restraint on each side in recognition of the interests of the other to the extent necessary to prevent sharp confrontation. While this general concept and approach were accepted by both sides, regrettably each side had differing conceptions of the proper restraint it – and the other side – should assume. This discrepancy led later to reciprocal feelings of having been let down by the other side. From the outset there was insufficient recognition of the need for more frank exchanges of views and collaboration in dealing with differences of interest. With time, these efforts collapsed. Both sides showed that they were not ready to accommodate the interests of the other. An additional complicating factor was the inability of the US leadership to manage and control its own state policy. But more important, on both sides there was a serious gap, even inability, to perceive the viewpoint and interests of the other. This gap grew, rather than lessened, with time and experience. As a consequence, trust – which was never very great – declined.

Both sides also showed themselves guilty of myopia. One additional broad and significant example illustrates this point well. Too little attention was paid, on both sides, to the important interrelationships that derived from the interplay of their political *strategies*. The Carter administration saw rapprochement with China as contributing to the containment of the Soviet Union, and therefore as reinforcement in restraining Soviet policy. If failed to consider whether the tightening noose of a grand encirclement (the United States, NATO, China, and Japan), as seen in Moscow, might have *impelled* the Soviet Union toward more active measures to prevent that encirclement (as in Afghanistan and potentially in Iran) and to leapfrogging to accomplish a counter-encirclement (as in Vietnam against China, and in Syria, Yemen, and Ethiopia in the Middle East). The Soviet Union in turn underestimated the extent to which actions it regarded as defensive and counterencir-cling (largely the same list) in fact – and not just in propaganda – were perceived in the West and China as offensive moves and thus contributed to the development of the very coalition of encirclement they were intended to counter.

One important change in the American strategy of global competition exacerbated this inattention to the interplay of strategies. The transition from Kissinger's strategy of détente in the period from 1969 to 1976 to that of Brzezinski in 1978–9 (continued in the post-détente strategies of 1980 and 1981–4) was characterized by a shift from a contest of maneuver in a system with two predominant powers to a positional conflict of two sides. Relations with China can illustrate. Kissinger avoided aligning the United States with either the Soviet Union or China against the other and secured a balancing position in triangular diplomacy. Under this approach, the United States could improve relations with both powers and improve its overall position in the process. After 1978 the United States shifted to a relationship with China designed to place pressure on the Soviet Union by aligning China with the United States in a coalition the latter would dominate. Thereafter, if the United States improved relations with either power, it would make its relations with the other worse. Moreover, the Chinese, once freed of the fear of

American–Soviet alignment, in the 1980s reasserted their own independence from alignment with the United States and to an extent gained
the balancing position in a reordered triangle.

Intentions, Perceptions, and Perspectives

Many developments during the period under review bear witness to the
importance of evaluating correctly the intentions, and not merely the
capabilities or ambitions, of the other power. As noted, it is now clear
that in 1979 the Soviet leaders saw a real threat to their own security
in Afghanistan. Judgment of the intentions of the Americans and
Chinese, coupled with the internal vulnerability of the Amin regime in
Afghanistan itself, led them reluctantly to decide to intervene militarily
to replace the Amin leadership and bolster socialist rule within the
country, while preventing the United States, China, and Islamic funda-
mentalists from gaining from the collapse or defection of the Amin
regime. The Carter administration's evaluation of the Soviet motivation
for intervention imputed expansionism and a threat to the Gulf and its
oil. Therefore the United States stressed the need to deter further Soviet
movement by strong punitive retaliation. This American reaction
merely reinforced the Soviet belief that a real threat had existed, and it
did not deter further moves that had not been planned.

If one side is in fact motivated by an expansionist impulse, then a
forceful advance stand in opposition or retaliatory response is called for
and can sometimes be effective. If, however, the action – no matter how
reprehensible and forcible – is motivated by fear of a threat or loss, a vigorous show of strength and threats of counteraction may in fact contribute to the perceived threat and hence to the very moves that the
other side wants to deter. By contrast, measures to allay the unfounded
fears might have been a more effective course. It thus becomes highly
important to assess, and assess correctly, the intentions and motivations
of the other side.

The importance of assessment is that it not only applies to a specific
situation, but also affects the lessons drawn from that experience. The
easy conclusion often reached about Soviet moves adverse to American
interests (especially by critics but sometimes also by incumbent administrations) was to question whether the United States possessed sufficient strength and had demonstrated clearly enough its readiness to use
it. Sometimes that may have been the relevant question. But the record
strongly suggests that more often it was not American strength and
resolve that Soviet leaders doubted, but American restraint and recognition of Soviet interests.

If international tension is seen as the product of perceived threats, détente can be characterized as the reduction of threat perceptions. In the latter half of the 1970s both sides perceived growing threats from the military programs, and political actions, of the other. Afghanistan in 1979 appeared to the Soviet leaders as a threat, not an opportunity. But the American leadership did not recognize that perception, despite earlier attempts by the Soviet side to indicate to the American government its aims in Afghanistan.

Both powers were also reluctant to acknowledge, even to recognize, failures of their own political systems. Instead, they were only too ready to project responsibility onto the other side. Thus, for example, Soviet claims of American responsibility for internal opposition in Afghanistan and Poland served (among other things) as an alibi for failures of Soviet-style socialism. American charges of Cuban and Soviet responsibility for revolution in Central America were similarly more convenient than acknowledging failures of reactionary regimes to provide for needed peaceful change. In addition to reflecting genuine fears based on perceived vulnerabilities, it was simply easier to project hostile intervention than to admit failures to facilitate or permit peaceful change within respective areas of predominant influence.

Thus, apart from differing conceptions of détente, there were very important differences in perceptions not only of the motivations of the other side, but of the very reality of world politics. Détente should have been recognized as one complex *basis* for a competitive relationship, not as an alternative to competition. That was the reality, and the fact should have been recognized.

During much of the 1970s American perceptions of what was occurring in the world failed to reflect reality. One example was the failure of the United States to see that it was waging a vigorous competition along with the Soviet Union. And the US leadership to varying degrees was more aware of the realities than the public (Nixon was the most aware, Carter the least). But even the practitioners of hardheaded détente often failed to recognize the whole reality. Political critics also either did not see, or did not wish to acknowledge, reality. The desire to sustain public support for policy by using a myth of détente (and of conformity with idealistic goals) also inhibited public awareness that the United States was competing as much as the Soviet Union. The result was a shift of public opinion as détente *seemed* not to be safeguarding and serving American interests. Ronald Reagan's challenge to President Ford in 1976 marked the first significant political manifestation of this shift. Although the challenge did not succeed, it did lead Ford to shelve SALT and to jettison the very word détente. By 1980 this shift contributed (along with domestic economic and other concerns, and President

Carter's ineptness and plain bad luck) to Reagan's victory and open American renunciation of détente.

Naïveté was charged to the advocates of détente. But while some may have had unrealistic aims and expectations, the American leaders and practitioners of détente (Nixon, Ford, Kissinger, Brzezinski, and Vance) were not as naïve as were the critics and challengers who preferred to remain blind both to the strength and vigor of US global competition and to the limits on Soviet power and policy. The critics of détente saw both American and Soviet power and its exercise from opposite ends of a telescope – a greatly exaggerated image of relentless Soviet buildup and use of power in a single-minded offensive expansionist policy, and a grossly distorted image of US innocence, passivity and even impotence in the world.

This US perspective contributed to American–European differences and frictions. The European powers (and most other countries in the world as well) had a much more balanced perception. Although they still exaggerated the Soviet threat, at least they recognized more accurately the active American role in competition – indeed, often they were concerned over what they saw as excessive American competition. For the Europeans had a very different view of the cooperative element in détente, valuing more highly than most Americans the potential for economic, political, social, and arms control gains and the realities of cooperation under détente. Hence, when the United States threw much of the substance of détente overboard after Afghanistan in favor of a policy of containment, and then, after the election of the Reagan administration, jettisoned even the aim of détente for a confrontational crusade, the Europeans balked, and East–West détente in Europe survived. Further US attempts to push and pull its Western European allies off détente and onto a course of confrontation through such means as attempting to compel economic sanctions only intensified the gap. Even as such key European countries as Britain and West Germany turned to conservative governments in the early 1980s, support for East–West détente (and criticism of American confrontational policies, for example in the Caribbean basin) continued, to the perplexity, dismay and sometimes anger of leaders in Washington.

An additional reason for European satisfaction with détente, and a diverging American view, was that one important but little remarked consequence of détente in Europe from 1969 through 1979 was that the focus of US–Soviet and general East–West competition shifted from Europe to the Third World. The Europeans welcomed this shift, which they correctly (if not usually articulately) perceived as a fruit of détente. The United States, with little European support in the Third World competition, was less grateful to détente.

The principal gap in perceptions was the broader and deeper one between the Soviet Union and the United States, and more generally between East and West. The inability to empathize with the other side or to consider the perceptions of the other side as real (even if not necessarily valid) was an important perceptual failing. Nonetheless, in addition to improving the American perception of reality it was also clearly desirable to seek to reduce Soviet and Western misperceptions of one another. There was also a strong tendency to attribute to the other side exaggerated *strength*, *control* over events, and *consistency* both in purpose and in implementation of policy. What made this irony dangerous was that each side acted on its perceptions of the intentions and power of its adversary in ways that tended to make those perceptions self-fulfilling prophecies.

The Arms Race and the Military Balance

A fourth cause of the decline in confidence in détente in the 1970s was the view widely held on both sides that the other side was acquiring military capabilities in excess of what it needed for deterrence and defense, and therefore was not adhering to détente. This is a complex question. For example, the limits under SALT reduced some previously important areas of concern and uncertainties in projecting the military balance – notably with respect to strategic defenses (ABMs). But another effect was that the rather complex *real* strategic balance was artificially simplified in the general understanding (and not just of the general public) to certain highlighted indexes, thereby increasing sensitivity to a symbolic arithmetical "balance." And national means of intelligence, which were given high credibility when it came to identifying a threat, were regarded with a more jaundiced eye when called upon to monitor and verify compliance with arms limitation agreements.

In any event, during the latter half of the 1970s concern mounted in the United States over why the Soviet Union was engaged in what was termed a relentless continuing arms buildup. At the same time US military programs were justified as meeting that buildup. In turn, the Soviet Union saw the American buildup as designed to restore the United States to a position of superiority.

Throughout the preceding two decades of Cold War and cold peace, the United States had maintained a clear strategic nuclear superiority. As the Soviet Union continued to build its strategic forces, despite earlier agreed strategic arms limitations, new fears and suspicions arose in the United States. Unfortunately, the actual consolidation of parity in the latter 1970s was not in synchronization with the political acceptance and public impression of parity in the early 1970s. What the Soviets saw as finally closing the gap through programs of weapons deployment, which they saw as fully consonant both with the terms of the SALT agreement and with achievement of parity, many in the United States saw as a Soviet pursuit of advantages that violated at least the spirit, if not the letter, of SALT and that threatened to go beyond parity to superiority. The real inconsistency was between the continuing Soviet deployments and the American public's *expectation* derived from SALT. The interim freeze of 1972 had set a level with respect to the deployment of forces, including some construction under way that had not yet been completed by the Soviet Union. In addition, it had limited only the level of strategic missile launchers, not of warheads, and the Soviets, who were behind in terms of arming their strategic missile force with MIRVS, sought to catch up in the years following. If the Soviet strategic deployments had occurred more nearly at the time of American deployment, and both countries had agreed to accept parity and stop at the same time (and not merely at the same level), the public perception would have been quite different.

While a desire to influence public opinion played a part in inflating presentations of the military threat posed by the other side, there were real buildups on both sides. In part, then, perceptions on both sides of a hostile arms buildup were genuine. But both sides were unduly alarmist in exaggerating the military capabilities – and imputed intentions – of the other.

The US misestimate of the pace of Soviet military outlays in the period from 1976 into the 1980s also contributed to the exaggerated impression of a relentless Soviet buildup. The fact of a deliberate cut in Soviet military expenditure from an annual real increase of 4–5 percent in the first half of the 1970s to only 2 percent from 1976 until 1983, with a stagnation at zero percent annual increase in military procurement for those seven years, was not recognized until 1983. While the Soviet military program continued at a high level, and indeed was a heavier burden on the Soviet economy than was then recognized, the significance of this Soviet reduction of their military outlays was missed. And from the Soviet standpoint, the US public insistence that there was a continuous Soviet increase, and use of that allegation to justify a real American and NATO buildup in the late 1970s and early 1980s, was perceived as a malevolent design rather than a mistaken intelligence assessment.

The Soviet Union did not serve its own best interests or the interests of détente by continuing to be so secretive about its military forces and programs. The case of the US misestimate of Soviet military spending is one clear illustration. To cite but one other significant example, the

Soviet argument that its SS-20 intermediate-range ballistic missile deployment represented only modernization of a long-standing theater missile force, and timely indication that it would replace a like number of older, larger-yield weapons, might have convinced some in the West who were uncertain and fearful as to the purpose behind the Soviet deployment. A strategic dialogue before rather than after NATO decided on a counterdeployment might have permitted some preventive arms control without the heightened tension and ex post facto attempt at arms limitations on intermediate-range nuclear forces (INF).

The INF deployments and the failed attempt at INF arms control in the late 1970s and early 1980s illustrate the close connection between arms control and political as well as military relationships. The INF situation became a major political issue between East and West, and also within the West. What the Soviet leaders had intended to be military modernization was perceived instead as a political-military challenge, and it spurred a Western counteraction. The NATO counteraction, which in turn was intended to reassure Western opinion and to ensure deterrence, instead was perceived in Moscow as an American threat that tied Western Europe more closely into US designs to regain overall military superiority with which to intimidate the Soviet Union. This perception of the American purpose led the Soviet leaders to attempt to head off the NATO deployment altogether – and when that attempt failed, to mount demonstrative military countermeasures through new deployments. The alliance maintained the consensus to proceed with deployment, defeating the Soviet attempts to head it off. But it was a pyrrhic victory, as the issue weakened the basic social-political support for the alliance, while the resulting renewed Soviet buildup did not allay the concerns that had led to the NATO deployment. Neither side added to its security, only to the strain on political relations. The later successful negotiation of an elimination of all intermediate-range missiles (in 1987) only underlined the futility and lack of useful purpose in the buildups of those missiles on both sides over the preceding decade.

Failures in Relating Détente to Internal Politics

In addition to major gaps in mutual understanding of such key elements of détente as behavior in international politics and in managing the arms race, a fifth cause of the decline of détente was a failure to understand its crucial relationship to the internal politics of the two countries. In part this failure was reflected in errors, in particular by the Soviet Union, in comprehending the domestic political processes and dynamics of the other country. There was also some failure by political leaders, especially in the United States, to gauge the degree of their own authority. The Soviet leaders also put too much trust in the ability of an American president to carry out policy. This situation was true in the whole matter of normalization of trade from 1972 on and repeatedly with SALT II from 1975 to 1980. While Nixon, Kissinger, and Ford were careful to relate linkages to foreign policy issues, Congress attempted to make its own linkages with Soviet internal affairs. If failed in the effort, creating in the process new issues in US–Soviet relations and reducing support for détente in the United States. The Soviet leaders also had difficulty understanding the sudden changes and discontinuities between (and occasionally within) administrations. On the other hand, American leaders, especially President Carter (and later President Reagan), had little understanding of the Soviet political leadership or of Soviet political processes. President Carter was especially insensitive to the necessary limits on détente as a medium for influencing the internal political affairs of the Soviet Union.

Leaders on both sides, especially the Soviet leaders, frequently and seriously underestimated the impact of their own actions on the perceptions and policy of the other side, and the extent to which the actions of one side had been responses to real or perceived challenges. And again, Soviet secrecy, and self-serving justifications on both sides, compounded this problem.

Finally, the failure in the United States to sustain a political consensus in support of détente also ranked as a major cause of its collapse. This conclusion is particularly clear when the role of domestic political factors in the United States in torpedoing the attempt at détente is considered. Most blatant, but far from unique, was the attempt to tie trade, and thus the whole economic dimension of détente, to what amounted to interference in the internal affairs of the Soviet Union. The approach was all the more tragic but no less lethal because of the high moral motivations of many of the supporters of the effort. In this respect, the Soviet leaders were more successful in the less difficult, though not easy, task of maintaining a consensus in their quite different political process.

One reason for the disintegration of the consensus in favor of détente in the United States was the failure of the leadership to explain its limits as well as its promises to the public. To the extent that the leaders themselves failed to gauge the differences in conceptions about détente and were prisoners of their own view of the world order, they could not make this limitation clear to others. But Nixon and Kissinger did understand very well at least that there was a continuing active competition – not only in the Soviet conception, but in their own policy – a competition that was, however, masked by too much talk about a new structure of peace. When the expectations of the public, aroused by the hyperbole about the benefits of peace and détente, were not met, disillusion set in – and so did a natural temptation to blame the other side. This reaction against détente, based on disillusionment (in the pure meaning of the term), was thus in part engendered by both Nixon's and Kissinger's over-estimation of their ability to manipulate and manage both international and national affairs. Nixon himself in a reflective mood several years later acknowledged that "the failure was not of détente but rather of the management of détente by United States policymakers" – of whom he was preeminent.[1] It should also be noted that the public (including the broader congressional and active political constituencies) was little aware of or prepared to understand the subtleties of international politics, or even the basic idea of a political relationship of mixed cooperation and competition with the Soviet Union. In addition, the political process in the United States not only did not provide a tradition of continuity or cushion against sudden changes in foreign policy, but it invited domestic political exploitation of apparent and actual adversities in the course of international relations.

Conclusion

The decade of détente in American–Soviet relations was in fact one of mixed confrontation and détente, of competition and cooperation, with a remarkable if ill-starred attempt to build – too rapidly – a structure for peaceful coexistence between powerful adversaries. Détente was not tried and failed. Nor was détente betrayed by one side or one event. The United States and the Soviet Union continued to coexist in a mixed rela-tionship of cooperation and competition. As the 1980s succeeded the 1970s, a period of renewed confrontation had begun. Yet as became evident by the mid-1980s, a policy of confrontation was no easier or more successful in serving American interests than one of détente. And from 1985 to 1989 a new détente developed, although for political reasons (and for Reagan even psychological reasons) that term remained anathema.

Détente could have been more successful with better understanding of its potentialities and limitations by leaders and publics in the United States and the Soviet Union. It could not, however, have been more than a moderated mix with greater cooperation and less friction in con-tinuing competition. A real alleviation of an adversarial relationship

1   Richard Nixon, "Hard-Headed Détente," *New York Times*, August 18, 1982, p. 20.

would only have been possible after a change in the basic underlying framework established by the worldviews of the two sides – both, in a sense, grounded in the Marxist–Leninist fundamental ideological assumption of an underlying conflict of class-based socialist and capitalist systems. Such a transformation occurred, unforeseen and with unexpected swiftness, in the late 1980s. But that is another, the final, stage in the history of American–Soviet relations.

Part IV

The End of the Cold War

Introduction to Part IV

One of the most astonishing aspects about the sudden end of the Cold War some time between the breaching of the Berlin Wall in November 1989 and the dissolution of the Soviet Union in December 1991 is the fact that hardly anyone predicted it. Despite the legions of professional experts employed by the governments in East and West and the thousands of academics in places of higher learning all over the world, almost everyone was taken by surprise. As the contributions by H. W. Brands and Arthur Schlesinger make clear, the reasons for the end of the Cold War have been debated almost as much as the controversial origins of the East–West conflict. While, as Schlesinger contends, it ultimately may not matter that much who is primarily to blame for the beginning of the Cold War or who is to be given credit for overcoming it, both questions will undoubtedly continue to arouse tremendous interest. Indeed the illumination of the factors involved will help us to obtain a clearer understanding of the nature and characteristics of this unique conflict which, after all, lasted for almost five decades or, as some scholars maintain, even decisively shaped the entire "short" twentieth century (from 1917 to 1991).

In general three reasons have been put forward to explain the unexpected end of the Cold War. Most conservative and neo-conservative commentators believe that it was President Reagan's huge rearmament effort including his Strategic Defence Initiative (SDI) which undermined the Soviet Union's economic viability. The attempt to compete in the arms race of the early 1980s caused havoc to the USSR's economy; ultimately it led to the country's collapse. More liberal and left-wing experts focus on the long-term trends. They believe that the détente of the 1970s including West German *Ostpolitik* and the consequences of the Helsinki conference of 1975 must be given credit for gradually undermining the authority of Soviet ideology and policies from within by fostering a spirit of dissent and support for democracy. Finally, commentators from all ideological spectra often assert that the Soviet Union's structural domestic problems led to its breakdown; according to this view the influence of external factors was only marginal. Gorbachev's economic and democratic reforms (Perestroika and Glasnost), which aimed at modernizing the Soviet Union's economic, social and political system, are held responsible for the development of an increasingly chaotic situation in the USSR which ultimately resulted in the country's collapse. It is, however, obvious that elements from all three positions contributed to the end of the Cold War. Yet, the question remains what weight should be attached to each of the factors. For example, increasingly Reagan's SDI programme is regarded as having been of crucial importance in motivating Gorbachev to embark on the economic restructuring of the USSR which in turn probably hastened his country's demise.

There are also a plethora of other questions which still need to be anwered. Why, for example, did Reagan change from his role as an unreformed cold warrior until 1983/4 to a supporter of negotiations with Gorbachev? Although it may ultimately be impossible to arrive at any clear answers, Henry Brand's article attempts to arrive at a differentiated picture. Among his conclusions is the contention that the Cold War's "conceptual simplicity" helped the United States to view themselves as a beacon of "relative goodness" and democratic role model for the rest of the world. This situation became much more difficult to maintain with the disappearance of the "evil empire" as Reagan once called the Soviet Union in his cold warrior days.

Thus, the triumphalism of Francis Fukuyama and others regarding the demise of the Soviet Union and the American "victory" in the Cold War including the prediction that the entire world had begun to move towards liberal democracy as practised in the USA may well have been inappropriate. After all, outside western and central Europe and North America only very few countries can be regarded as truly liberal democratic states. In general to qualify for the label liberal democracy requires a society dominated by law and order, the regulated but competitive use of the forces of the free market, and effective democracy in practice as exemplified by democratic elections and the clear division of powers between the executive, the legislature and the judiciary.

Still, there are lessons to be learnt from the Cold War, as Arthur Schlesinger explains in his contribution, which may well help to prevent the emergence of a similar conflict between big powers (e.g. China) or big interests in the years to come. Schlesinger concludes that each side perceived its respective enemy in the Cold War as endowed with much greater power and more evil intentions than was warranted. This led to the development of mutual misperceptions and misunderstandings which continued to prolong the Cold War mindset. What one side saw as defensive, e.g. the build-up of American military bases in Europe, the other side viewed as an aggressive strategy of encirclement. Moreover, the Cold War seems to have been over-institutionalized: there was great resistance in the governmental bureaucracies in East and West to incorporate changes and maintain sufficient flexibility to allow international affairs to be viewed in a less simplistic way. Instead, certainty and self-righteousness appear to have dominated the thinking of the leading political and economic hierarchies in East and West. In particular in the 1950s and 1960s, and to a lesser extent in the 1970s and 1980s, the Cold War was often viewed as a bipolar game. However, it was in fact a multilateral contest and although the countries of Western Europe were indeed under the hegemonic oversight of the USA, they were much more than just passive observers.

Most importantly, Schlesinger makes clear that the Cold War was not a "zero-sum game" where a success for one side equalled a loss for the other side. Yet, throughout its history the Cold War was viewed by most politicians in East and West as such a "zero-sum game"; consequently they had little interest in embarking on fruitful negotiations. Yet, with hindsight it must be regarded as doubtful if it was an unrelenting "policy of strength" which brought about the end of the East–West conflict. It appears that the carefully designed negotiating tactics from the détente of the 1970s to Reagan's and Bush's "summit diplomacy" with Gorbachev between the Geneva summit in November 1985 and the September 1990 summit in Helsinki contributed decisively to the winding down of the Cold War. In addition, the Soviet Union's inherent democratic deficit and the country's economic and political problems made the country's survival ultimately almost impossible. However, by then the Cold War had already come to an end; albeit a much better "new world order" as predicted by President George Bush Senior in 1990 has not materialized.

8

Who Won the Cold War?
1984–1991

H. W. Brands

Originally appeared in *The Devil we knew: Americans and the Cold War*.
Oxford University Press, © 1993 H. W. Brands.

The Limits of Belligerence

Americans like strong characters, but by the end of the movie they
usually prefer to see the hero smile and soften a little. They want their
leads to be tough when conditions require, when the bad guys allow no
other choice, but they like to know that good ultimately triumphs, and
that the hero can eventually let down his guard.

By 1984, Reagan had been playing the tough guy for three years.
With an election approaching, he and his handlers decided to lighten
up. The president commenced the campaign season with a reassessment
of where America stood with respect to the Soviets. "We've come a long
way," he declared, "since the decade of the 1970s – years when the
United States seemed filled with self-doubt and neglected its defenses,
while the Soviet Union increased its military might and sought to
expand its influence by armed force and threats." The ground covered
was the result, naturally, of the efforts of the present administration.
"Three years ago we embraced a mandate from the American people to
change course, and we have. With the support of the American people
and the Congress, we halted America's decline. Our economy is now in
the midst of the best recovery since the 1960s. Our defenses are being
rebuilt. Our alliances are solid, and our commitment to defend our
values has never been more clear." Though the Soviets, who had
expected the Americans to wallow in their weakness, initially had not
known what to make of the American turnaround, by now the Kremlin

was getting the message. This was good for the United States and for the peace of the world. "One fact stands out: America's deterrent is more credible, and it is making the world a safer place – safer because now there is less danger that the Soviet leadership will underestimate our strength or question our resolve."

Having regained its feet, the United States must move forward. "Deterrence is essential to preserve peace and protect our way of life," Reagan said, "but deterrence is not the beginning and end of our policy toward the Soviet Union." American leaders must establish a dialogue with the Soviet government, with the goal of achieving a constructive working relationship between the two countries. Whatever ideological differences divided the Soviet Union from the United States, the peoples of the two countries shared an interest in avoiding war and reducing the level of armaments.

Reagan cited three areas of relations as being both needful and susceptible of improvement. The first involved regional conflicts in such places as the Middle East, South and Southeast Asia, Central America, and Africa. The president conceded that most of these conflicts had originated in local disputes, and he doubted that the United States and the Soviet Union could terminate them. But he believed that Washington and Moscow could undertake "concrete actions" to reduce the risk that local conflicts would spread and suck in the superpowers.

The second area of necessary and possible improvement was the global arms race. "It is tragic to see the world's developing nations spending more than $150 billion a year on armed forces – some 20 percent of their national budgets." (Why it wasn't tragic to see the United States by itself spending more than $225 billion on armed forces – some 34 percent of the American national budget – the president didn't explain.) The United States and its allies had agreed to remove thousands of nuclear weapons from Europe. (The president declined to point out that many of these weapons were being replaced by more powerful weapons, such as Pershing II missiles.) "But this is not enough. We must accelerate our efforts to reach agreements that will greatly reduce nuclear arsenals, provide greater stability, and build confidence."

The third area was the general tone of Soviet–American communications. Exchanging insults would get the world nowhere. Washington and Moscow should seek to establish "a better working relationship with each other, one marked by greater cooperation and understanding." Reagan granted, albeit obliquely, that he had sometimes spoken of the Soviet Union in language that was less than diplomatic. "I have openly expressed my view of the Soviet system. I don't know why this should come as a surprise to Soviet leaders, who've never shied from expressing their view of our system." But an inclination to frankness needn't prevent the two sides from dealing fruitfully with each other. "We don't refuse to talk when the Soviets call us 'imperialist aggressors' and worse, or because they cling to the fantasy of a communist triumph over democracy. The fact that neither of us likes the other's system is no reason to refuse to talk. Living in this nuclear age makes it imperative that we do talk." The Soviets recently had broken off discussions on limiting intermediate-range nuclear forces in Europe, and had refused to set a date for a previously expected new round of talks on strategic and conventional weapons. (The president neglected to mention that the Soviet walkout had followed the deployment of the first Pershing IIs, which, as the Kremlin complained, could reach Moscow, while Soviet intermediate missiles couldn't reach Washington.) The Soviets' refusal to talk was regrettable, Reagan said, and should be corrected. "Our negotiators are ready to return to the negotiating table to work toward agreements," he added. "We will negotiate in good faith. Whenever the Soviet Union is ready to do likewise, we'll meet them halfway."

Actually, the administration had no intention of meeting the Soviets halfway, and, as events proved, all the significant concessions of the Reagan years came from the Kremlin. Nor did the speech offer anything Soviet leaders could hang their hats on in the other areas Reagan specified. Yet if the speech lacked substance, its style marked something of a turning point in Reagan administration policy. The president apparently had decided he had played the get-tough-with-Moscow role for about everything it was worth. Now he was adopting a more conciliatory approach. "Our two countries have never fought each other," he said (eliding the American intervention in Russia at the end of World War I). "There is no reason why we ever should." The Reagan of 1981 had thought he knew a very good reason why the United States and the Soviet Union might fight: because the Soviets were bent on conquering the world. The Reagan of 1984 – "a year of opportunities for peace," he said – left the world-conquest paragraphs on the editing-room floor. He spoke to Soviet leaders, not as enemies of humanity, but as potential partners in the quest for human betterment. "Together we can strengthen peace, reduce the level of arms, and know in doing so we have helped fulfill the hopes and dreams of those we represent and, indeed, of people everywhere. Let us begin now."[1]

Even if 1984 hadn't been an election year, Reagan would have felt pressure to moderate his confrontational posture of the previous three years. The governments of the European allies had largely resisted the return to the Cold War, and NATO meetings during the early 1980s

---

1   Reagan speech, January 16, 1984, *Public Papers of the Presidents of the USA: Ronald Reagan.*

repeatedly turned into wrangling sessions, with the American delegates attempting to write a desire for detente out of joint communiques, and the Europeans attempting to write it in. The Europeans generally won, though not without allowing the Americans to insert the qualifier "genuine" before the offending noun. Other manifestations of inter-allied annoyance, such as the quarrel over the Soviet gas pipeline, similarly indicated that detente would go to its grave in Europe, if in fact it did, more slowly and far less quietly than it had in America.

While the governments of the allies experienced difficulty accepting Washington's reversion to Cold War form, opposition parties on the far side of the Atlantic had even more trouble. The British Labour party and West Germany's Social Democrats found it convenient to take Reagan at his bombastic word, and the image of the gun-slinging cowboy became a staple at rallies of the West European socialists. The Labourites flirted with unilateral nuclear disarmament – an idle threat at the time, considering Labour's political unpopularity (traceable in part precisely to this threat), but a position that indicated the wide-spread dissatisfaction with the worsening state of superpower relations. Like Labour, the German Social Democrats opposed the deployment of the American Pershing IIs and Tomahawk cruise missiles, with both parties complaining that the new weapons would place Soviet nuclear forces on even hairier triggers than at present, and would, in the bargain, make the launching sites of the missiles prime targets for Soviet rockets. Though Margaret Thatcher's Conservatives and Helmut Kohl's Christian Democrats overruled the opposition and ordered deployment to commence, the demonstrations and other disruptions that sur-rounded the deployment caused it to be a sensitive political topic for both London and Bonn.

The European anti-nukers had plenty of company in the United States. Carter's demise and Reagan's ascendancy had driven American détentists into the shadows, with elected officials and persons aspiring to office voicing broad support for a big defense budget and other signs of Cold War enthusiasm. But individuals and groups with no particular desire to stay within the tightening bounds of orthodoxy preached an alternative vision. Some opponents of Reagan administration policies were past the age of caring what was currently fashionable in Washington's power circles. In 1982, *Foreign Affairs* ran an article by former government officials George Kennan, McGeorge Bundy, Robert McNamara, and Gerard Smith advocating a shift in American nuclear policy to one of no-first-use. Ever since the early Cold War, the United States and its NATO allies had reserved the right to use nuclear weapons to counter a conventional offensive by the communists. This policy reflected the same influences that had given rise to Eisenhower's New

Look, namely, a desire to defend Western Europe on the cheap. By adhering to a possible-first-use policy, the Reagan administration was breaking no fresh ground. Yet the bellicose tenor of various administration statements had alarmed Kennan and company, who worried that much of the world was getting the impression that a gang of warmongers controlled America's nuclear arsenal. By promising not to be the first country to hit the button, the United States would reassure those who wished to think better of America. At the same time, a no-first-use policy would reinforce global security by keeping the conceptual firebreak between conventional and nuclear weapons free of the clutter of improbable plans for limited nuclear war, which some persons associated with the Reagan administration had been talking about. "It is time to recognize that no one has ever succeeded in advancing any persuasive reason to believe that any use of nuclear weapons, even on the smallest scale, could reliably be expected to remain limited," the four authors stated. "Any use of nuclear weapons in Europe, by the Alliance or against it, carries with it a high and inescapable risk of escalation into general nuclear war which would bring ruin to all and victory to none."[2]

Less authoritative voices than those of Kennan, Bundy, McNamara, and Smith swelled the anti-nuclear chorus. Journalist Jonathan Schell provided *New Yorker* readers a graphic description of what a nuclear bomb could do to Manhattan. . . .

Predictably, the Reagan administration's supporters rejected the anti-nuclear argument. The neoconservatives poured scorn on what they judged the simplemindedness of the no-nukers. Charles Krauthammer scored Schell for forgetting the accomplishments of nuclear deterrence. "Deterrence has a track record. For the entire postwar period it has maintained the peace between the superpowers, preventing not only nuclear war but conventional war as well." Krauthammer censured the nuclear-freezers for advocating what amounted to unilateral disarmament. Their pressure could prevent the United States and the Western allies from updating their arsenals, but who would enforce the freeze on the Soviets and the Chinese? The freeze movement played on people's fears of nuclear war, but it offered nothing constructive to substitute for the current system of great-power relations. "The freeze is not a plan; it is a sentiment," Krauthammer said. "The freeze continually fails on its own terms. It seeks safety, but would jeopardize deterrence; it seeks quick action, but would delay arms control; it seeks real reductions, but removes any leverage we might have to bring them about."[3]

2 Bundy, Kennan, McNamara, and Smith, "Nuclear Weapons and the Atlantic Alliance," *Foreign Affairs*, Spring 1982.
3 Krauthammer, "In Defense of Deterrence," *New Republic*, April 28, 1982.

Krauthammer likewise derided the no-first-use counsel of Kennan et al. Dubbing the four authors the "auxiliary brigade of the antinuclear movement," Krauthammer contended that unless a no-first-use policy were accompanied by a politically implausible upgrading of conventional forces, it would mean "the end of the Western alliance and the abandonment in particular of West Germany to Soviet intimidation and blackmail." Though the "four wise men" – Krauthammer made plain that he used the phrase ironically – acknowledged the need for conventional strengthening, they didn't give this need the emphasis it deserved. The hoi polloi of the anti-nuclear movement could be counted on to ignore it entirely. Irresponsible demagogues would appropriate the prestige of the four, and attach it to the disarmament agenda. Kennan and the others should have seen that this would happen. Hence, their raising of the first-use issue was perverse and dangerous. "The result of their highly publicized, grossly imbalanced proposal is predictable: another support in the complex and highly vulnerable structure of deterrence has been weakened. The world will be no safer for it."[4]

New Kid on the Bloc

Despite the neoconservatives' spirited defense of deterrence, of peace-through-strength, and of the Cold War, the Reagan administration continued to gravitate toward accommodation with Moscow. By the middle of 1984, Reagan's re-election was in the bag, and the president, like most White House second-termers, especially those of advanced years, began looking to the history books. Eisenhower, in the late 1950s, had taken the easing of superpower tensions to be his primary goal – a quest facilitated by the departure of John Foster Dulles, who died in 1959. In Reagan's case, the shift to a less confrontational posture was similarly eased by a change at the State Department. George Shultz wasn't less disposed than Alexander Haig, Reagan's first secretary of state, had been to use military force when conditions required, but Shultz was considerably less disposed than General Haig to make combative statements and martial gestures. In October 1984, Shultz outlined his understanding of the appropriate method for dealing with the Soviets. Shultz gave the necessary nod to the "profound differences" between the American and Soviet approaches to world affairs, saying that the American government, embodying the will of the American people, respected the rights of other peoples to pursue their legitimate objectives undisturbed, while the Soviet government, embodying a totalitarian ideology,

4   Ibid.

attempted to impose its will on other countries and peoples. But then Shultz got to the meat of his message. "Despite these profound differences, it is obviously in our interest to maintain as constructive a relationship as possible with the Soviet Union. For better or worse, the Soviet Union wouldn't soon disappear. Nor did Shultz think this was entirely for the worse. "Its people are a great and talented people, and we can benefit from interchange with them." In any event, the United States couldn't ignore them or their government.

The essential issue, Shultz declared, was the degree to which Soviet bad behavior in one area of relations required American sanctions elsewhere. Shultz didn't entirely reject linkage of this sort, but he thought it easy to overdo. "Linkage as an instrument of policy has limitations," he asserted. "If applied rigidly, it could yield the initiative to the Soviets, letting them set the pace and the character of the relationship." The secretary of state reminded listeners that American negotiators didn't negotiate for the fun of it. "We negotiate when it is in our interest to do so." For this reason, the United States would err to break off negotiations on one topic to register disapproval of Soviet policy on another. The Carter administration had fallen into this error after the invasion of Afghanistan, and neither Americans nor Afghans had benefited. (This was quite a statement coming from a top Reagan official – criticizing Carter for being too tough on the Russians.) Shultz quoted Winston Churchill on the subject of linkage: "It would, I think, be a mistake to assume that nothing can be settled with the Soviet Union unless or until everything is settled." (Shultz didn't add that Eisenhower and Dulles had rejected Churchill's argument and vetoed the British prime minister's proposal for a summit with the new post-Stalin leadership.)

Some persons contended that negotiations with the Kremlin would forever fail because the Soviets could never be trusted. "But the truth is," Shultz countered, "successful negotiations are not based on trust. We do not need to trust the Soviets; we need to make agreements that are trustworthy because both sides have incentives to keep them." Shultz also rejected the argument that the United States should keep building weapons until negotiations became unnecessary. "Our premise is that we should become strong so that we are *able* to negotiate." Progress would take time, but it was definitely possible. "The way is wide open to more sustained progress in US–Soviet relations than we have known in the past."[5]

One reason Shultz adduced for his optimism was a recent remark by Soviet party boss Konstantin Chernenko (who succeeded Yuri Andropov,

5   Shultz speech, October 18, 1984, *Bulletin of the Department of State*, December 1984.

who had followed Brezhnev briefly), that Moscow likewise desired a constructive dialogue. Perhaps Chernenko's actions would have justified Shultz's optimism. But the Soviet leader didn't live long enough for the world to find out. In March 1985, politburo primacy passed to Mikhail Gorbachev, a younger and much more energetic man. Under the twin rubrics of *glasnost* (openness) and *perestroika* (restructuring), Gorbachev swiftly set out to revolutionize Russian domestic and foreign policy as no one had since Lenin.

Gorbachev's impact on American foreign policy was hardly less. By instigating the remaking of the Soviet Union, and by allowing the remaking of Eastern Europe, Gorbachev challenged the assumptions on which American Cold War policy had rested for forty years. In a stunningly short period, he deprived Americans of the only major enemy most of them had ever known, and, like the half of a two-person tug-of-war who unwarningly lets go, he threw America's Cold War apparatus abruptly off balance. He forced American leaders and the American people to devise new definitions of American national interests, and to design new methods of securing these interests. It was arduous work, and would take time.

The Reagan administration responded to Gorbachev's reforms by pursuing its policy of accommodation toward the Soviet Union. For decades, American representatives had complained of Moscow's slowness in negotiations. The Russians carried patience to the point of psychological warfare, wearing down their interlocutors not by argument but by tedium. Gorbachev reversed the situation overnight, firing off a salvo of new proposals, which he followed up with a parade of ideas during subsequent months. For starters, he offered to extend the 1963 partial nuclear test ban to a prohibition of all nuclear testing, underground as well as in the atmosphere. He announced a unilateral Soviet moratorium on tests, suggesting that Washington might respond in kind. He forwarded a plan to reduce the strategic nuclear arsenals of the superpowers by 50 percent, in exchange for an agreement by the United States to stop work on strategic defenses and for other lesser concessions.

The unaccustomed motion in Moscow caught the Reagan administration by surprise. The Defense Department did what the Kremlin had done for years when confronted with the unexpected: it said no, and later provided reasons. The opposition by Pentagon officals to Gorbachev's new approach reflected a variety of considerations. In the first place, the Pentagonists suspected a trick, on the zero-sum thinking that anything the Russians would suggest must, ipso facto, be bad for the United States. In the second place, even if the offers contained no hidden booby traps, the Soviets seemed to be in a compromising mood.

The United States should hold firm and see what Moscow would offer next. Third, the specific offers put on the table thus far would work to America's peculiar disadvantage. The United States relied on nuclear weapons to offset the Soviet edge in conventional forces. A test ban would inhibit America's ability to maintain a high condition of reliability in present weapons, and to develop more-effective future weapons. As for strategic defense, the United States evidently held an advantage in this crucial area of military technology. It would be foolish to relinquish the advantage.

What went without saying, and perhaps even without thinking among the truest believers in the Pentagon, was that the kinds of curbs the Kremlin suggested would cut seriously into the military buildup that was making the generals, admirals, and defense contractors happier than they had been since the flush times of the early 1950s. Whether or not arms control would stabilize world affairs, it would *de*stabilize, bureaucratically and economically, all those involved in the operation of the world's largest purchasing organization. A test ban would slow or halt the development of the next generation of nuclear weapons, thereby slowing or halting the development of the next generation of military officers, civilian government officials, scientific researchers, business executives, union leaders, and production workers employed in the various phases of the weapons' progress from design to deployment. A reduction in nuclear strategic forces would lead to a reduction in the administrative and labor battalions the nuclear forces required. A shelving of SDI would slam the door on the most promising project the military-industrial-scientific complex had seen since the atom bomb.

The Pentagon took extraordinary measures to prevent the president from accepting Gorbachev's new thinking. On the eve of a November 1985 Geneva summit meeting, Caspar Weinberger sent Reagan a letter warning against the dangers the summit entailed. At this stage, the State and Defense departments were arguing about how far America should continue to honor previous arms-control agreements and near-agreements, in the face of alleged Soviet violations. The defense secretary cautioned the president:

> In Geneva, you will almost certainly come under great pressure to do three things that would limit severely your options for responding to Soviet violations. The first is to continue to observe SALT II. The second is to agree formally to limit SDI research, testing and development to only the research allowed under the most restrictive interpretation of the ABM treaty, even though you have determined that a less restrictive interpretation is justified legally. The Soviets doubtless will seek assurances

that you will continue to be bound to such tight limits on SDI development and testing that would discourage the Congress from making any
but token appropriations. Third, the Soviets may propose communique or
other language that obscures their record of arms control violations by
referring to the "importance that both sides attach to compliance."

The president must dodge these dangers, Weinberger declared. "Any or
all of these Soviet proposals, if agreed to, would sharply restrict the
range of responses to past and current Soviet violations available to
us."[6]

Perhaps to ensure that the president paid proper attention to this
advice, someone with access to the letter leaked it to the press. Not surprisingly, the maneuver did not conduce to profitable negotiations with
Gorbachev, which was precisely the point. White House aides were
furious. One top-level official, asked by a reporter if the Weinberger letter
had been "sabotage," replied, "Sure it was."[7]

Much of the reason for the intra-administration sniping – aside
from the fact that the State Department and the National Security
Council lacked the Defense Department's proprietary interest in a big
army, navy, and air force – was that the president hadn't made up his
mind about arms control. Some question existed whether Reagan
had the essential issues entirely in hand. Comments spoken in all
apparent sincerity suggested either that the president was confused
about the relationship between SDI and other weapons systems, or that
he was playing an exceedingly deep game. At the end of October, he told
a group of Soviet journalists that the deployment of SDI would come
only after the elimination of offensive missiles. As he phrased it, "I have
said and am prepared to say at the summit that if such a weapon is possible, and our research reveals that, then our move would be to say to
all the world, 'Here, it is available.' We won't put this weapon, or this
system, in place, this defensive system, until we do away with our
nuclear missiles, our offensive missiles." These remarks sent shock
waves across the Potomac to the Pentagon, where they raised the specter
of an easy Soviet veto of SDI, accomplished merely by refusing to
eliminate offensive weapons.[8]

A week later, after some frantic re-briefing by defense officials, the
president clarified his position – or muddied it, depending on one's point
of view. He denied what certain persons had inferred from his earlier
statement. Speaking of SDI, he said, "Someone just jumped to a false
conclusion when they suggested that I was giving a veto to the Soviets

6   Weinberger to Reagan, October 13, 1985, New York Times, October 16, 1985.
7   New York Times, October 17, 1985.
8   Reagan interview, October 31, 1985, Weekly Compilation of Presidential documents.

over this." The United States wouldn't let Soviet stonewalling stop deployment.

> Obviously, if this took place, we had the weapon – I keep using that term; it's a defensive system – and we could not get agreement on their part to eliminate the nuclear weapons, we would have done our best, and, no, we would go ahead with deployment. But even though, as I say, that would then open us up to the charge of achieving a capacity for a first strike. We don't want that. We want to eliminate things of that kind. And that's why, frankly, I think that any nation offered this under those circumstances that I've described would see the value of going forward. Remember that the Soviet Union has already stated its wish that nuclear weapons could be done away with.[9]

Another week later, Reagan further refined his position. Asked whether he still intended to share the results of SDI research with the Russians, the president said,

> Maybe I didn't make it clear. That's what I meant in my earlier answer – not just share the scientific research with them. Let me give you my dream of what would happen. We have the weapon. We don't start deploying it. We get everybody together, and we say, "Here, here it is. And here's how it works and here's what it'll do to incoming missiles." Now, we think that all of us who have nuclear weapons should agree that we're going to eliminate the nuclear weapons. But we will make available to everyone this weapon. I don't mean we'll give it to them. They're going to have to pay for it – [laughter] – but at cost. But we would make this defensive weapon available.[10]

Whatever uncertainty his pre-summit remarks may have sown, by the time Reagan got to Geneva, he had his position straight. He wouldn't abandon work on strategic defense. "I simply cannot condone the notion of keeping the peace by threatening to blow each other away," he told Gorbachev. "We must be able to find a better way." Reagan explained that the United States didn't intend for SDI to destabilize deterrence, nor to provide a cover for achieving nuclear superiority. He reiterated his desire to share defensive technology with other countries, and he promised to allow Soviet scientists access to American research facilities, in order to verify the defensive nature of the work going on there.

Gorbachev wasn't buying. The general secretary contended that though the Americans might call SDI purely defensive, it could just as

9   Reagan interview, November 6, 1985, ibid.
10   Reagan interview, November 12, 1985, ibid.

easily yield "offensive nuclear weapons circling the earth." The talk of sharing technology was so much eyewash. The United States was plotting, as it had plotted repeatedly in the past, to achieve a "one-sided advantage" over the Soviet Union. Responding to Reagan's reminder that the United States hadn't abused its nuclear monopoly after World War II, and to the president's question, "Why don't you trust me?," Gorbachev asked why Reagan didn't trust *him*. When Reagan said that as American president he had an obligation to take into account the capabilities of the Soviet Union, as well as the intentions of its leaders, Gorbachev countered that as Soviet general secretary he himself could be no less vigilant. Whatever America's present intentions, Gorbachev said, SDI would give the United States enormous destabilizing capabilities. The Soviet government could never allow the threat of such destabilization to arise.[11]

In the end, the Geneva summit produced nothing beyond handshakes and smiles. Reagan held to SDI tighter than ever, and the anti-arms-controllers in the Pentagon breathed more easily.

Yet Gorbachev hadn't run out of ideas. In January 1986, the Soviet leader laid out a breathtaking scheme for nothing less than the total elimination of nuclear weapons by the end of the century. The scheme amounted to an attempt to call the Americans' bluff. Reagan had been plumping SDI as a means for making offensive nuclear weapons obsolete, and now Gorbachev was going the president one better by offering to make them not merely obsolete but nonexistent. Needless to say, the proposal was principally a propaganda ploy, since no one seriously expected that either superpower would agree to reduce itself militarily to the status of an India or a Brazil. All the same, the proposal threatened to steal much of Reagan's peacekeeping thunder.

Washington had dealt with Soviet propaganda before, and it was not totally unprepared for this round. Yet a subsidiary part of Gorbachev's proposal occasioned considerable concern. At the time when the Reagan administration had been attempting to persuade the Europeans to accept the Pershing IIs and Tomahawks, American officials – led by Assistant Defense Secretary Richard Perle – had offered what came to be known as the zero option. Under this scheme, the United States and its allies would forgo deployment of the Pershings and Tomahawks, in exchange for the Soviet Union's dismantling of its own SS-20 intermediate-range missiles. The result would be no NATO intermediate missiles and no Soviet intermediate missiles. Few persons on either side took the zero option at face value. The Soviets rejected it because it

11　Strobe Talbott, *The Master of the Game: Paul Nitze and the Nuclear Game* (New York 1988), 285–86; Donald T. Regan, *For the Record* (San Diego, 1988), 317.

required them to trade their own missiles already in place for missiles the Americans hadn't deployed and might never. The Americans knew that the Soviets would reject it, and some, like Perle, were happy they did. Perle's objective was not so much to get the SS-20s out of Europe as to get the Pershings in. After all – as the Soviets endlessly complained – the Pershings targeted Moscow, while the SS-20s targeted merely Bonn, Paris, and London. The basic aim of the zero option was to provide political plausibility to the position of the European governments who wanted to deploy the American missiles, but had to deal with vocal opposition groups who didn't.

By 1986, when hundreds of the American intermediate missiles had been placed in Europe, the zero option had gained substantial appeal for Moscow, and lost a great deal for Washington. Now a zero solution would involve trading real threats for real threats, rather than real for hypothetical. As a consequence, when Gorbachev announced that the Soviet Union accepted the zero principle, the Reagan administration began backing and filling. Though the zero option originally had focused on Europe, American officials reminded everyone listening that the plan had called for the elimination of Soviet SS-20s in Asia as well, since these mobile missiles could be moved to Europe in a crisis. The Pentagon tried to divert attention from the now relatively realistic zero option for intermediate nuclear forces, by pushing a proposal for outlawing all ballistic missiles – a measure as unrealistic and therefore safe as Gorbachev's scheme for the total elimination of nuclear weapons.

Simultaneously, the Soviets continued to pound away at SDI. They denounced it as a new form of warmongering, and productive only of an unprecedentedly expensive round of the arms race. A growing number of Americans came to agree. Congress, realizing that the budget deficit wouldn't vanish on its own, and recognizing that the president was now a lame duck, began to question whether the country could afford a defensive system judged impractical by some of America's best scientists. In addition, the fresh image of Soviet leadership Gorbachev was cultivating – reasonable, non-threatening, more inter-ested in domestic reform than foreign adventures – was having its desired effect. Brezhnev had made a convincing bogey, but Gorbachev didn't.

In response to the growing opposition, SDI's American supporters launched a counterstrike. A group denominating itself the Coalition for SDI warned the president against bargaining away America's advantage in strategic defense. Another organization, the Center for Peace and Freedom, decried the danger of an "SDI sellout." The so-called "laser lobby" on Capitol Hill pressed for a commitment not simply to SDI research but to full development and deployment. Congressman Jack

Kemp, whose previous support for the zero option was returning to haunt him, especially now that he was preparing a run for the 1988 Republican presidential nomination, complained publicly about persons in the State Department who were trying to get Reagan to step back from SDI. Matters reached such a pass that Paul Nitze found himself branded a dove for expressing less than unrestrained enthusiasm about SDI. Nitze could hardly believe what he heard and read. "It gets me down," he told a friend, "to be identified as a giveaway artist."[12]

Reagan tried to calm the fears that he would let the Soviets come between the star warriors and their baby. Replying to reports that in a letter to Gorbachev he had suggested a "grand compromise" offering to swap SDI for major reductions in offensive weapons, the president told a news conference, "Let me reassure you right here and now that our response to demands that we cut off or delay research and testing and close shop is: No way. SDI is no bargaining chip; it is the path to a safer and more secure future. And the research is not, and never has been, negotiable." Reagan slammed opponents of SDI for playing into Soviet hands. Efforts in Congress to curtail SDI funding "could take away the very leverage we need to deal with the Soviets successfully." Persons who claimed that SDI wouldn't work suffered from "clouded vision." "Sometimes politics gets in your eyes," the president said. If SDI was as big a waste as opponents claimed, why were the Soviets so interested in blocking it? Closing his argument with an anecdote, he told how Robert Fulton had tried to sell his steamboat to Napoleon. The emperor had scoffed at the notion of boats defying wind and current, Reagan said. "Let's not make the same mistake."[13]

Gorbachev guessed that he might have better luck dealing with the president personally than working through the divided American bureaucracy. He suggested a tête-à-tête. Reagan and Gorbachev already had a summit slated for Washington in December, but the general secretary thought a quiet weekend without all the summit fanfare might facilitate cooperation. How about Iceland in October? Gorbachev doubtless appreciated that a pre-election summit would appeal to Reagan. The Geneva meeting of 1985 had given the president's ratings a boost, and with the Republicans suffering from Americans' chronic sixth-year political itch, Gorbachev believed that Reagan would be glad for anything that might help his party hold the Senate. Reagan was.

American officials hadn't yet gotten used to Gorbachev's style of negotiation, and his actions at Reykjavik again took the administration by surprise. Reagan and his advisers flew to Iceland chiefly prepared to

12   Talbott, *Master of the Game*, 311–12.
13   Reagan briefing, August 6, 1986, *Weekly Compilation*.

talk about the intermediate nuclear forces, but at the first session, the general secretary suggested that the two leaders think big, that they "wrench arms control out of the hands of the bureaucrats." Gorbachev proceeded to describe what the wrenching ought to entail. He once more called for across-the-board cuts of 50 percent in strategic offensive weapons, but this time specified that the cuts should include "substantial – I don't mean trivial, but substantial" reductions in heavy missiles, the ones the United States deemed so threatening. He offered to accept American definitions of strategic weapons (a previously sticky point), and he dropped the condition that British and French strategic weapons be counted as part of the American stockpile. He restated his acceptance of the zero option, indicating that a solution to the European-versus-Asian aspect of the issue could be worked out. He said he'd allow the American SDI project to proceed, subject only to a pledge that neither side would overturn the ABM treaty for ten years.

Over that night, Gorbachev's and Reagan's spear-carriers tussled about the precise form the proposed cuts should take, and about exactly what the ABM treaty said regarding anti-missile defenses. They came close to agreement, and their work laid the basis for the eventual accord on intermediate nuclear forces. But the talks stuck on SDI, specifically on whether SDI research had to take place within laboratories. The Soviets wanted to keep SDI indoors, while the Americans wanted the freedom to try out promising ideas in the atmosphere or in space.

At the final session of Reykjavik meeting, Gorbachev attempted to break the deadlock by reiterating his desire for total de-nuking. "I would favor eliminating all nuclear weapons," the general secretary declared. Reagan perked up. That was what he had been aiming for all along, the president replied. "Then why don't we agree on it?," Gorbachev asked. "Suits me fine," Reagan said.

Then came the hook. "But this must be done in conjunction with a ten-year extension of the ABM treaty and a ban on the development and testing of SDI outside the laboratory," Gorbachev said.

In subsequent weeks, Reagan's agreement to the elimination of nuclear weapons occasioned a minor controversy. Was the president speaking in general terms of a nuclear-free world, or in particular of the kind of ten-year timetable Gorbachev proposed? Administration officials assured worried European leaders, who cringed at the thought of facing all those Soviet tanks without an American nuclear shield, that the president was merely expressing a someday wish for humanity.

One thing Reagan's assent clearly did *not* encompass was the required constraint on SDI. "There is no way we are going to give up research to find a defense weapon against nuclear missiles," Reagan told Gorbachev. On this rock the meeting broke up. "We tried," Paul Nitze told journalists as the president and the general secretary headed for their planes. "By God, we tried. And we almost did it." But only almost.[14]

Because it's There – and Ollie's Not

Reagan returned from the Reykjavik meeting and walked smack into the Iran-contra scandal. Not much connected the two events causally, although many of the same people were involved. But each contributed to the de-escalation of the Cold War. While the Iceland summit failed to produce the kind of sweeping arms control agreement the two principals batted around during their weekend at Hofdi House, it demonstrated definitively that, in Gorbachev, the Soviets had a leader willing and able to deal. It also suggested that the hard-liners in the Reagan administration wouldn't be able to block arms control forever. Gorbachev was saying yes faster than they could think of reasons to say no, and at some point they would have to accept victory.

The Iran-contra affair eroded the foundation of the Cold War from another direction. Previous presidents had crossed the line into activities that most Americans, in most circumstances, probably would have considered unethical or immoral, such as trying to assassinate Castro and Lumumba. But because Congress had granted the executive branch great discretion in waging the Cold War, the dirty tricks involved (at least the ones played outside the United States) weren't illegal. The Iran-contra affair was different. The questionable pedigree and checkered performance of the Nicaraguan guerrillas had put off sufficient numbers of senators and representatives that Congress had decided to pull the plug on lethal American aid. But just as the Reagan White House wouldn't (yet) take yes for an answer from Moscow on arms control, it wouldn't take no from Congress on Nicaragua. It set about funding the contra war by extra-congressional means. Legal counsel to the administration's intelligence oversight board advised the president that though the Boland amendment prohibited the CIA and the Defense Department from funding the contras, the measure didn't apply to the National Security Council. Unsurprisingly, the administration declined to inform Congress of this advice. As the counsel, Bretton Sciaroni, circumspectly conceded to the Iran-contra committee later, "It would seem to be the implication that if Congress found out about the legal opinion, it would move to prevent NSC officials from acting." When word eventually surfaced that the Reagan administration might have violated the

14   Regan, *For the Record*, 337–55; Talbott, *Master of the Game*, 315–26; Ronald Reagan, *An American Life* (New York, 1990), 677.

law, Congress had no choice but to investigate. The Democrats on Capitol Hill were happy to.[15]

The Iranian connection in the contra-supply business rendered an investigation even more necessary. If the administration hadn't been caught in the exceedingly compromising position of trying to barter arms to Iran for American hostages, and if the president hadn't been caught lying about the matter, the public might well have shrugged at the Nicaraguan side of the fiasco. Polls consistently showed a lack of strong feeling one way or the other about Nicaragua, and although the administration may have failed to heed congressional strictures on aid to the contras, the American people didn't exactly hold Congress in the highest esteem.

As matters turned out, the unearthings the Iran-contra committee accomplished did surprisingly little political damage to Reagan personally. Oliver North may or may not have masterminded the operation, but his televised flag-waving deterred the committee from delving too deeply into the affair. More to the point, most Americans didn't desire to see Reagan disgraced. He was a nice old man, entirely unlike that shifty Richard Nixon, whose Watergate pecadillos afforded the obvious parallel. Besides, after six years of a conspicuously casual style of leadership in the Oval Office, many Americans were willing to believe that the president really didn't know what some of his closest advisers were doing.

All the same, as the muck of the Iran-contra fiasco rose around his administration, Reagan couldn't help recognizing that further summiteering would tend to lift him above the mess. By the beginning of 1987, Gorbachev was the most attractive politician in the world – if not necessarily in the Soviet Union – and foreign leaders were lining up to be photographed with him. Reagan could reasonably hope that some of the good ink Gorbachev was receiving would rub off. Moreover, concluding a landmark arms-control agreement with the Soviet Union would go far toward making people forget the venial violations of the Iran-contra affair.

The path to an agreement was made easier by the departure of key Cold Warriors in the administration. Richard Perle, known around Washington as the "Prince of Darkness," both for his brooding visage and for his unrelenting opposition to arms control, announced his resignation in March. As he told a friend in leaving, it was "getting to be springtime for arms control around here," and he preferred to quit uncompromised. Kenneth Adelman, the director of the Arms Control

15   William S. Cohen and George J. Mitchell, *Men of Zeal: A Candid Inside Story of the Iran-Contra Hearings* (New York, 1988), 123.

and Disarmament Agency, and Perle's partner in opposition, bailed out a few months later. Caspar Weinberger, sensing a shift toward tighter budgets, decided that telling the generals and admirals they couldn't have everything they wanted would be less fun than telling them they could, and gave notice in November.[16]

An even more important roadblock to an INF agreement disappeared in February, when Gorbachev detached the issue of intermediate missiles from the question of star wars. The White House praised Gorbachev's action, and sent the pro-arms control George Shultz to Moscow to work out details. Some American officials still feared a trap. The soon-to-retire – but hardly retiring – American commander of NATO, General Bernard Rogers, warned of the dangers of a denuclearized Europe in which Warsaw Pact conventional forces would continue to outnumber those of the Atlantic alliance. Rogers went on to excoriate unnamed "preemptive conceders in high positions in the United States government" who were rushing to agreement chiefly for the sake of agreement. Shultz, on the verge of vanquishing the anti-arms-controllers, wasn't about to let a rogue general kill the INF deal. The secretary of state declared Rogers "way out of line," and asserted that his suggestion that an INF agreement would endanger American security was "entirely incorrect." Such an agreement would make America more secure, not less.[17]

From here, it was smooth sailing. In September, following additional conversations between Shultz and Soviet foreign minister Eduard Shevardnadze, Reagan announced tentative concurrence on an INF accord. The finalized treaty formed the centerpiece of a December Reagan–Gorbachev summit in Washington. A few bitter-enders in the Senate still found reason to oppose the treaty, but in May 1988 the upper chamber ratified the INF pact by a vote of 93 to 5, delivering its approval just in time for another summit, this in Moscow.

Reagan couldn't get enough of summitry. In all, the president met Gorbachev five separate times. This was more than any of his predecessors had met Soviet leaders, more than anyone would have guessed during Reagan's evil-empire phase, and far more than suited those conservatives and neoconservatives who still clung to the Cold War. By the last meeting, the two presidents (Gorbachev having been elevated to Soviet head of state) were best buddies. "Since our first summit in Geneva three years ago," Reagan said, "we've traveled a great journey that has seen remarkable progress, a journey we continue to travel together." The distance traveled since the early days of the Cold War was

16   Perle in Talbott, *Master of the Game*, 346.
17   Rogers in *Washington Post*, June 18, 1987; Shultz in *New York Times*, June 21, 1987.

even greater. "The decades following World War II were filled with political tensions and threats to world freedom. But in recent years, we've seen hopes for a free and peaceful future restored and the chance for a new US–Soviet relationship emerge." So taken was Reagan with what he and Gorbachev had accomplished that he described the current period as "the brightest of times."[18]

Is It Over Yet?

Reagan didn't quite consign the Cold War to the ash heap of history, but he came close. Gorbachev left him little choice. In February 1988, the Soviet leader announced that Soviet troops would begin to evacuate Afghanistan by May, and would complete their pullout by the following February. In March, he ordered his defense minister to get together with the American defense secretary to discuss military doctrine, with an eye to reducing superpower tension further. At the Moscow summit in May, he and Reagan concluded a variety of agreements for Soviet–American cooperation, covering activities ranging from nuclear-power research to the rescue of fishermen in distress. In September, he offered to close the Soviet naval base at Cam Ranh Bay in Vietnam, if the United States agreed to close its facilities in the Philippines. At the same time, he proposed to place the controversial Krasnoyarsk radar station (seen by some American experts as violating the ABM treaty) under international supervision, and to convert it to a space science station. In December, he ordered the dismantling of two other radar installations that had raised similar questions.

Meanwhile, throughout the year, the internal reforms Gorbachev had set in motion within the Soviet Union gained momentum. Dissenters spoke more freely, both inside the Communist party and outside it, and for the first time in their careers, party officials faced the prospect of competitive elections. *Glasnost* and *perestroika* began to spill over into Eastern Europe after Gorbachev encouraged the allies to design "innovative policies" to deal with the stagnation left over from the bad old days of his predecessors. Poland's government agreed to negotiations with Solidarity. Hungary sacked Janos Kadar and nearly half the country's Central Committee. Ten thousand Czechs gathered in Wenceslas Square to commemorate the "Prague spring" of 1968.

As the evidence accumulated that Gorbachev was a phenomenon fundamentally different from anything the Kremlin had housed since the October Revolution, some American commentators were more than

18   Reagan address, December 10, 1988, *Weekly Compilation*.

happy to declare the Cold War over. George Kennan stated that containment was now "irrelevant." In fact, he said it had been irrelevant for quite some time. With the possible exception of the period of the Berlin blockade of 1948–9, the Soviet Union had never posed a serious military threat to the United States. The more important Soviet ideological challenge had largely disappeared after the European countries on the American side of the Elbe had regained their economic and political feet in the 1950s and 1960s. Recent developments within the Soviet Union indicated that the ideological challenge had vanished for good, since it was evident that not even the communists believed in their ideology any longer. Marxism–Leninism was "a stale and sterile ritual," Kennan wrote. Soviet leaders might pay lip service to the old icons for awhile yet, since the icons provided the sole legitimation for the leaders' continued hold on government. But commmunist ideology no longer moved the leaders or their country. The United States should bear this in mind in relations with the Soviet Union. "The communist aspect of it all has very little to do with the Soviet Union today."

Kennan had long criticized America's over-emphasis on military matters in dealing with Moscow, and now he denied that the military buildup of the 1980s had had much to do with the changes in the Soviet Union. If anything, he asserted, Washington's hard line had strengthened the hand of hard-liners in the Kremlin who opposed the changes Gorbachev was trying to implement. The mellowing of the Soviet system was "primarily the result of forces operating within Soviet society." The most important of these forces were disillusionment at the failure of communism to deliver the material benefits it had promised, disgust at the brutality of life under a form of government still operating by essentially Stalinist principles, and dissatisfaction among ethnic minorities at their subordination to the Russian majority. As the Soviet people grew increasingly aware of conditions outside their country, and of the gap that separated them from the advanced nations of the West, the more insightful Soviet leaders – outstandingly Gorbachev – were deciding that only major reform could prevent the Soviet Union from falling by the wayside.

If America's Cold War mindset had ever served a useful purpose, it no longer did. Kennan conceded that the American ideology of the Cold War had provided a psychological relief valve for that sizable segment of the American population that needed "to cultivate the theory of American innocence and virtue, which must have an opposite pole of evil." But it was time to grow up. "The extreme military anxieties and rivalries that have marked the high points of the Cold War have increasingly lost their rationale. Now they are predominantly matters of the past. The Cold War is outdated." The Soviet Union was ahead of the

United States in recognizing this fact. Americans had better follow Russia's example. "The Soviets dropped the Cold War mentality. Now it's up to us to do the same thing."[19]

The neoconservatives disagreed. While granting that something was happening behind the Iron Curtain, the intelligentsia of the Reagan Cold War weren't ready to declare their services dispensable. Jeane Kirkpatrick remained to be convinced that events in the Soviet Union were proving her wrong about the distinction between totalitarianism and authoritarianism. "While there is evidence to suggest that totalitarian states are capable of change," Kirkpatrick remarked at the end of 1988, "there is so far no example of such a regime evolving into something different." Kirkpatrick admitted that communist ideology in the Soviet Union no longer possessed the persuasiveness it once had, but she held that the crumbling of communism, if such was what was at hand, didn't necessarily imply the end of totalitarian rule. "The Russian tradition of the theocratic state is a discouraging prologue to *perestroika*. Orthodox doctrine has been married to the sword for a very long time. Before communist ideology was joined with state power, the Czar and the Russian Orthodox Church were the omnipotent authority." Which way would Gorbachev jump next? Kirkpatrick, less confident predicting the future than she had been a decade earlier, said she awaited new developments with "rapt attention."[20]

Charles Krauthammer adopted a similar view. Krauthammer noted a statement by Britain's Margaret Thatcher – normally a neoconservative favorite – that the Cold War was over, and said, "Uncharacteristically, she is wrong. Such thinking is wishful until the Soviets leave not just Afghanistan but Central America, until they not only talk about 'defensive sufficiency' but practice it by making real cuts in defense spending and by reconfiguring their offensive force structure in Europe." Yet Krauthammer didn't claim that nothing had changed. Much had, and more might. "For the first time in the postwar period it is possible to foresee an end to the Cold War – on Western terms."

Krauthammer perceived two routes leading beyond the Cold War. One ran from totalitarianism to authoritarianism. (Krauthammer had less residual faith in the Kirkpatrick doctrine than the doctrine's author.) "It is conceivable that in the foreseeable future the USSR will have been transformed into a merely authoritarian one-party state, not terribly more illiberal than most of the 19th century monarchies." In this case, its ideological engine out of fuel, the Soviet Union would conduct its

19   George Kennan, "Obituary for the Cold War," *New Perspectives Quarterly*, Summer 1988.
20   Jeane Kirkpatrick, "The Withering Away of the State?" *New Perspectives Quarterly*, Winter 1988–89.

foreign relations much like other major powers. "Not a guarantee of peace, by any means, but a respite from the prospect of unending, irreconcilable hostility" – in other words, though Krauthammer didn't utter them, detente as envisaged by Nixon and Kissinger.

The other possible route leading beyond the Cold War would traverse the wreckage of *glasnost* and *perestroika*. If Gorbachev's reforms failed, the Kremlin, probably under a successor regime, might desire to continue the Cold War, but would lack the capacity. A recognition of this fact, Krauthammer asserted, was precisely what had inspired the present changes. "The Soviets know that their historic achievement of the last forty years – being able to match a coalition of the greatest powers in history: the United States, Britain, France, Germany and Japan – is slipping out of their reach. Soviet rethinking on this score is not due to any great soul-searching. It is merely a response to objective reality." Regardless of the cause, the failure of reform would leave the Soviet Union worse off than ever. "The old system will likely not be able to sustain itself and certainly not be able to maintain a policy of imperial expansion."

Krauthammer held that with the Kremlin on the ropes, now wasn't the time to ease the pressure or declare the Cold War over. "Indeed, declaring it over or being willing to offer the other guy a draw is one way of blowing it." The Soviets were suing for peace, because they knew that otherwise they'd lose. "By challenging Soviet acquisitions, by leading a worldwide economic resurgence, by launching an arms race that the Soviets have had great trouble matching, the United States has convinced the Soviets that, if things continue, they can no longer win the twilight struggle." On the eve of victory, the United States must remain firm.

Krauthammer wasn't sure that victory, assuming it did come, would be an unalloyed blessing. "Nations need enemies," he wrote. "Take away one, and they find another." Why? For purposes of self-identification and motivation. "Parties and countries need mobilizing symbols of 'otherness' to energize the nation and to give it purpose." Examining the history of the Cold War, Krauthammer detected a disquieting tendency toward confusion in American foreign policy during periods when the national enemy hadn't been clearly defined. In the decade and a half after 1945, Americans almost unanimously agreed that the Soviet Union was America's chief and mortal enemy. The Vietnam War undermined this consensus, and American policy floundered. Americans after Vietnam lacked an obvious and appropriate outlet for the natural hostilities all persons feel. They turned their hostilities toward lesser evils, toward what Krauthammer called America's "ugly friends": Pinochet in Chile, Park in Korea, Marcos in the Philippines,

Pahlavi in Iran, Somoza in Nicaragua. During this period of cognitive and moral disarray, the Soviets made significant advances, to the extent that the Kremlin could dream of winning the Cold War. But the Reagan-era "recovery from Vietnam" restored direction and perspective to American policy, and "abolished the brief communist fantasy of a Pax Sovietica."

Now, with the overly optimistic already declaring the Cold War ended, Americans had to face the problem of finding another enemy. Krauthammer worried that if the 1988 presidential campaign offered any guidance, Americans again would take to bashing their allies. Richard Gephardt had suggested economic sanctions against Japan, as a means of countering what he considered unfair trading practices. Other candidates had followed suit. Krauthammer judged this a very disturbing, though predictable, development.

Yet such problems remained the business of the future. At present, the United States must concentrate on winning – not just ending – the Cold War. "It would be a historic tragedy," Krauthammer concluded, "to settle for anything less than victory now that it is in sight for the first time."[21]

Zbigniew Brzezinski wasn't going to settle for less than victory either, although not from neoconservative skepticism (Brzezinski being no neoconservative), but from a belief that nothing less than victory was at all likely. The Cold War was as good as over, the former Carter administration hawk declared, because communism had entered its "terminal crisis." Within a short time, communism would be "largely irrelevant to the human condition," and would hereafter be remembered primarily as "the twentieth century's most extraordinary political and intellectual aberration." Brzezinski described Gorbachev's reforms in terms of trying to remove three layers of communist dogma and practice. Removal of the first layer, that of the Brezhnev era, was well under way. Work on the second, Stalinist, layer had begun. The deepest, Leninist, layer so far remained beyond the reach of the chippers. Gorbachev hadn't conceded the need to tackle Lenin's legacy, and he would find it exceedingly difficult to do so, for Leninism provided the foundation of Communist party rule. "Any rejection of it would be tantamount to collective psychological suicide," Brzezinski wrote.

Yet the same forces that had prompted the attack on Brezhnevism and Stalinism would require erasing Leninism as well. The problem with all three isms, especially Leninism, was their common inheritance from grandfather Marxism: the belief, or predisposition to believe, that the economic and political development of large numbers of people could

21 Krauthammer, "Beyond the Cold War," *New Republic*, December 18, 1988.

be entrusted to the virtues and abilities of a small elite. Hard Soviet – and Chinese – experience had proved this belief false. However well-intentioned an elite might be, it lacked sufficient wisdom for all the decisions that had to be made in a modern economy and society, and however well-intentioned the founding generation of an elite, declension invariably followed the passing of the founders. "In the final analysis," Brzezenski asserted, "Marxist–Leninist policies were derived from a basic misjudgment of history and from a fatal misconception of human nature." The end of the communist experiment was at hand. As a consequence, the end of the Cold War was at hand too.[22]

Francis Fukuyama took Brzezinski's theme of communism's failure and pushed it considerably further. Fukuyama, who worked for George Kennan's old outfit, the State Department's policy planning staff, suggested that the world was witnessing not merely the end of communism or the end of the Cold War, but the end of history. Curiously, considering his employer, Fukuyama's notion of history had little to do with the mundane business of relations among governments. Nor was Fukuyama's history chiefly a matter of wars or elections or migrations of people or capital, or any of the activities and issues that fill 90 percent of the pages of the world's history books. To Fukuyama, the history that counted was the history of ideas, and indeed a special subset of the history of ideas. At the core of history, he argued, was the struggle among intellectual paradigms for ordering relations among individuals. For nearly two hundred years, the leading paradigm had been Western liberalism, with its emphasis on personal and property rights. For the majority of those two centuries, history had been a matter of testing alternatives to liberalism. The most important alternatives had been communism and fascism. Fascism had lost out during World War II, when liberalism and communism combined to defeat it. After the war, at the beginning of the Cold War, liberalism and communism advanced to the finals.

For a time, communism gave liberalism a stiff challenge. The conversion of China to communism in 1949 enormously enhanced the credibility of the doctrines of Marx and Lenin, especially among the Third World peoples who were in the process of choosing between the liberal and communist paradigms. But communism ultimately failed on the crucial issue: economics. "The past fifteen years," Fukuyama wrote, "have seen an almost total discrediting of Marxism–Leninism as an economic system." From this discrediting, general disillusionment followed. In China, the government had allowed, even encouraged, a

---

22   Zbigniew Brzezinski, *The Grand Failure: The Birth and Death of Communism in the Twentieth Century* (New York, 1989), 1, 47–48, 242.

transition away from centralized control of the economy, and though China's rulers were trying to maintain their grip politically even as they devolved economically, Fukuyama believed they would encounter increasing difficulty doing so. In the Soviet Union, the retreat from communism had gone further in the political sphere than in the economic, but there, as in China, the loosening of communism's control in one area of national life would loosen it in other areas as well.

Fukuyama didn't claim that the Soviet Union and China would become liberal democracies on the Western model in the near future. This wasn't his point. His point was that the paradigm that once had energized Soviet and Chinese political and economic life was dead. "At the end of history it is not necessary that all societies become successful liberal societies, merely that they end their ideological pretensions of representing different and higher forms of human society." Communism's pretensions were dying fast. With the death, history ended.

Like others looking beyond the Cold War (and in his case, beyond history), Fukuyama viewed the future with something less than undiluted optimism. "The end of history will be a very sad time." Struggle was what gave life meaning, and the great struggles were nearly over. "The struggle for recognition, the willingness to risk one's life for a purely abstract goal, the worldwide ideological struggle that called forth daring, courage, imagination and idealism, will be replaced by economic calculation, the endless solving of technical problems, environmental concerns and the satisfaction of sophisticated consumer demands. In the post-historical period there will be neither art nor philosophy, just the perpetual caretaking of the museum of human history." Fukuyama confessed "a powerful nostalgia" for the time of struggle, and as a concluding obiter dictum he held out the possibility that "the prospect of centuries of boredom at the end of history" somehow would get history started again.[23]

The German Question, and Other Chestnuts

Fukuyama needn't have worried about boredom. During the autumn of 1989, history hopped a fast train West, and within six months, the Cold War order in Europe vanished. The watershed event was the opening of the Berlin Wall in November, which not only undid the division of Europe, the most obvious manifestation of the Cold War, but also resurrected the German question – the issue that had triggered the Cold War in the first place. The desire to crush Nazi Germany had led to the

23   Francis Fukuyama, "The End of History?," *National Interest*, Summer 1989.

initial partitioning of Hitler's Reich, and the failure of the wartime Allies to agree on what to do about postwar Germany had made the partition permanent – or at least long-lasting. The rearming of the West's portion of Germany, and Bonn's admission to NATO, had precipitated the creation of NATO's mirror image, the Warsaw Pact. This completed the conversion of what had begun as a diplomatic dispute between Washington (and London) and Moscow into the armed faceoff at Germany's heart that epitomized the Cold War.

As it became clear in the latter part of 1989 that the Brezhnev Doctrine for the Eastern European countries – once socialist, always socialist – had given way to what a Gorbachev spokesman called the Sinatra doctrine – they do it their way – American leaders and commentators remembered that the American presence in Europe, besides being designed to keep an eye on the Soviets, served the additional purpose of keeping an eye on the Germans. The historically minded recalled a statement by John Foster Dulles in 1954 explaining the caution with which the West should approach the subject of German (at the time, West German) sovereignty. Dulles declared that everyone, including the Germans, wished to avoid the danger of "resurgent militarism" in Germany. To prevent this, German rearmament must take place within the framework of a "collective international order." The collective order at hand was the North Atlantic alliance, although Dulles hoped for the evolution of a more comprehensive structure of European unity.[24]

During subsequent years, the European Economic Community came to complement the Atlantic alliance as an encouragement to German civility. But the Common Market lacked the crucial element required to keep the Germans satisfied with incomplete sovereignty: nuclear weapons. So long as the United States pledged to defend Germany, with American nuclear weapons if necessary, Bonn denied itself the big bombs and satisfied itself with the status of a second-rate power.

The arrangement worked well enough as long as the threat from the East persisted. Americans accepted the need for a strong commitment to Europe, and Germans accepted the need for American protection. As the Soviet threat diminished, though, at the end of the 1980s, the major parties to the arrangement began rethinking the deal. In the United States, would-be spenders of a post-Cold War "peace dividend" challenged the indispensability of stationing hundreds of thousands of American soldiers in Germany. Germans, who for a generation had put up with NATO maneuvers that trampled fields, clogged

24   Dulles statement, August 31, 1954, *Bulletin*, September 13, 1954.

roads, rattled windows, and produced the impression that Germany was still an occupied country – which it was, albeit by friendly forces – looked toward the end of the Cold War as affording some peace and quiet.

Yet the sobering thought of an unattached Germany, especially one augmented by the reunification that appeared increasingly inevitable, worked to counteract the American inclination to pull back from Europe. The Cold War might be over, and the Soviet threat might be dissipating – although one could never be completely confident about a country that, economic ruin or not, possessed more than ten thousand nuclear weapons – but the system of international relations that had undergirded the Cold War still promised a measure of comfort for the uncertain years ahead. American officials refrained from voicing fears that Germany might again prove Europe's loose cannon. They left the voicing of such fears to less reticent types in the media and the think tanks (and to a British cabinet officer who got the boot for saying what many people on both sides of the Atlantic were thinking). As a consequence of this delicacy, Washington's demand that a unified Germany be a member of NATO seemed at times to be informed more by inertia than by logic. Logic there was, though, for whatever the defects of the Cold War, while it lasted one knew what to expect of much of the world from one day to the next. As the Cold War ended, each day brought fresh surprises. For the time being, most of the surprises were pleasant, for the West. But one could only guess how long the pleasantness would last. The American insistence on holding Germany within NATO represented an effort to keep the surprises within bounds.

The Soviets initially objected, although whether from wounded pride, sincere concern at a unified Germany in the enemy camp, or a desire to drive up the price of later concession, was hard to say. Eventually the Kremlin decided it might as well accept with reasonable grace what it couldn't reasonably prevent. The Soviet leadership may also have decided that a Germany under NATO's watch, and therefore not feeling pressured to develop such disconcerting emblems of independence as nuclear weapons, was preferable to a Germany all alone. Whatever the reasoning, in the summer of 1990, Moscow cut a deal with Bonn (already preparing to relocate to Berlin, everyone guessed) discreetly tying Soviet acquiescence in German NATO membership to German economic aid to the Soviet Union and some face-saving promises about not positioning troops from other NATO countries in the soon-to-beformer German Democratic Republic.

If the re-knotting of the Germanys convinced nearly everyone that the Cold War was over, the Persian Gulf crisis that began in August

1990 convinced the rest. By invading Kuwait, Saddam Hussein accomplished the heretofore nearly inconceivable feat of arraying both Americans and Soviets on the same side in a war-threatening situation in the Middle East. With rare and fleeting exceptions like the Suez crisis of 1956, Washington and Moscow previously had taken great pains to assume conflicting positions whenever the principal powder keg (and petroleum barrel) of the world threatened to explode. When the United States backed the Israelis, the Soviet Union backed the Arabs. When the United States cultivated Iran, the Soviet Union cultivated Iraq. When the United States wooed Egypt, the Soviet Union wooed Syria. When the United States supported Saudi Arabia, the Soviet Union supported Yemen. But following the Iraqi invasion of Kuwait, Washington and Moscow joined hands in condemning Saddam Hussein and guiding sanctions through the United Nations Security Council.

Only the very optimistic ascribed this diplomatic conjunction to a Russian conversion to America's kind of right-mindedness on the need for inviolable frontiers and the protection of the small and weak against the large and strong. For that matter, it required almost equal optimism to believe in the White House's complete conversion to such views. In fact, Washington and Moscow arrived at the same destination in the Persian Gulf by different routes. The Americans wanted to keep Hussein's hand off the oil spigot of Kuwait and Saudi Arabia as least as much as they wanted to guarantee self-determination (of an autocratic sort) to the Kuwaiti people. The Soviets wanted to act the part of responsible world citizens in order to ensure a supply of Western capital to underwrite their leap to a market economy.

Yet whatever the origins of the conjunction, there it was. How long it would hold was another question. As an oil exporter, the Soviet Union had nothing against the higher prices Hussein was aiming for. As an oil importer, the United States did. As a longtime opponent of monarchy and Western imperialism, the Soviet Union had no philosophical interest in guaranteeing borders devised by Kuwaiti emirs and British colonialists. As a longtime (if not perfectly consistent) supporter of international legal forms, the United States did. At a couple of moments, just before the diplomatic crisis gave way to war in January 1991, and again before the anti-Iraq air offensive was succeeded by a ground invasion, Gorbachev started to waffle. Conservatives at home pressured him to put some distance between his government and the United States, and he did. But not much. In each case, the advantages to be gained by sticking with the majority of United Nations opinion seemed to outweigh the advantages of taking Iraq's point of view, and the Kremlin remained on the American side of the issue.

Past Due

Though the anti-Iraq coalition held, Gorbachev's domestic position didn't. In August 1991, a group of disgruntled apparatchiks and worried military officers attempted to reverse five years of reform by arresting Gorbachev and seizing control of the Soviet government. The coup failed, almost farcically. Yet while Gorbachev regained his position as president of the Soviet Union, the net result of the affair was to shift the political center of gravity in the country to advocates of republican (that is, provincial) autonomy. Boris Yeltsin, president of the Russian republic, led a mass exodus from the Soviet Union. By the end of the year, the union was no more, replaced by a loose and seemingly tenuous Commonwealth of Independent States.

The dissolution of the Soviet Union convinced even those few who still doubted that the Cold War was over. If the Soviet government couldn't keep its own territory together, it didn't pose much of a threat to anyone else's. As the fissures began to develop in the edifice of Soviet power, some observers in the West feared a nuclear civil war between seceding Soviet republics. But nothing of the sort happened, and the creation of Lenin and Stalin went to its grave with a whimper, rather than a bang.

In the immediate aftermath of the opening of the Berlin Wall – the event, it looked increasingly clear, that future generations would recognize as marking the end of the Cold War – most Americans had been happy to celebrate a brilliant victory over their foe of forty years. In many ways, it was indeed a brilliant victory. The United States had gone head-to-head with the Soviet Union for nearly two generations, in Europe, Asia, Africa, and Latin America. The contest had been both geopolitical and ideological. The weapons of combat had been military, economic, and diplomatic. Sometimes the fight had been carried on in open view of the world, sometimes in the shadows of the international nether realm. At the end, the Soviet Union was utterly vanquished. What once had been a superpower lay shattered in more than a dozen pieces. Its motivating ideology was completely discredited, abandoned by all but a declining handful of stubborn Stalinists in China, North Korea, Vietnam, and Cuba.

Yet, as the buzz of watching Berliners dance atop the wall wore off, Americans increasingly asked themselves just what they had won. The end of the Cold War hadn't brought peace to the world, not even to Americans. On the first anniversary of the opening of the Berlin Wall, half a million American soldiers and sailors were in the Persian Gulf region or on their way there. Within two months more, they were engaged in the largest American military operation since before the Cold

War began. The Persian Gulf War of 1991 didn't last long, and claimed relatively few American lives. For the first time since the 1940s, a Middle Eastern conflict hadn't threatened to drag in the superpowers on opposite sides. Even so, despite the thrashing Saddam Hussein received, the outcome of the war was disappointing. Hussein remained in power in Baghdad, as obstreperous, if not as dangerous, as ever. The Arab–Israeli dispute remained unresolved (although the parties were talking off and on). The industrialized nations remained dependent on the oil of the Persian Gulf. This last problem appeared likely to get worse, as the collapse of the Soviet Union turned the world's largest oil producer into a net importer. The successor states, along with the countries of Eastern Europe, soon would be competing on the world market for petroleum.

Nor had the end of the Cold War brought prosperity to the United States. On the contrary, the beginning of the 1990s witnessed a recession in America, the first in a decade. The timing was partly coincidental. All economic expansions run out of steam sooner or later. But the large cutbacks in weapons procurement consequent to the Cold War's end exacerbated the downturn, and in defense-oriented communities from New England to Southern California, people began to remember the bad old days fondly. Few were so blunt as to say that the Pentagon ought to keep buying weapons merely to provide jobs for defense workers (although candidate for re-election George Bush came close in 1992), but there was much talk of the need to proceed carefully – that is, slowly – in converting the economy to a post-Cold War footing.

For awhile, it had looked as though the Pentagon might not have to cut back much at all. Since the period when Gorbachev had commenced accepting American positions on arms control, the American military establishment had been on the lookout for ways to ensure that it would continue to be supported in the style to which it was accustomed. Perennial bears in the market of international relations, the generals and admirals and their civilian attachés found the bullish post-Cold War world environment distinctly unsettling. A measure of the Pentagon's concern was its agreement to enlist in America's war on drugs, which it previously had dismissed as distracting from the military's main mission. But drugs were small potatoes, and not even the Defense Department's best pitchmen could justify star wars and aircraft-carrier battle groups as necessary to neutralize the Medellin cocaine cartel.

Saddam Hussein arrived just in time, or so it seemed. More convincingly than the Pentagonists could ever have done on their own, Baghdad's bully demonstrated that there remained a role for American military power. Indeed, the Defense Department could hardly have devised a better demonstration. The campaign against Iraq allowed the Pentagon to show off its high-tech weaponry, including radar-evading Stealth aircraft, ground hugging cruise missiles, Patriot anti-missile missiles, and laser-guided bombs, as well as planes, helicopters, and tanks equipped with infra-red, fight-in-the-night viewers. Merely preparing for the war stretched America's sealift and airlift capacity to the maximum, which reminded Congress that the less sexy items of the defense budget mattered as much as the sleek and shiny.

An argument could even be made, and was, that the war in the Persian Gulf underlined the need for star wars. When technical studies had revealed – to the satisfaction of most, though not all, observers – the impracticality of building a shatterproof bubble that would protect the United States from a massive Soviet nuclear attack, SDI proponents suggested that a space shield was still worth building as a defense against stray shots from minor nuclear powers. At first, this was a tough sell, since the only minor nuclear powers were Britain, France, China, probably Israel, maybe India, and conceivably South Africa – none of which seemed motivated to go after the United States in the likely future. But Iraq was a potentially different story. Hussein didn't bother to disguise his desire for nuclear weapons, nor his disdain for much that Americans held dear. To be sure, although Baghdad appeared to be within a few years of developing usable nuclear warheads, no one expected Iraq's rocketeers to produce intercontinental missiles before the century's end. On the other hand, star wars wouldn't be ready much before then either. When America's hightech weapons worked better in the six-week war against Iraq than most people had predicted, the case for star wars seemed stronger still.

In certain respects, however, American weapons worked too well. By destroying Hussein's capacity to make war, the Pentagon fought itself out of that part of its job. As the recession-aggravated federal deficit ballooned during the year after the Persian Gulf War, the Bush administration couldn't resist demands for substantial slicing in defense programs.

The demands to cut defense were one sign of the trepidation with which many Americans viewed the future at the end of the Cold War. A large part of the trepidation centered on the prospects for the American economy. Though the early and middle years of the Cold War had seen the economy surge forward, the last decade of the contest had witnessed a decline in America's economic health. The most obvious symptoms of the decline were the country's twin deficits: the federal budget deficit and the trade deficit. In the pre-Keynes era, a country's economy had customarily been considered much like the weather: everyone talked about it, but no one could do much about it. In the early 1990s, the federal deficit seemed to have fallen into a similar category. Politicians and editors expounded ceaselessly on the burden a large and chronic deficit would place on the shoulders of future generations of American taxpayers, with interest on the federal debt, now the largest single budget item, being the one that would have to be paid first. They decried the deleterious effects of the deficit on American international competitiveness, with safe government bonds drawing dollars away from risky but potentially rewarding, and productivity-raising, investments in the private sector. They wrung hands regarding even America's independence, with the world's largest debtor nation having to think carefully about actions that might frighten the foreign money required to roll over the federal debt. But despite all the talk, American politicians made precious little progress trimming the deficit, for the simple reason that cutting the deficit threatened to generate more politically mobilizable pain than politically mobilizable relief. The pain would hurt in the present, while the relief would ease matters only over the long term. Since 87 percent of American federal legislators (435 representatives and 33 or 34 senators, out of 535 total lawmakers) face election every two years, there is a strong bias in favor of the short term.

While the federal deficit indicated a failure of the American political system, the trade deficit reflected a more fundamental faltering of the American economy. At the beginning of the Cold War, American producers had been the most efficient in the world, and the free-trade regime the United States had sponsored worked significantly to their benefit. By the 1980s, however, American costs of manufacturing commonly exceeded those of foreign competitors. In one industry after another, Americans lost primacy to the Japanese, the Germans, or the newly industrializing countries of the Pacific rim. Whether America could run a large trade deficit indefinitely occasioned as much debate as how long the federal budget deficit could persist. Indeed, the twin deficits were Siamese, in that the trade deficit provided the foreign dollars that helped finance the budget deficit, while the budget deficit diverted investment capital that might have alleviated the trade deficit.

What no one could debate, however, was the fact that the two deficits revealed a considerable slippage of American power since the beginning of the Cold War. Though America's economy remained the world's largest, it was losing ground. If the European Community achieved effective economic integration as anticipated, the American economy would fall to second place for the first time during the twentieth century. Already the United States lacked the kind of discretionary wealth it had commanded early in the Cold War, when it could simultaneously fight the Korean War, rebuild the American military, and reconstruct

Western Europe and Japan. Significantly, when the reform governments of Eastern Europe and the Soviet Union appealed for help in making the transition from command to market economies, it wasn't the Americans but the Europeans and Japanese who had the most cash on hand to help finance the switch. And when George Bush sent American troops, ships, and planes to the Persian Gulf, the American secretary of state, James Baker, toured the capitals of the world soliciting funds to finance the operation.

America's economic woes weren't entirely hangover effects from the Cold War. The budget-bingeing of the 1980s included growth in federal programs that had nothing to do with defense, programs that proved even more resistant than the Pentagon's pets to trimming. Moreover, anyone with historical perspective, viewing the world situation in 1945, would have declared America's decline relative to other countries to be inevitable. Eventually, those countries flattened by the world war – especially Germany and Japan – would pick themselves up and regain their places of prominence in the international community. In addition, industrializing countries – whether re-industrializing, like Germany and Japan in the 1950s, or newly industrializing, like Korea and Taiwan in the 1960s and 1970s – naturally tend to grow faster than already industrialized countries like the United States. Increases in productivity come more easily at low levels of production than at ones already high, and more readily in manufacturing than in the service activities that typify mature economies. The low-wage regimes in the newly industrializing countries worked to high-wage America's detriment as well.

Yet if a combination of factors produced the predicament Americans found their economy in at the beginning of the 1990s, the Cold War counted considerably in the combination. The military buildup of the 1980s had contributed significantly to the federal deficit, both in plain monetary terms and in the political sense of breaking government spending loose from the constraints of a broad feeling that budgets ought to balance, at least during prosperous times. By the mid-1980s, budget numbers that would have buried previous administrations were optimistic targets for would-be deficit-reducers. Moreover, the deficit became addictive. Economically, it fueled the expansion of the 1980s, and in the process entered into American expectations about the future direction of the economy, to the extent that mere talk of a balanced budget brought on withdrawal symptoms: that is, fears of recession. Politically, American officials and candidates for office got used to telling voters they could have what they wanted without having to pay for it. The voters responded by electing the candidates who promised most persuasively.

Meanwhile, the military emphasis of the American economy under-mined American international competitiveness. For nearly two genera-tions, the demands of the American military had channeled some of the most capable minds and personalities in the country into activities that did little for the long-term growth of the economy. That little wasn't nothing. The Manhattan Project and its Cold War successors had fos-tered the creation of the commercial atomic-power industry. Production for the American air force subsidized manufacturers of civilian aircraft. Various technologies crossed into the private sector from work done for the Pentagon and the space program (the latter itself a manifestation of the Cold War, beat-the-Russians mindset). But military-driven research and development yielded civilian-useful advances only inefficiently – and reluctantly, in that most of the cutting-edge work was originally secret. It wasn't coincidental that Germany and Japan, freed by the United States from the necessity to defend themselves by their own efforts, demonstrated particular aptitude at developing products for the more economyexpanding civilian market.

In the final accounting, a country can only support the foreign policy its economy can finance. At the beginning of the Cold War, the Ameri-can economy could finance almost any kind of foreign policy the American people and government chose. The people and government chose an enormously ambitious policy, one that projected the United States vigorously into every time zone and every inhabited latitude. By the 1990s, the American economy could finance nothing so ambitious, partly because the economy itself lacked the resilience and dynamism it had possessed half a century earlier, partly because demands unrelated to foreign policy were claiming a larger share of the economy's output, and partly because other wealthy countries were bidding up the price of power. At the century's midpoint, $12 billion in Marshall Plan aid had rebuilt much of Western Europe. In the century's last decade, the same amount might have purchased a few blocks of downtown Tokyo. Even after adjusting for inflation and the overheated character of the Japa-nese real-estate market, the difference in purchasing power was enor-mous. The result was that United States was reduced from being head, shoulders, and torso above the rest of the world to being perhaps head above the rest. And some bumptious countries among that rest were growing fast, while the United States wasn't.

The Passing of an Age

The ambivalence that characterized much American thinking at the end of the Cold War reflected more than the troubled economy. It indicated a sense that Americans were witnessing the end of an era, an era that in many respects had been a golden age for the United States. The country had never experienced such a period of prosperity. With but a few glitches, the years of the Cold War had seen Americans grow wealthier and wealthier. The American standard of living at the Cold War's end was higher than it had ever been, and if pockets of poverty persisted, and if the country's growth rate had tailed off toward the present, nothing in life is perfect. Nor had America ever been more powerful in world affairs than during the Cold War. Indeed, no country in history had ever been more powerful than the United States had been, especially during the Cold War's early phase. It can make a nation giddy to bestride the world, as America had done from the mid-1940s to the 1960s. Heightening the giddiness was a recognition of the apparent irresistibility of American culture, which persisted into the 1990s. On every continent, in nearly every society, wherever one looked, people were emulating American styles of dress, watching American television shows and movies, eating and drinking American foods and beverages. At least outwardly, the world was becoming more like America all the time.

Yet perhaps the most important feature of the Cold War era, and that which would be missed most, was its conceptual simplicity. Charles Krauthammer was probably right when he argued that nations need enemies. During the Cold War, America had an enemy that could hardly have been improved upon. The Soviet Union was officially atheistic, which earned it the hostility of America's semi-official Christian majority. It was dictatorial, which offended American democratic sensibilities. It was socialistic, which threatened the private-property rights most Americans enjoyed or aspired to. It was militarily powerful, which endangered America's physical security. It was ideologically universalist, which set it in direct opposition to the United States, which was too. It was obsessively secretive, which precluded knowing just how dangerous it was. Should interest or inclination inspire one to inflate the threat, or simply to err on the side of safety, disproof or convincing correction was almost impossible.

While the Soviet Union remained a credible foe, Americans could congratulate themselves on their own relative goodness. Only the most morally chauvinistic thought America had a corner on the world's supply of *absolute* goodness, but so long as the Kremlin played its malevolent part, Americans merely had to be better than their Soviet rivals to feel virtuous. If America's record on race relations contained flaws, at least those who protested weren't packed off to gulags. If the American political system was sometimes superficial, at least Americans got to vote in genuine elections. If America occasionally settled for less than democratic perfection from its allies and clients, at least it held up a democratic example for them to follow.

Beyond the realm of moral psychology, the Cold War framework simplified the problem of understanding international relations. The bipolar scheme of world affairs reduced the need to delve closely into the motives and objectives of other countries, since a country's position regarding communism served, in the predominant American view, as a litmus test for that country's policies as a whole. To be sure, this test sometimes yielded false results. Neutralists like India often found themselves treated as fellow-travelers, while some right-wing dictators were accorded Free World membership. Moreover, those American officials who made their careers in foreign policy never took the litmus results very seriously. But for Americans who desired a quick and dirty division of the world into friends and foes, the communism-versus-democracy test did the job.

The communist issue served a similar purpose in American domestic politics, although here the problem of spurious results was even worse. Few American voters cared to take the time to educate themselves to the nuances of the possible positions candidates might adopt on issues relating to national security. For that majority who didn't, the question of whether an individual was reassuringly hard or suspiciously soft on communism simplified the sorting process. The trouble was that once candidates caught on to the game, almost everyone passed the test.

The Cold War simplified matters for particular groups in other ways. The forty years of the Cold War were a glorious time for the American defense industry, which might have been accused of colluding with the Soviet defense industry had the latter enjoyed any ability to collude across borders. Collusion or not, the armorers of the two sides shared an interest in heavy defense spending, and they benefited from each other's arms-racing actions. In the absence of such a readily identifiable and consistently threatening enemy as the Soviet Union, American weapons-producers never would have achieved the growth they did during the post-1945 period. Their vested interest in the Cold War appeared in their bottom lines.

Persons and organizations that had hidden behind the Cold War to oppose social reform – regarding race, for example – had a less compelling interest in keeping the chill on East–West relations. For them, the Cold War had been a handy distractive device, but should it be taken away, they would find another – secular humanism, perhaps. All the same, redbaiting would be hard to match for its capacity to change the subject, and to throw advocates of reform on the defensive.

Just as the Cold War had simplified matters for many in the United States, its end promised to complicate things. Psychologically,

Americans would have to adjust to a world lacking an agreed-upon focus of evil against which they could favorably contrast themselves. Possible alternative focuses fell short in one respect or another. Saddam Hussein served the purpose for awhile, but he didn't have the staying power required of a real solution to the problem. Japan took some heavy beating on the issue of trade and jobs, but even many Americans thought their country's economic woes were chiefly homegrown. Neither was as soul-satisfying as the Soviets.

Politically, American candidates and public officials would have to come up with a more imaginative national-security agenda than reactive anti-communism. Bush promoted his "new world order" for a time, but acceptance levels were disappointing. Japan-bashers in Congress ran up against the difficulty that Americans liked the goods Nissan and Sony were sending east.

Economically, advocates of high defense spending would have to devise new rationales for keeping the production lines humming. Hussein helped, but not for long. And in the absence of a new threat, the peace-dividenders likely would slash deeply into profits and jobs.

Strategically, American planners would have to figure out how to deal with a world unlike that which they had come to know over forty years. While the demise of the Soviet Union diminished the likelihood of a civilization-shattering thermonuclear war, other sources of tension quickly ruled out a nail-biting moratorium. The Persian Gulf crisis and war demonstrated that troubles would persist into the post-Cold War era. Strikingly, the fact that Washington and Moscow were cooperating in the affair, a fact often cited as evidence of the new possibilities for peace opened up by the Cold War's end, actually deprived Washington of a potentially important diplomatic lever. In previous regional conflicts, when the United States and the Soviet Union had backed opposing parties, American leaders could pressure Moscow to restrain its allies, in the interest of preserving or improving broader superpower relations. The pressure didn't always work as well as Washington hoped, as the Nixon administration's efforts to get Moscow to help stop the Vietnam War short of a North Vietnamese victory demonstrated. Yet even in the Vietnamese case, Hanoi accepted a ceasefire. And, generally, a client's desire for continued Soviet aid acted to moderate its behavior somewhat. In cases where the two superpowers took the same side, the Kremlin card lost its value.

In Europe, the Soviet withdrawal from the center of the continent, accomplished in principle if not in detail during the summer of 1990, rendered the American guarantee of German security almost worthless. The Germans were too business-minded to go on long paying something for nothing. This implied major changes in the structure of European

and Atlantic relations. German reunification per se had little to do with
the issue, if only because for the near future the annexation of East
Germany by West Germany would cost rather than benefit the Germans.
Nor did one have to suppose another nasty turn by German nationalism to predict that sooner or later Germany would begin to act more
independently. Perhaps the European Community would provide the
supra-national framework the Cold War previously had. Perhaps
not. The latter possibility was what had Germany-watchers worried.
Germany's insistence on swift recognition of the independence of
Slovenia and Croatia during Yugoslavia's civil war, while the other
European governments and the United States urged caution, didn't
lessen the worries.

Future American relations with Japan raised similar concerns. Like
the Germans, the Japanese had been persuaded to devote their considerable energies and ingenuity to perfecting the performance of their
economy. Matters of defense and foreign affairs they left primarily to the
Americans. Although a few nationalist-minded Japanese, and a somewhat larger number of cost-conscious Americans, had complained at
the arrangement, it substantially satisfied both parties so long as Cold
War Russia presented a plausible danger to Japanese and American
interests. As the Soviet threat diminished, however, many Japanese grew
less inclined to follow America's lead internationally, and many Americans grew less inclined to pay for Japan's defense. Analogously with the
German case, one didn't have to assume a return to the militarism of
the 1930s to wonder about the effects of the re-emergence of Japan as
an independent East Asian great power. A trade war between the United
States and Japan, the first rumblings of which already were echoing
through Congress, would be bad enough.

Was Hitler Normal?

The sudden end of the Cold War, succeeded in short order by the collapse
of the Soviet Union, raised some fundamental questions regarding what
it had been all about. The most obvious question was whether it had been
necessary for Americans to get so worked up over an enemy that proved
to be a shell – a large country, to be sure, with formidable-looking
weapons, but one with a decrepit economy and a political will insufficient to keep it from breaking apart at the first wind of honest reform.
Had the Soviet threat *ever* been very great? How much of the perceived
threat had been genuine and how much a figment of American imagi-
nations? Was "cold war" useful, or misleading, as a description of the
rivalry between the United States and the Soviet Union?

The "cold war" metaphor had first gained general currency with Walter Lippmann's 1946 book, *The Cold War*. At the time Lippmann wrote, the metaphor was plausible enough. Americans had just fought the biggest war in history, and found themselves confronting circumstances that resembled, in certain respects, those that had preceded the war. Stalin was as much a dictator as Hitler had been, and the Red Army was indisputably powerful. Communist ideology was potentially as expansionistic as that of the Nazis, if less explicitly bellicose. Undeniably, Stalin was a person to keep an eye on.

But the cold-war metaphor worked better as a literary device than as a description of international reality. Wars, at least as Americans historically have understood and fought them, are relatively brief affairs, with readily distinguished enemies and concrete objectives. Sometimes Americans had gained their wartime objectives: independence from Britain, subjugation of the Confederacy, destruction of Hitler. Sometimes they hadn't: acquisition of Canada, preservation of secession and slavery. But in every instance, the enemies and the goals had been clear, and Americans could tell whether they had attained the goals or not.

The objectives of the Cold War were considerably more nebulous, as was the nature of the enemy. Was the enemy communism? Or was it the Soviet Union? Was China an enemy? Then how could it become a friend? Was the United States fighting for territory, or for political and moral principles? Was containment sufficient to America's needs, or must the United States roll back communism?

Had Americans been less beguiled by the Cold War metaphor – had it not served so many purposes beyond the realm of foreign affairs – they might have recognized that the Cold War was no war at all, but simply the management of national interests in a world of competing powers. Because Americans defined their interests globally, and because America's foremost rival possessed mighty military weapons, American interest-management involved incessant effort and careful weighing of the possibility of armed conflict. Yet, though it was new to Americans, this was the sort of thing great powers had done as long as there had been great powers. It wasn't the comparatively placid and uneventful peace Americans had gotten used to in their many years of relative insulation from world affairs, but neither was it war.

Whatever the validity of the Cold War metaphor, Americans during much of the post-1945 period operated according to the premise that the only way to prevent the Cold War from flaring into World War III was to prevent a replay of the events that had led to World War II. This premise rested on a second, more basic premise: that Hitler wasn't an aberration but an archetype, that the model of escalating aggression he had used would be used by other ruthless, ambitious, and powerful national leaders. As it pertained to Stalin and the Soviet Union, this premise was made explicit in the "red fascist" imagery of the early Cold War. But essentially the same idea at various times infused American thinking about such countries as China, North Korea, Vietnam, Cuba, Indonesia, Egypt, and Iraq. The thrust of the argument was that dictators are insatiable, that aggression feeds on weakness, that appeasement merely postpones the day of reckoning.

Without doubt, power creates a certain community among those who wield it. And those who employ force as their primary instrument of policy tend to respond more readily to counterforce than to less direct kinds of appeals. Even so, the Hitler analogy obscured at least as much as it illuminated. Prior to the outbreak of World War II, Stalin showed none of the territorially expansionist compulsions that made Hitler Hitler. If anything, Stalin's reign produced a retreat from the world-revolutionism of Lenin's era, and the Georgian strongman's chief contribution to Marxist–Leninist theory was the notion of "socialism in one country." Neither did Stalin's actions after the war demonstrate much beyond a stubborn desire to prevent a repeat of the recent ruination. The Red Army refused to withdraw from where the war's end found it, but the Kremlin captured no new territory by force. The only significant Soviet military actions after 1945 were the crushings of reform in Hungary in 1956 and Czechoslovakia in 1968, and the Afghanistan war of 1979 and later. The Hungarian and Czech operations, though brutal and morally repugnant, were plainly designed to bolster a tottering status quo, to hold what Moscow had, rather than to extend the Russian writ to fresh territory. The Afghanistan fighting was largely defensive as well, intended to ward off the advance of Islamic fundamentalism toward the Soviet Union's Muslim provinces.

For forty years, the United States and its NATO allies devoted tremendous effort to preparations for the defense of Western Europe against a Soviet attack. During all that time, the attack never came. Why not? Did the Kremlin decide, in the face of the Western preparations, to forget about adding West Germany or France to its European empire? Or had it never intended such additions?

There is no way of knowing. Stalin, like many dictators, took his secrets with him to his tomb. Certainly, the Soviet military had contingency plans for an attack against the West, but planning is what planners get paid to do, and many plans have almost nothing to do with reality. (Until the 1930s, American strategists were drafting contingency plans for a war against Britain.) Besides, attacks can be defensive. If you are convinced that the enemy is going to hit you, you'll probably want to hit first. While it is impossible to prove that Stalin did *not* intend to attack the West, neither has it been shown that he *did*.

In the early years of the post-1945 period, when the memories of World War II's horrendousness were still raw, when the Western European countries were in a comparatively exposed position, and when American resources almost overmatched the rest of the world combined, American leaders understandably preferred to err on the side of caution. Less understandably, they continued to err long after circumstances had changed. By the 1960s or 1970s or 1980s, one might have thought, the burden of proof should have been on the alarmists. But by then, of course, the Cold War had been thoroughly domesticated and bureaucratized, providing benefits only barely involving American national security.

If the Hitler analogy obscured what Stalin and the Soviets were up to, it made a mash of what other communists were about. Tito's nose-thumbing at Stalin should have demonstrated that communists could be as fractious among themselves as in relations with capitalists. And anyone with the least sense of Chinese history, or the slightest understanding of the traditional Chinese disdain for most things foreign, could have guessed that the Chinese would follow Moscow's line exactly as long as they discerned advantages to themselves from doing so.

But because it served other purposes – political, economic, psychological – to treat communism as a global conspiracy, and to liken a failure to confront this conspiracy to the failure to halt Hitler, anti-appeasement became the touchstone of American Cold War policy. In anti-appeasement's name, Americans fought a bloody war in Korea, believing they were frustrating the Kremlin's planet-devouring designs. While the Korean War yielded mixed results for South Korea – the fighting devastated the country, but left it beyond Kim Il Sung's obnoxious reach – the cost far exceeded anything Americans would have accepted simply for South Korea's sake. In anti-appeasement's name, the United States fought another bloody war in Vietnam, failing this time to achieve even the preservation of a non-communist government. As if to drive home the lesson that fighting in Vietnam to contain China had been wrongheaded, communist China and communist Vietnam soon fell out, to the point of war in 1979.

Comparisons to Hitler had the perverse effect of overblowing the communist military threat, which was largely nonexistent, and consequently understating the communist political threat, which wasn't. To their credit, some American officials in fact understood that the threat the communists posed was principally political. To their discredit, they did relatively little to share their insight with the wider American public. The Cold War climate in America wasn't conducive to nuance regarding communism. A few brave souls tried to explain such matters as that a communist China needn't be a China unalterably wedded to Moscow and irretrievably antagonistic to the United States, but the personal calumny and professional banishment these few suffered for their efforts alerted their colleagues and successors to the consequences of divergence from the party line. Most American officials chose the safer route of looking on communism as a hungry beast poised to devour the world as soon as America's guard let down. Measures designed to counter the communist political threat – for instance, by improving the economic and political performance, and thereby the attractiveness, of the countries of the "Free World" – were occasionally enacted, with the Marshall Plan being the outstanding example. But for every dollar Washington spent on economic aid, and for every meaningful exhortation American officials made to allies to respect democratic rights, Washington spent a hundred dollars on weapons, and American officials gave a score of speeches calling for staunch resistance to communist aggression.

Most perversely, the call to arms against communism caused American leaders to subvert the principles that constituted their country's best argument against communism. In 1945, the United States stood higher in the estimation of humanity than ever before, arguably higher than any country had ever stood in history. American soldiers and sailors had played a central role in the recent defeat of the almost universally detested fascists. Unlike the British and French, the Americans had no extensive colonial holdings that gave the lie to their professions of support for self-determination – the Philippines were slated for (and received) independence in 1946, and Puerto Rico didn't appear to want it. Unlike the Russians, the Americans treated the peoples of the countries they liberated with respect, and rather than seeming scarcely an improvement over the Wehrmacht, as Red Army troops often did, American GIs brought hope of an end to strife and oppression.

Within a short time, however, world opinion of the United States began to slide. The better to contain communism, Washington aligned itself with colonial and reactionary regimes that flouted the principles Americans had just fought a war to vindicate. Since comparatively few persons outside the North Atlantic region considered communism a greater enemy than colonialism and institutionalized inequality, what appeared a necessary tradeoff to many Americans appeared self-serving and hypocritical to most foreign observers of American actions. People of the Third World – which earned its sobriquet precisely because of its inhabitants' determination to resist the two-worlds framework of the Cold War – often deemed America's alliance-building tantamount to imperialism, of which they had had more than enough. American intervention in the Korean War looked to be misguided meddling in an Asian civil conflict. The war in Vietnam was widely viewed as a case of neo-colonial repression of indigenous nationalism. American backing for rightist regimes elsewhere in Asia, Africa, and Latin America seemed to fit the imperialist pattern.

Self-described "realists" in the United States could ignore the Third World carping – How many divisions did Nehru have? – and contend that any illusions anyone harbored of meaningful American moral superiority were better off debunked. The Cold War, they held, like all great-power conflicts, was essentially amoral. The strong did what they wanted, the weak what they were required, and there was little of right or wrong about the matter. This was the Doolittle philosophy: beat the devil at his own game. And it was the philosophy that, slightly disguised, informed the Kirkpatrick doctrine of support for right-wing dictators and antagonism to left-wing dictators.

The flaw in this philosophy was that it didn't suit the American people. Whatever the objective merits of "realism" as a description of behavior among nations, and whatever its appeal or lack thereof to Germans, Brazilians, Chinese, Nigerians, or anyone else, Americans have from the beginning of their national existence demonstrated an incurable desire to make the world a better place. Sometimes they settled for the stand-offish exemplarism of John Quincy Adams. Sometimes they insisted on the missionary interventionism of Woodrow Wilson. But almost always they believed that America had important lessons to teach their fellow human beings: about democracy, about capitalism, about respect for individual rights and personal opportunity and the rule of law.

This save-the-world inclination was largely responsible for the fervor with which Americans waged the Cold War. It provided much of the impetus behind the Marshall Plan: Americans were going to rescue Western Europe from starvation, disease, and despair. It lay beneath the commitment of American lives to Korea and Vietnam: the United States would preserve those vulnerable countries from the depredations of dictatorship. It motivated the appropriation of billions of dollars in aid to countries of Asia, Africa, and Latin America: American funding would help bring prosperity and dignity to the downtrodden of the planet. To be sure, the rhetoric of American concern for the welfare of other peoples and countries usually involved some hypocrisy, and in back of every important Cold War initiative there lurked careful considerations of self-interest. Yet the very fact that self-interest had to be dressed up in selfless clothing testified to the importance of moral factors in American politics, and consequently in American foreign relations. The staying power of the Cold War paradigm resulted in no small part from its capacity to combine the selfless with the self-interested.

Sometimes the twain parted, though, and when the parting became undeniable, as during the Vietnam–Watergate era, it rent the American Cold War consensus. All but the most hard-bitten Americans found sorely trying the discovery that the United States government had actively sought to assassinate leaders of foreign countries, countries not at war with the United States, whose principal crime consisted of being caught in the crossfire between the White House and the Kremlin. Americans of every political persuasion recoiled from the televised images of South Vietnamese citizens immolating themselves to protest the policies of the government the United States was supporting, from the photographs of naked Vietnamese children running screaming from napalm attacks by American planes, from the descriptions of Vietnamese villages destroyed that they might be "saved." Liberals and conservatives alike resented the corruption of the American political and legal process in the name of national security.

Defenders of American Cold War policies held that compromises were necessary to defend basic American values. Whether they really *were* necessary is impossible to tell. Conceivably, had American agents not conspired in the overthrow of popularly based governments in Iran and Guatemala; had they not tried to assassinate Lumumba and Castro; had they not tampered with elections in the Philippines and Syria and elsewhere; had they not destabilized leftist regimes in Chile and other countries; had they not bombed Indonesian islands and mined Nicaraguan harbors; had the United States not provided arms and money to a score of repressive juntas from Cuba to Pakistan to Zaire; had the FBI not disrupted the lawful activities of legitimate political groups in the United States; had the CIA not violated its own charter and engaged in domestic espionage; had American armed forces not lost 50,000 dead in Korea and nearly 60,000 in Vietnam – conceivably, had the United States not committed these acts, along with other acts presumably more constructive, communism might have conquered the world, or enough of it to render America significantly poorer, unhappier, and less secure.

In the real world, however, what counts isn't the conceivable but the likely. From the vantage point of the 1990s – which, of course, isn't the vantage point of the late 1940s and 1950s – the internal weaknesses of communism seem to have been sufficiently great to have made anything approaching the world-conquest scenarios of NSC 68 and similar manifestoes exceedingly improbable. Although conservatives claimed that American pressure was responsible for finally buckling the Soviet system in the late 1980s, as reasonable a case can be made that American antagonism actually *prolonged* the Cold War. For almost forty years, while Soviet leaders could plausibly cite an American threat to the security of their country – and, considering Washington's success in ringing Russia with American allies, considering the large and ever-growing size of the American nuclear arsenal, and considering the "massive-retaliation" and "evil-empire" language American leaders recurrently resorted to, the threat must have seemed quite plausible – Moscow could put off dealing with the problems inherent in the communist scheme of government. Had the United States not cooperated in playing the villain (just as the Soviet Union played the villain to the United States), the Kremlin might have been forced to confront its true problems sooner.

Similar considerations apply to America's dealings with other communist countries. By backing Chiang in China's civil war, for nearly a generation after that war otherwise would have ended, the United States handed Beijing's new mandarins an issue with which to divert the Chinese masses from their overwhelming domestic difficulties. Washington was consistently Fidel Castro's best friend by being his worst enemy. If Castro had ever had to justify his one-man rule in Cuba on its own merits, rather than on the demerits of the superpower across the Florida Strait, whose leaders still tried to strangle the Cuban economy thirty years after the Cuban revolution, he would have found the going a great deal harder. A principal consequence of American involvement in the Vietnamese war – aside from the millions of deaths, maimings, and displacements the fighting in Indochina produced – would seem to have been the postponement of the day when the Vietnamese communists had to stop fighting, at which they were very good, and start governing, at which they were a disaster.

The fact is that communism – not capitalism or democracy – has been the communists' worst enemy. But nations have had to discover this for themselves. External force has usually succeeded only in delaying the discovery.

Had attempts to force the discovery been costless, the delay might not have meant much. But the cost to America, not to mention to the delayed nations, was very high. More than 100,000 Americans died fighting wars that had almost nothing to do with genuine American security. The American economy, in 1945 the envy of the earth and the engine of global growth unprecedented in history, by the 1990s sputtered and faltered under the weight of four decades of military spending inconceivable before the Cold War. The chronic deficits that were a primary legacy of that military spending prevented the federal government from addressing many of the serious problems that crowded in on the country. Perhaps worst of all, American leaders, sometimes without the knowledge of the American people, sometimes with the people's approval, consistently cut moral corners in the Cold War, contradicting the ideals America was supposed to be defending. In 1945, nearly all Americans and probably a majority of interested foreigners had looked on the United States as a beacon shining the way to a better future for humanity, one in which ideals mattered more than tanks. During the next forty years, American leaders succeeded in convincing many Americans and all but a few foreigners that the United Stats could be counted on to act pretty much as great powers always have. If Americans felt ambivalent about their victory over the Soviet Union, they had reason to.

9

Some Lessons from the Cold War

Arthur Schlesinger, Jr.

Originally appeared in J. M. Hogan (ed.), *The End of the Cold War: Its meaning and implications.* Cambridge University Press, 1992.

In those faraway days when the Cold War was young, the English historian Sir Herbert Butterfield lectured at Notre Dame on "The Tragic Element in Modern International Conflict." Historians writing about modern wars, Butterfield said, characteristically start off with a "heroic" vision of things. They portray good men struggling against bad, virtue resisting evil. In this embattled mood, they see only the sins of the enemy and ignore the underlying structural dilemmas that so often provoke international clashes.

As time passes and emotions subside, history enters the "academic" phase. Now historians see "a terrible human predicament" at the heart of the story, "a certain situation that contains the element of conflict irrespective of any special wickedness in any of the parties concerned." Wickedness may deepen the predicament, but conflict would be there anyway. Perspective, Butterfield proposed, teaches us "to be a little more sorry for both parties than they knew how to be for one another." History moves on from melodrama to tragedy.[1]

Butterfield made a pretty good forecast of the way Cold War historiography has evolved in the more than forty years since he spoke. In the United States the "heroic" phase took two forms: the orthodox in the 1940s and 1950s, with the Russians cast as the villains, and the revisionist in the 1960s, with the Americans as the villains. By the 1980s, American Cold War historians discerned what one of the best of them,

---

1   Herbert Butterfield, "The Tragic Element in Modern International Conflict," was published in *Review of Politics*, April 1950, and reprinted in Butterfield, *History and Human Relations* (London, 1951), 9–36.

John Lewis Gaddis, called an "emerging post-revisionist synthesis."[2] History began to pass from a weapon in the battle into a more analytical effort to define structural dilemmas and to understand adversary concerns. *Glasnost* permitted comparable historiographical evolution in the former Soviet Union.

Quite right: The more one contemplates the Cold War, the more irrelevant the allocation of blame seems. The Second World War left the international order in acute derangement. With the Axis states vanquished, the Western European allies spent, the colonial empires in tumult and dissolution, great gaping holes appeared in the structure of world power. Only two nations – the United States and the Soviet Union – had the military strength, the ideological conviction, and the political will to fill these vacuums.

But why did this old-fashioned geopolitical rivalry billow up into a holy war so intense and obsessive as to threaten the very existence of human life on the planet? The two nations were constructed on opposite and profoundly antagonistic principles. They were divided by the most significant and fundamental disagreements over human rights, individual liberties, cultural freedom, the role of civil society, the direction of history, and the destiny of man. Each state saw the other as irrevocably hostile to its own essence. Given the ideological conflict on top of the geopolitical confrontation, no one should be surprised at what ensued. Conspiratorial explanations are hardly required. The real surprise would have been if there had been no Cold War.

And why has humanity survived the Cold War? The reason that the Cold War never exploded into hot war was surely (and by providential irony) the invention of nuclear weapons. One is inclined to support the suggestion (Elspeth Rostow's, I think) that the Nobel Peace Prize should have gone to the atomic bomb.

At last this curious episode in modern history is over, and we must ask what lessons we may hope to learn from a long, costly, dark, dreary, and dangerous affair; what precautions humanity should take to prevent comparable episodes in the future. I would suggest half a dozen fallacies that the world might well forego in years to come.

The first might be called the fallacy of overinterpreting the enemy. In the glory days of the Cold War, each side attributed to the other a master plan for world domination joined with diabolical efficiency in executing the plan. Such melodramatic imagining of brilliant and demonic enemies was truer to, say, Sax Rohmer, the creator of Dr. Fu Manchu, than to shuffling historical reality.

2   John Lewis Gaddis, "The Emerging Post-Revisionist Synthesis on the Origins of the Cold War," *Diplomatic History* 7 (Summer 1983): 171–90.

No doubt Soviet leaders believed that the dialectic of history would one day bring about the victory of communism. No doubt Western leaders believed that the nature of man and markets would one day bring about the victory of free society. But such generalized hopes were far removed from operational master plans.

"The superpowers," as Henry Kissinger well put it,

> often behave like two heavily armed blind men feeling their way around a room, each believing himself in mortal peril from the other whom he assumes to have perfect vision. Each side should know that frequently uncertainty, compromise, and incoherence are the essence of policy-making. Yet each tends to ascribe to the other a consistency, foresight, and coherence that its own experience belies. Of course, over time, even two blind men can do enormous damage to each other, not to speak of the room.[3]

The room has happily survived. But the blind men meanwhile escalated the geopolitical/ideological confrontation into a compulsively interlocked heightening of tension, spurred on by authentic differences in principle, by real and supposed clashes of interest, and by a wide range of misperception, misunderstanding, and demagoguery. Each superpower undertook for what it honestly saw as defensive reasons actions that the other honestly saw as unacceptably threatening and requiring stern countermeasures. Each persevered in corroborating the fears of the other. Each succumbed to the propensity to perceive local conflicts in global terms, political conflicts in moral terms, and relative differences in absolute terms. Together, in lockstep, they expanded the Cold War.

In overinterpreting the motives and actions of the other, each side forgot Emerson's invaluable precept: "In analysing history, do not be too profound, for often the causes are quite simple."[4] Both superpowers should have known from their own experience that governments mostly live from day to day responding to events as they come, that decisions are more often the result of improvisation, ignorance, accident, fatigue, chance, blunder, and sometimes plain stupidity than of orchestrated master plans. One lesson to be drawn from the Cold War is that more things in life are to be explained by cock-up, to use the British term, than by conspiracy.

An accompanying phenomenon, at first a consequence and later a reinforcing cause of overinterpretation, was the embodiment of the Cold

3   Henry Kissinger, *White House Years* (Boston, 1979), 522.
4   Ralph Waldo Emerson, *Journals*, ed. E. W. Emerson and W. E. Forbes (Boston, 1908–1914), 4:160.

War in government institutions. Thus our second fallacy: The fallacy of overinstitutionalizing the policy. The Soviet Union, a police state committed to dogmas of class war and capitalist conspiracy and denied countervailing checks of free speech and press, had institutionalized the Cold War from the day Lenin arrived at the Finland Station. In later years the Cold War became for Stalin a convenient means of justifying his own arbitrary power and the awful sacrifices he demanded from the Soviet peoples. "Stalin needed the Cold War," observed Earl Browder, whom Stalin purged as chief of the American Communist party, "to keep up the sharp international tensions by which he alone could maintain such a regime in Russia."[5]

In Washington by the 1950s the State Department, the Defense Department, the Central Intelligence Agency, the Federal Bureau of Investigation, and the National Security Council developed vested bureaucratic interests in the theory of a militarily expansionist Soviet Union. The Cold War conferred power, money, prestige, and public influence on these agencies and on the people who ran them. By the natural law of bureaucracies, their stake in the conflict steadily grew. Outside of government, arms manufacturers, politicians, professors, publicists, pontificators, and demagogues invested careers and fortunes in the Cold War.

In time, the adversary Cold War agencies evolved a sort of tacit collusion across the Iron Curtain. Probably the greatest racket in the Cold War was the charade periodically enacted by generals and admirals announcing the superiority of the other side in order to get bigger budgets for themselves. As President John F. Kennedy remarked to Norman Cousins, the editor of the *Saturday Review*, in the spring of 1963, "The hard-liners in the Soviet Union and the United States feed on one another."[6]

Institutions, alas, do not fold their tents and silently steal away. Ideas crystallized in bureaucracies resist change. With the Cold War at last at an end, each side faces the problem of deconstructing entrenched Cold War agencies spawned and fortified by nearly half a century of mutually profitable competition. One has only to reflect on the forces behind the anti-Gorbachev conspiracy of August 1991.

A third fallacy may be called the fallacy of arrogant prediction. As a devotee of a cyclical approach to American political history, I would not wish to deny that history exhibits uniformities and recurrences. But it is essential to distinguish between those phenomena that are predictable and those that are not. Useful historical generalizations are mostly

5 Steven G. Neal, "A Comrade's Last Harrumph," *Philadelphia Inquirer*, 5 August 1973.
6 Norman Cousins, *The Improbable Triumvirate* (New York, 1972), 114.

statements about broad, deep-running, long-term changes: the life-cycle of revolutions, for example, or the impact of industrialization and urbanization, or the influence of climate or sea power or the frontier. The short term, however, contains too many variables, depends too much on accident and fortuity and personality, to permit exact and specific forecasts.

We have been living through extraordinary changes in the former Soviet Union and in Eastern Europe, in South Africa and in the Middle East. What is equally extraordinary is that *no one foresaw these changes.* All the statesmen, all the sages, all the savants, all the professors, all the prophets, all those bearded chaps on "Nightline" – all were caught unaware and taken by surprise; all were befuddled and impotent before the perpetual astonishments of the future. History has an abiding capacity to outwit our certitudes.

Just a few years back some among us were so absolutely sure of the consequences if we did not smash the Reds at once that they called for preventive nuclear war. Had they been able to persuade the US government to drop the bomb on the Soviet Union in the 1950s or on China in the 1960s . . . but, thank heaven, they never did; and no one today, including those quondam preventive warriors themselves, regrets the American failure to do so.

The Almighty no doubt does know the future. But He has declined to confide such foresight to frail and erring mortals. In the early years of the Cold War, Reinhold Niebuhr warned of "the depth of evil to which individuals and communities may sink . . . when they try to play the role of God to history."[7] Let us not fall for people who tell us that we must take drastic action today because of their conjectures as to what some other fellow or nation may do five or ten or twenty years from now.

Playing God to history is the dangerous consequence of our fourth fallacy – the fallacy of national self-righteousness. "No government or social system is so evil," President Kennedy said in his American University speech in 1963, "that its people must be condemned as lacking in virtue," and he called on Americans as well as Russians to reexamine attitudes toward the Cold War, "for our attitude is as essential as theirs."[8] This thought came as rather a shock to those who assumed that the American side was so manifestly right that self-examination was unnecessary.

Kennedy liked to quote a maxim from the British military pundit Liddell Hart: "Never corner an opponent, and always assist him to save his face. Put yourself in his shoes – so as to see things through his eyes.

---

7   Reinhold Niebuhr, *The Irony of American History* (New York, 1952), 173.
8   John F. Kennedy, *Public Papers, 1963* (Washington, 1964), 460–1.

Avoid self-righteousness like the devil – nothing is so self-blinding."[9] Perhaps Kennedy did not always live up to those standards himself, but he did on great occasions, like the Cuban missile crisis, and he retained a capacity for ironical objectivity that is rare among political leaders.

Objectivity – seeing ourselves as others see us – is a valuable adjunct to statesmanship. Can we be so sure that our emotional judgments of the moment represent the last word and the final truth? The angry ideological conflicts that so recently obsessed us may not greatly interest our posterity. Our great-grandchildren may well wonder what in heaven's name those disagreements could have been that drove the Soviet Union and the United States to the brink of blowing up the planet.

Men and women a century from now will very likely find the Cold War as obscure and incomprehensible as we today find the Thirty Years War – the terrible conflict that devastated much of Europe not too long ago. Looking back at the twentieth century, our descendants will very likely be astonished at the disproportion between the causes of the Cold War, which may well seem trivial, and the consequences, which could have meant the veritable end of history.

Russians and Americans alike came to see the Cold War as a duel between two superpowers, a Soviet–American duopoly. But the reduction of the Cold War to a bilateral game played by the Soviet Union and the United States is a fifth fallacy. The nations of Europe were not spectators at someone else's match. They were players too.

Revisionist historians, determined to blame the Cold War on an American drive for world economic hegemony, have studiously ignored the role of Europe. Washington, they contend, was compelled to demand an "open door" for American trade and investment everywhere on the planet because American capitalism had to expand in order to survive. The Soviet Union was the main obstacle to a world market controlled by the United States. So, by revisionist dogma, American leaders whipped up an unnecessary Cold War in order to save the capitalist system.

No matter that some fervent open door advocates, like Henry A. Wallace, were also fervent opponents of the Cold War. No matter that the republics of the former Soviet Union now want nothing more than American trade and investment and full integration into the world market. And no matter that most Western European nations in the 1940s had Socialist governments and that the democratic socialist leaders – Clement Attlee and Ernest Bevin in Britain, Leon Blum and Paul Ramadier in France, Paul-Henri Spaak in Belgium, Kurt Schu-

9   Arthur M. Schlesinger, Jr., *A Thousand Days: John F. Kennedy in the White House* (Boston, 1965), 110.

macher, Ernst Reuter, and Willy Brandt in West Germany – had powerful reasons of their own to fear the spread of Stalinist influence and
Soviet power.

Such men could not have cared less about an open door for
American capitalism. They cared deeply, however, about the future of
democratic socialism. When I used to see Aneurin Bevan, the leader of
the left wing of the British Labour party, in London in 1944, he doubted
that the wartime alliance would last and saw the struggle for postwar
Europe as between the democratic socialists and the Communists. "The
Communist party," Bevan wrote in 1951, "is the sworn and inveterate
enemy of the Socialist and Democratic parties. When it associates with
them it does so as a preliminary to destroying them."[10] Many in the
Truman administration in the 1940s espoused this view and, dubbing themselves (in private) NCL, favored American support for the
non-Communist Left.

The democratic socialists, moreover, were in advance of official
Washington in organizing against the Stalinist threat. Despite his above-
the-battle stance at Notre Dame, Herbert Butterfield himself wrote in
1969, "A new generation often does not know (and does not credit the
fact when informed) that Western Europe once wondered whether the
United States could ever be awakened to the danger from Russia."[11]
The subsequent opening of British Foreign Office papers voluminously
documents Sir Herbert's point.

Far from seeing President Truman in the revisionist mode as an
anti-Soviet zealot hustling a reluctant Europe into a gratuitous
Cold War, the Foreign Office saw him for a considerable period as an
irresolute waffler distracted by the delusion that the United States could
play mediator between Britain and the Soviet Union. Ernest Bevin,
Britain's Socialist foreign secretary, thought Truman's policy was "to
withdraw from Europe and in effect leave the British to get on with the
Russians as best they could."[12] A true history of the Cold War must add
European actors to the cast and broaden both research nets and analytical perspectives.

The theory of the Cold War as a Soviet–American duopoly is
sometimes defended on the ground that, after all, the United States and
the Soviet Union were in full command of their respective alliances. But
nationalism, the most potent political emotion of the age, challenged the
reign of the superpowers almost from the start: Tito, Mao, and others
vs. Moscow; De Gaulle, Eden and others vs. Washington. Experience has

10   Aneurin Bevan, foreword, *The Curtain Falls*, ed. Denis Healey (London, 1951).
11   Herbert Butterfield, "Morality and an International Order," in *The Aberystwith Papers: International Politics, 1919–1969*, ed. Brian Porter (Oxford, 1972), 353–4.
12   Alan Bullock, *Ernest Bevin: Foreign Secretary, 1945–1951* (London, 1983), 216.

adequately demonstrated how limited superpowers are in their ability to order their allies around and even to control client governments wholly dependent on them for economic and military support. Far from clients being the prisoners of the superpower, superpowers often end as prisoners of their clients.

These are lessons Washington has painfully learned (or at least was painfully taught; has the government finally learned them?) in Vietnam, El Salvador, Israel, Saudi Arabia, Kuwait. As for the Soviet Union, its brutal interventions and wretched Quislings in Eastern Europe only produced bitterness and hatred. The impact of clients on principals is another part of the unwritten history of the Cold War. The Cold War was *not* a bilateral game.

Nor was it – our sixth and final fallacy – a zero-sum game. For many years, Cold War theology decreed that a gain for one side was by definition a defeat for the other. This notion led logically not to an interest in negotiation but to a demand for capitulation. In retrospect the Cold War, humanity's most intimate brush with collective suicide, can only remind us of the ultimate interdependence of nations and of peoples.

After President Kennedy and Premier Khrushchev stared down the nuclear abyss together in October 1962, they came away determined to move as fast as they could toward détente. Had Kennedy lived, Khrushchev might have held on to power a little longer, and together they would have further subdued the excesses of the Cold War. They rejected the zero-sum approach and understood that intelligent negotiation brings mutual benefit. I am not an unlimited admirer of Ronald Reagan, but he deserves his share of credit for taking Mikhail Gorbachev seriously, abandoning the zero-sum fallacy he had embraced for so long, and moving the Cold War toward its end.

And why indeed has it ended? If the ideological confrontation gave the geopolitical rivalry its religious intensity, so the collapse of the ideological debate took any apocalyptic point out of the Cold War. The proponents of liberal society were proven right. After seventy years of trial, communism turned out – by the confession of its own leaders – to be an economic, political, and moral disaster. Democracy won the political argument between East and West. The market won the economic argument. Difficulties lie ahead, but the fundamental debate that created the Cold War is finished.

Index